Praise for *The PBIS Team Handbook*

"*The PBIS Team Handbook* is the new go-to guide for PBIS coaches and administrators. It not only gives you step-by-step instructions on how to fully and successfully implement the program in your building, but it also breaks it down and humanizes the process. It provides many practical forms that can be used by PBIS teams and coaches. The handbook makes you think of not only the impact on your students, but also the impact on members of your team and teachers and staff in your building. This is a must-read—no matter what stage you are at in PBIS implementation."

—Cristina Dobon-Claveau, district PBIS coordinator,
Western Placer Unified School District in Lincoln, California

"This book is a very accessible summary of the process of implementing and sustaining schoolwide PBIS. It addresses the best practices in PBIS from the perspective of people who have been involved with it on the ground level and who are willing to offer advice on issues that implementers often face. Teachers and others involved in implementation will find the insights of the authors helpful as they undertake their own journey to support meaningful behavioral outcomes for students. A must-have for PBIS team members in schools."

—Kevin J. Filter, Ph.D., associate professor of psychology,
Minnesota State University, Mankato

"Changing behaviors in students can be difficult; however, changing the way adults view those behaviors is a challenge. This book takes teams through a step-by-step process that not only implements but also provides the tools needed to sustain a schoolwide behavioral support system in order to build an environment in which teachers can teach and students can learn."

—Amy Piotrowski, special education coordinator at Chanhassen Elementary,
Chaska Middle School East, and Integrated Arts Academy

The PBIS Team Handbook

Setting Expectations and Building Positive Behavior

Beth Baker, M.S.Ed., and Char Ryan, Ph.D.

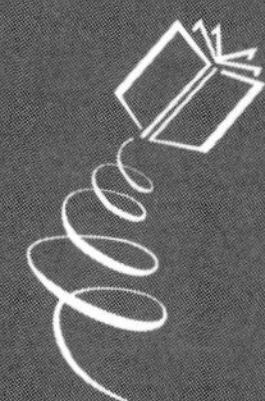

free spirit
PUBLISHING®

Library of Congress Cataloging-in-Publication
Baker, Beth.
The PBIS team handbook : setting expectations and building positive behavior / Beth Baker, Char Ryan.
pages cm
Includes index.
ISBN 978-1-57542-469-9 (paperback) — ISBN 1-57542-469-X 1. School psychology—United States. 2. Behavior modification—United States. 3. School children—United States—Discipline. 4. Students—United States—Psychology. 5. School management and organization—United States. I. Ryan, Charlotte A. II. Title.
LB1060.2.B34 2014
370.15—dc23

2014001088

ISBN: 978-1-57542-469-9

Edited by Meg Bratsch and Cathy Broberg
Cover and interior design by Michelle Lee

Photo credits, cover: Blend Images–JGI/Jamie Grill/Getty Images (kids) and © Anankkml/Dreamstime.com (sign); page 7: © Monkey Business Images/Dreamstime.com; page 97: © Zurijeta/Dreamstime.com; page 149: © Zurijeta/Dreamstime.com; author photos: Sarah Whiting.

10 9 8 7 6 5 4 3
Printed in the United States of America

Free Spirit Publishing Inc.
6325 Sandburg Road, Suite 100
Golden Valley, MN 55427-3629
(612) 338-2068
help4kids@freespirit.com
www.freespirit.com

Dedication

From Beth: I dedicate this book to Mark, Dylan, and Isabella for being patient and keeping me on task; and to my parents, Jim and Mary Jo, for giving me a place to write and feeding me.

From Char: I dedicate this book to my family and many friends and colleagues who believed that I could do this very big task. With unconditional support, they asked me continuously how the book was progressing, which kept me on the road despite the numerous distractions that arose.

Acknowledgments

From Beth: Thank you to the following people for reading what I wrote and engaging in conversations: Heidi Andermack, Sarah Whiting, Rebecca Thielman, LaTonya Dupree, and Enitan Yarbrough; to Ann Dillard for helping me shape my vision; to our wonderful editor Cathy Broberg; and to Judy Galbraith and Meg Bratsch at Free Spirit Publishing for guiding our work and being patient.

From Char: I'd like to give a special thank you to Rob Horner, Kent McIntosh, and Kevin Filter who generously read parts of this manuscript and offered their input and support to the finish line. In addition, thank you to PBIS colleagues in Minnesota and across the country who so quickly and willing gave their permission to use materials they or their agencies developed. Thank you to MiBLSi, Missouri PBIS, Maryland PBIS and others for sharing your accomplishments and examples; and to the Osseo Public Schools for their support of this project. Though I have always experienced generous sharing among SW-PBIS founders and implementers, the support from this community of people is priceless. Thank you to Cathy Broberg for her editorial expertise and ability to move this forward at all the right times; and to Judy Galbraith and Meg Bratsch for believing in our idea and providing the patience, support, and expertise to assist us in completing this book.

Contents

List of Figures

List of Reproducible Forms

Download these forms and the PDF presentation at freespirit.com/PBIS-forms. Use the password 2bpositive.

Introduction

Historically, many educators have relied on reactive practices to improve student behavior. We hand out a detention or a visit to the principal for a disruptive behavior. If the behavior doesn't change, maybe the next time we call home and issue another detention. If that still doesn't work, we call home again and issue a suspension. These practices will work for some students, yet others seem unaffected by behavioral interventions such as these. After all this work, the behavior isn't changing, and the teacher gives up trying. Given the number of office referrals and suspensions, these students become what we call "high flyers." Although they've been suspended multiple times, their behavior is still far from stellar.

Another way to deal with behavior is proactively. We teach and model for students exactly how we want them to behave and intervene swiftly and often until they grasp it—ideally before a harsh reactive practice is required. The guidelines provided by Schoolwide Positive Behavioral Interventions and Supports (SWPBIS) were created for this approach. Schoolwide PBIS (hereafter referred to as PBIS) has emerged as a powerful organizing framework that supports school staff in their efforts to move from reactive to proactive behavioral interventions. Supported by decades of research, PBIS is strongly rooted in behavioral theory and practice. By combining evidence-based practices with a systems approach to implementation, PBIS has created a model that has widespread adoption and lasting success.

Using the PBIS framework, schools develop practices to prevent problem behavior and to teach and reinforce expected behaviors consistently across school settings. The system supports all school staff using data to monitor the outcomes. Consistent data collection enables schools to determine whether the interventions are working for students and whether staff members are receiving the support they need to use the interventions effectively. PBIS, when implemented with fidelity across school systems and grades, has been shown to improve student outcomes (academic skills, pro-social behaviors, graduation rates, attendance, etc.). A school that has fully implemented PBIS will demonstrate a continuum of practices for students with typical needs all the way through practices for students who have high-intensity needs.

Implementation of PBIS occurs in progressive stages, or tiers, with Tier 1 being implemented before Tiers 2 and 3 of the framework. It may take your school two or three years to get a firm foundation in place for Tier 1, during which you establish the universal system. This book will help you develop a sound understanding of PBIS and walk you through the process of implementing Tier 1 of the framework. The book closes by briefly discussing how to prepare for implementing Tiers 2 and 3.

Why We Wrote This Book

We wrote this book to explain the components of PBIS and its implementation in user-friendly terms and to offer examples and lessons learned from our experience. The following describes Beth's early experience with PBIS:

> I was teaching middle school students with emotional-behavioral disorders, and one day during a math lesson a student said to me "You're a (insert expletive)." I am not sure why he said it, but I didn't like it. I responded, "That's it! You are suspended! You can go

home!" and went to find an administrator. Instead I found the school psychologist and told her what had just happened in my classroom. She asked me, "What do you hope to get by suspending this student?" I told her that he couldn't speak to me that way and he needed to go home. "Do you really think suspending him one more time for the behavior he's been doing for six years is going to change anything?" I thought about it for a minute and then sheepishly replied, "No." But I felt exasperated and defeated—what else could I do but suspend him? The school psychologist gave me a social skills curriculum she had received from a mental health treatment center and suggested that it might be helpful to use with my students. She asked her intern to lead the curriculum's lessons with my class.

Schoolwide PBIS (hereafter referred to as PBIS) has emerged as a powerful organizing framework that supports school staff in their efforts to move from reactive to proactive behavioral interventions.

Over the coming months, the intern taught my students how to use calming strategies. He talked about different sources of anger and how the students could release their anger in healthy ways. As a class, we developed common language to discuss feelings and how we react to those feelings. For my part, the curriculum prompted me to work toward understanding my students better. As I learned more about their backgrounds, I realized that the feelings and behaviors they demonstrated in class probably had little to do with me, and more to do with anxiety and reacting to their environments. They were simply displaying the same behaviors they had always used to cope with anger, hurt, and frustration. The student who called me a name wasn't really angry at me—he was angry at the world (and eventually told me as much when we discussed the incident). In the past, swearing at a teacher had brought him an automatic suspension, a way to escape school. But this consequence had not served to change his behavior. Once I understood this, I wanted to keep the students in the building and work on developing healthier ways of expressing anger.

I remember this incident quite vividly and how it made me rethink my purpose in teaching students with challenging behaviors. It was no longer just about the academics; now I saw how focusing on the social-emotional aspect of my students' lives could also improve their everyday experiences over the long term. I began allowing behavioral "do-overs" in my classroom. We talked about feelings and processed disruptive behaviors, and I reinforced positive behaviors that students displayed.

With these changes, I no longer felt like a gatekeeper, sending kids back and forth to the behavior room. Now I felt more involved and connected with my students and I enjoyed watching them grow emotionally—they could share with me what they were frustrated about and then together we could come up with a solution. The atmosphere in my classroom became calmer.

The changes didn't happen overnight. There was a lot of work involved—relationships built by taking baby steps—and some kids weren't interested in talking about their feelings. Even so, I remember running into a parent of one of these students a few years after their family had moved to a different district. She gave me a hug and told me that her son was doing really well and that his anger was no longer causing him significant trouble. Was it what he had learned in my classroom? Maybe. Was it maturity? Possibly. Does it matter? Not to me. What matters to me is that he figured out a way to cope with his behaviors that worked for him and were not disrupting everyone around him.

That was my introduction to PBIS, although I was yet to fully understand the theories and principles involved and the potential of PBIS to improve an entire school's culture. Eventually, I enrolled in graduate school to earn a master's degree in education, and part of my program required that I do an action research project (implement a project and collect data on it over time). The middle school where I was teaching had just started a schoolwide behavioral program for students and I knew it would be a perfect setting to collect data for my project. While conducting research on social-emotional learning, I kept bumping into articles on PBIS. When I started reading them, I realized that although the program at my school was a great start, it did not include interventions for students who were being continually referred out of class and in need of more intensive supports. It also didn't emphasize data collection.

I started looking at our data and determined which students were having trouble, not just names but also demographics, grades, attendance, behavioral strengths, and patterns. The school's handling of behavior and discipline problems paralleled a scenario that is repeated across the country: A student would get referred out of the classroom and go to the behavior room; here he or she would complete a form agreeing not do the behavior again, get a lecture, and then return to class. For some students this process was repeated several times a day, day after day. Teachers were frustrated because behaviors weren't changing. Some students were actually choosing the behavior room over the classroom. Administrators were distressed with the number of students out of class, because we all know that students don't learn unless they are in class.

I began to memorize research and sound bites about PBIS, but I had a hard time really explaining the overall concept and its practices to my colleagues. If only I knew exactly what PBIS meant . . . If only there were a book that spelled everything out in simple language.

Eventually, our principal decided to adopt PBIS in our school. She began by gathering a PBIS team together. We registered for a two-year cohort training with our state department of education. It was at these trainings that I got to know Char, one of the trainers and the coauthor of this book. She was a great mentor to me while I took on the role of a PBIS coach and led my school through the implementation process.

In time, we began talking more about the layers and parts of PBIS and why implementation often seems difficult. By then, I had worked as a special education teacher (for students with emotional-behavioral disorders), as a behavior specialist, and as a PBIS coach. Char's expertise in PBIS included serving as the Minnesota PBIS coordinator and working as a coach, as an evaluation specialist, and as a trainer. We decided to collaborate on creating this guide to help educators who are considering PBIS understand how it operates and how to bring it into their own schools with success.

A word from Char about what brought her to PBIS:

> I have been in the education and mental health fields for my entire career. My primary focus has been on child, adolescent, and adult behavior. I taught, and I served in many other roles, including teacher, behavior specialist, program director, and psychologist. Over the decades, I have seen significant trends, some of which I would gladly distance myself from.
>
> Back in the 1990s, I was a specialist for students with emotional and behavioral disorders, for whom I have always been a strong advocate. We worked very hard to promote the use of positive interventions with individual students. Sadly, in those days, exclusionary and punitive practices were commonplace; seclusion and restraint were poorly used and often went undocumented. There was (and still is) significant

stigma and misunderstanding about students and their behavior, especially those with emotional and behavioral disorders. For one, it was widely assumed by some that students *chose* particular problem behaviors because they wanted to disrupt the school day for everyone. This belief in motive, and therefore justification for removal, was painful to observe in action.

My team and I promoted the use of function-based support and other progressive practices among those who worked with students with challenging behaviors. We tried to encourage acceptance and positive practices in the schools in general and with students with emotional and behavioral problems specifically. Unfortunately, change did not occur as fast as I had hoped for.

In hindsight, it is clear that our systems were not in order to support some of these changes. When I became involved with the SWPBIS initiative, it was incredibly rewarding for me. The system was coming together in a consistent way; what we were trying to do with students at the top of the PBIS tiered model was gaining a foundation schoolwide in a comprehensive, systematic way. As this change took root in schools, my brightest moments to this day came from an incredibly skilled and committed administrator and staff with whom I worked. Commonly, administrators and others tell me that with PBIS in place, they can better serve all students, including those who have more intensive needs. Indeed, PBIS has provided such a significant shift in practice and attitude that I readily agreed to join Beth in promoting it and recognizing all of the terrific work that has been done by the leaders in this field.

About This Book

The PBIS Team Handbook has been written primarily for district PBIS coordinators and new and emerging PBIS coaches—both internal (school-based) coaches and external (district) coaches—and for leadership teams, including administrators. Other school staff may also benefit from reading the book and learning the details of how PBIS works and how it is best implemented.

Part One: What Is PBIS? The first five chapters of this book present the components, roles, and expected outcomes of using the PBIS framework.

- **Chapter 1 PBIS 101** provides a detailed overview of PBIS, what it is, how it originated, how the tiers work, who is involved in using the strategies in a school setting, and what steps are necessary to begin implementing it with fidelity. You'll learn what this type of systems change may look like in your building and how these changes will lead to a safer, calmer school climate.

The sections, chapters, and resources in this book align with the Implementation Blueprint for Schoolwide PBIS that was developed by Rob Horner and George Sugai, with support from the U.S. Department of Education's Office of Special Education Programs (OSEP). Throughout this book, we refer to sections of the PBIS website (www.pbis.org). A nationwide network supports schools throughout the country with SWPBIS resources. Please take a look at the national OSEP Technical Assistance Center on the PBIS website to see all the contributors who have helped make PBIS the huge success that it is. Another foundational resource is *The Handbook of Positive Behavior Support*,[1] which details the history, depth, and breadth of this initiative.

[1] Sailor, Dunlap, Sugai, and Horner, 2009.

- **Chapter 2 The PBIS Leadership Team** details the role of a team in introducing and implementing PBIS, describes how to form an effective team, and identifies key roles and responsibilities for different team members. We also discuss how to prepare for, conduct, and evaluate team meetings to ensure that best practices are being followed, and we explore the specific role of administrators in PBIS.
- **Chapter 3 The PBIS Coach** describes the key role and tasks of this important leader in the implementation process, from the knowledge and skills a coach needs to specific steps in guiding the process. Ideas on how to grow and develop as a coach are also covered.
- **Chapter 4 Data and Assessment** explains the essential assessment and data collection piece of PBIS. It also identifies the key components in any behavior monitoring system used to track referrals, and summarizes the numerous assessment tools that are commonly used in PBIS.
- **Chapter 5 Effective Data-Based Decision Making** describes methods of data-based problem solving for PBIS Leadership Teams, including implementation progress, fidelity, and outcome data. It details methods of using office discipline referrals in problem solving and briefly introduces the model, Team-Initiated Problem Solving (TIPS).

Part Two: Implementing PBIS Tier 1. This section of the book offers a step-by-step guide through the five stages of implementation, explaining the main tasks of each stage, the individuals involved, and how to keep stakeholders informed.

- **Chapter 6 PBIS Stage 1: Exploration and Adoption** explains how to get started with PBIS, including how to determine need, collect baseline data, and take the first steps to get buy-in from school staff and administrators.

This book will help you develop a sound understanding of PBIS and walk you through the process of implementing Tier 1 of the framework.

- **Chapter 7 PBIS Stage 2: Getting Ready—Installing the Infrastructure** discusses the important task of establishing a PBIS Leadership Team and the initial work of the team as they develop an action plan. At this point, schools typically develop the three to five schoolwide expectations that will serve as the foundation for behavioral change in their schools and design an approach to teach and reinforce those expectations.
- **Chapter 8 PBIS Stage 3: Getting Going—Initial Implementation** explains how to put the eight key features of PBIS effectively in place. Special attention is focused on training staff at this stage.
- **Chapter 9 PBIS Stage 4: Up and Running—Full Implementation** explores what PBIS looks like once all of the features are in place and the strategies of reinforcement have become automatic to all school staff. The chapter discusses how to ensure that the strategies and principles of PBIS are being used as intended and with fidelity.
- **Chapter 10 PBIS Stage 5: Sustaining and Continuous Improvement** looks at how to sustain PBIS over the long term, when leadership and staff turn over and when momentum slows. The discussion includes adapting PBIS to changing circumstances, addressing common barriers at this stage, and identifying what actions will lead to continual improvement and support for PBIS throughout the school.

Part Three: Setting the Stage for PBIS Tiers 2 and 3. The final section of this book explores how to know when your school is ready to move beyond the first tier of PBIS, and what to do next.

- **Chapter 11 Are You Ready for Advanced Tiers?** offers questions to help you consider whether your school is comfortable enough to advance to the second and third tiers of PBIS to meet the needs of students with more pronounced behavioral challenges.

Glossary, Resources, and Appendix. At the end of this book is a glossary of relevant terms, a list of helpful resources, and an appendix filled with reproducible forms and lists to help you and your school with PBIS implementation. You will also find these forms in the digital download.

Digital Download. The digital download accompanying this book contains customizable versions of all of the reproducible forms as well as a PDF presentation that can be modified for use in your school to introduce the PBIS framework to your staff or district. We have done the research and created this tool to help you provide professional development in your school or district. See page x for details on how to access the download from Free Spirit's website.

PLC Guide. If you wish to use this book in a professional learning community or book study group, a PLC Guide with chapter-by-chapter discussion questions is available. You may download the free guide at freespirit.com.

How to Use This Book

Regardless of whether your school is already in the midst of implementing PBIS or has yet to commit to adopting PBIS, you will find information and resources in this book that apply to where you are on your journey. You may choose to read the book straight through or select specific sections or chapters that address where you are right now.

Professional learning communities (PLCs) and book study groups can use this book if your school is exploring or already using PBIS. These chapters will help you get caught up on the terminology and the process. (It took Beth about two years to catch on to some of the nuances of the model.) Also, principals may purchase copies of the book for the PBIS Leadership Team to have on hand during the implementation phase and to walk your team through the process. Staff members who are new to your building may also appreciate having a copy to catch up on what PBIS is all about.

We welcome you to this wonderful journey. It will likely be filled with pit stops, hills, and valleys. But with patience and perseverance, you can help lead your school to reduced behavioral problems and improved academics, fostering an environment in which teachers are teaching more, administrators are disciplining less, and students are more engaged and productive.

Beth Baker and Char Ryan

Part One

What Is PBIS?

Chapter 1
PBIS 101

Positive Behavioral Interventions and Supports (PBIS) is now being used in more than 18,000 schools across the United States and abroad in every school setting, from the lunchroom to the library, from the locker room to the individual classroom—and everywhere in between. The PBIS framework has been adopted by rural, suburban, and urban schools; by area learning centers (ALCs), charter schools, and separate site special education programs; and by preK schools through high schools. Some juvenile justice centers also use PBIS. The framework can be implemented in any school that is interested in improving behavioral and academic outcomes for all students. Many educators and other school staff are witnessing the benefits of this approach and seeing safer, calmer learning environments.

You may be a coach or PBIS team member looking for a way to communicate to others what PBIS represents. Or perhaps you are a staff member trying to figure out just what PBIS means to you. Regardless of your role, this chapter will provide you with a basic understanding of the PBIS approach and how it can be used in your school.

How Was PBIS Developed and How Does It Work?

In the 1980s, researchers at the University of Oregon began to research and develop interventions for use with students who have emotional-behavioral disorders. They noted success with the following practices:

- preventing unwanted behaviors
- using evidence-based practices to teach new behaviors
- teaching the new behaviors explicitly, mindfully, and step-by-step
- keeping data to track progress toward meeting social skills goals

In 1997, Congress renewed the Individuals with Disabilities Education Act (IDEA) and secured funding to establish the national Center on Positive Behavioral Interventions and Supports (www.pbis.org). Researchers from across the country contributed their research and implementation ideas. Finally, all the key studies and research involving behavioral change and supports for students with behavioral disorders were in one spot. The center also created partnerships with university researchers in Oregon, Florida, Missouri, and other states. This led to the expansion of the PBIS framework from special education classrooms to schoolwide programs. In 2004, Rob Horner and George Sugai, with support from the U.S. Department of Education's Office of Special Education Programs, wrote the PBIS Blueprints to guide practitioners in implementing PBIS.

Today, PBIS is sometimes incorrectly referred to as the behavioral side of Response to Intervention (RTI). As educators, we use RTI when reviewing the academic progress of students—tracking how many words students can read correctly in one minute, their knowledge of letter sounds, and their acquisition of math skills, for example. If students fail to meet annual reading or math targets, or to pass district and statewide tests, districts respond with interventions aimed at specific skill deficits to help students increase academic skills. PBIS does something similar in the area of social skills deficits. These two sides of the triangle model work together to help students be successful in school by improving academics and social behaviors.

Ultimately, PBIS is an organizing framework for schools to determine how they want to operate as a community—that is, what type of learning environment they want to create and what that means in terms of student behavior. PBIS is grounded in a continuum of evidence-based interventions that are used consistently throughout the school to prevent problematic behavior, to teach pro-social skills, and to reinforce new skills. The framework includes a set of clear practices that are embedded in a three-tiered support system for students. Teachers use specific techniques and procedures, while real-time data provides evidence to determine outcomes. A variety of measurement tools included in the framework are described in Chapter 4 and discussed in more detail in later chapters. The framework includes the following eight key features:

1. PBIS Leadership Team that guides the implementation
2. Statement of purpose
3. Three to five schoolwide positive behavioral expectations
4. Procedures for teaching the expectations, including a behavioral matrix explaining how those expectations will look in the school
5. Lesson plans that incorporate the behavioral expectations
6. Acknowledgment system that recognizes students using expected behavior—both within and outside the classroom
7. Flowchart of detailed procedures showing how to handle student misbehaviors schoolwide—both within and outside the classroom
8. Data-based system for monitoring implementation, fidelity, and outcomes

PBIS is implemented in stages, which enables the school to be fully prepared and trained for the interventions and system changes. The PBIS Leadership Team monitors the fidelity of implementation and completes surveys to ensure the process is on track to success. Staff members are surveyed to determine what school settings and behaviors may need extra attention (such as hallway behaviors) and what areas may simply need to maintain pro-social behaviors (for example, by posting expectations to remind adults and students about appropriate behaviors).

Ultimately, PBIS is an organizing framework for schools to determine how they want to operate as a community.

Educators have spent a lot of time, energy, and money figuring out the best way to teach kids reading, math, and other disciplines. PBIS helps schools figure out how to teach social-emotional learning skills. Teachers know that students who regularly disrupt class or who spend a lot of time in the principal's office aren't learning academic skills. What's more, we know that students who are aware of their emotions and can regulate when they are feeling frustrated will do better in school. As a special educator by training, Beth has written many goals for students about self-regulation and then spent a lot of time teaching those students how to recognize when they are frustrated or anxious and how to handle it in the classroom. We know that students learn the expected school behaviors if they see them modeled and are given time for practice, feedback, and skill reinforcement. Yet when it comes to social-emotional skills, many teachers don't want to spend time teaching behaviors they think their students should already know, despite the fact that some students haven't mastered the skills we want them to have.

A Tiered Model

PBIS offers three tiers of support to ensure all students get the help they need as they learn new skills. For teachers and other educators, the framework guides us to look at the practices we use and to identify new skills we may need to develop in order to fully support all students.

The three-tiered system of PBIS is based on a model of prevention from public health. The model says that 80 percent of the people will respond to general guidance or correction, about 15 percent will need a bit more treatment, and maybe the top 5 percent will need specialized treatment. PBIS replicates that model in terms of students demonstrating expected school behaviors. The model recognizes that not all problem behavior is the same, nor do all students respond to the same types of interventions. The PBIS framework guides schools in meeting the needs of students at all tiers through a continuum of interventions. This continuum is designed to help staff prevent disruptive behaviors while teaching and acknowledging pro-social behaviors.

Figure 1.1

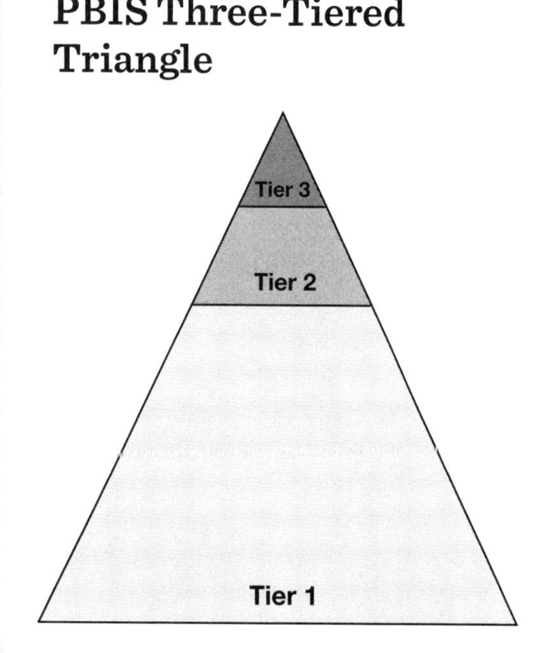

Figure 1.1 illustrates the PBIS three-tiered triangle. The bottom of the triangle (typically shown in green) represents schoolwide behavioral initiatives, what we call Tier 1 interventions. This is the primary level of prevention, and it involves setting schoolwide expectations and interventions for student behavior. Typically, 80 percent of students will be successful with Tier 1 interventions solidly in place. Some schools find that Tier 1 produces success with even more of their students, up to 90 percent or more. During one academic year, these students have zero or one referral out of the classroom for problem behavior.

The next layer of the triangle (typically yellow) adds Tier 2 interventions for about 15 percent of students—those who need a bit more assistance over and above the schoolwide interventions. Tier 2 interventions are designed for students who have received two to five office discipline referrals (ODRs) for behavioral issues. These students need more interventions, such as a social skills group or a check-in/check-out system.

Tier 3 at the top of the triangle (typically red) reflects the most intensive interventions for students with the highest level of need. Generally, Tier 3 interventions are used with about 5 percent of the school population. The students at Tier 3 require focused one-on-one interventions to learn expected school behaviors.

Outcomes Supported by Three Integrated Elements

The overarching goals for schools are to ensure the academic success and the social competence of all students. In the PBIS system, three integrated elements support the outcomes for social competence:

1. **Data to support decision making.** Data are used to develop plans and actions that respond to what is really occurring in the school rather than reaching at straws and saying things like, "I am pretty sure most of our students have never had a referral," or, "He said at the staff meeting that things are going well, so they must be." Data that are kept current provide a real-time look at your school climate.

Figure 1.2

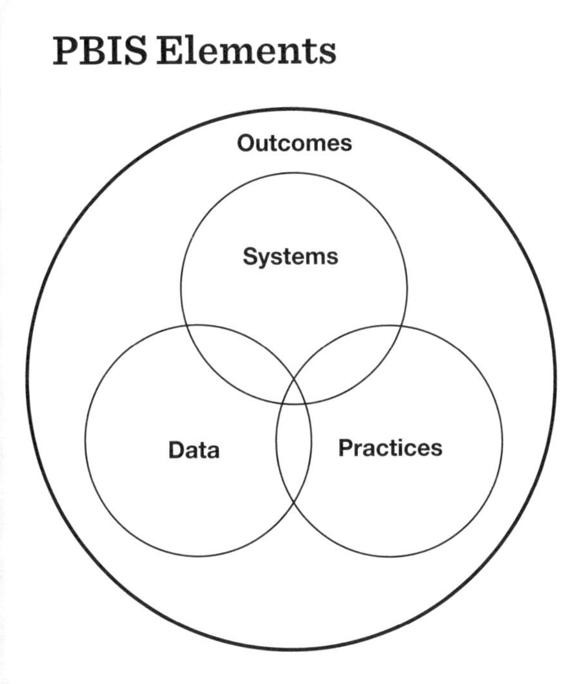

2. **Practices to support student behavior.** Expectations for student behavior are developed and clearly communicated to all students. Along with this, practices are in place for preventing students' disruptive behaviors from erupting in class or in the hallways, and for reinforcing positive behaviors.

3. **Systems to support staff behavior.** Staff are trained to prevent many student behavioral problems as well as to deal with disruptive behaviors in a more proactive and positive manner. Systems infrastructure includes creating routines that support and sustain new adult behavior.

These three elements are key to having a behaviorial model that is effective, efficient, and relevant. **Figure 1.2** illustrates the way they interact to produce positive outcomes.

How Is PBIS Implemented?

Anyone who has ever tried to make big changes or adopt new practices in a school knows that it is a complex process. An entire body of science has evolved that studies adoption and implementation of evidence-based practices across the fields of education, social services, medicine, and business. Today, the National Implementation Research Network (NIRN) offers a valuable resource to those who want to know more about the implementation science of evidence-based practices.

The new implementation science gives us an important perspective regarding the work we are doing. First, the process of adopting a new system of practice—no matter how popular—tends to take up to three to five years or more. From the onset, schools must make a long-term commitment to change.

The second big idea from the implementation science is that system change occurs in stages leading to full implementation. The stages portray implementation as a process rather than an event. This means that adoption occurs in a progressive, if not uneven, trend. This dimensional approach has implications for what we do as leaders, coaches, and team members. Understanding this progressive evolution of implementation helps us develop specific tasks for those involved in introducing and using PBIS in schools. The process, then, requires ongoing attention, commitment of resources, and *patience*. In Minnesota, where we work, administrators and schools are advised from the moment of PBIS application that they need to understand and commit to a multiyear process.

The following list summarizes the five stages schools move through as they plan for and then begin using PBIS in their buildings. Each chapter in Part 2 of this book details one of the five stages of PBIS implementation.

1. **Exploration and adoption:** Learning more about PBIS and whether it would be a good fit for your school. Does your school need it? How could it be helpful?

2. **Installation:** Getting commitments from your district, your school administration, and your school staff; setting up your PBIS Leadership Team and defining leadership and coaching roles; setting up a data management system such as Schoolwide Information System (SWIS) or another way to track office discipline referrals; choosing a universal, or schoolwide, social skills curriculum or teaching methods.

> The process of adopting a new system of practice—no matter how popular—tends to take up to three to five years or more.

3. **Initial implementation:** Training school staff and students, collecting baseline data, putting minimal features in place—such as teaching behavioral expectations schoolwide and setting up the behavioral referral process. The PBIS Leadership Team collects baseline data and starts completing the Team Implementation Checklist and setting some action plan steps.
4. **Full implementation:** All universal, or Tier 1, components are now operating completely. Behavioral expectations are taught schoolwide and the PBIS Leadership Team meets on a regular basis. At this point, districts may consider expanding PBIS to other schools.
5. **Sustainability and continuous improvement:** PBIS has become common practice, which is reflected in school or district policy and visibility. Schools have implemented systems that ensure continuous adaptation to fit local changes, while maintaining fidelity.

Who Is Involved with PBIS?

PBIS is a schoolwide initiative. This means that every adult on staff who encounters students during the school day—from hall monitors to teachers and administrators—is trained in using PBIS practices so that students receive the same message consistently in all school settings. Successful implementation of PBIS relies on at least 80 percent agreement from staff, or what we refer to as "staff buy-in." Buy-in is an important and constant consideration, both while PBIS is being implemented and during later stages in which sustainability and improvement are the focus.

When schools decide to implement PBIS, a coach and a representative PBIS Leadership Team are chosen to ensure that the practices of PBIS are being used with fidelity across all school settings. The coach might be a general or special education teacher, behavior specialist, school psychologist, social worker, counselor, or administrator. The PBIS Leadership Team should be composed of a cross-section of staff in your building.

Administrators, in particular, play a key role in providing leadership and garnering initial and long-term support for PBIS. This support takes many forms—including financial support for substitute teachers, full-time equivalent (FTE) staff allocations for coaches and for others in key roles, and public support for the initiative and its successes within the district and community. Indeed, systems change becomes possible in a school only when it is backed by a larger network of support.

Figure 1.3 identifies the essential components and their organization in a complete PBIS system. The chart can serve as a blueprint for teams at various levels—the school, district, region, state, and beyond. This graphic provides a macro look at the various school-based system components that need to be in place to support and sustain PBIS.

So how would this graphic organizer apply to a school team? Notice that the PBIS Leadership Team is at the center. This is consistent with PBIS being a team-implemented framework. As implementation progresses, the PBIS Leadership Team needs to address several supportive systems; these are situated along the top of the diagram:

- **Funding** at the school and district level is critical. The PBIS Leadership Team develops a plan to ensure ongoing funding.
- **Visibility** is crucial to telling your story from beginning to end: to staff in your school; to your district administration; to the school board, PTO, community, and so on.
- **Political support** refers to embedding the PBIS framework into the structure of the school and district so that key stakeholders support it.
- **Policy** includes multiple levels, from revising local school policies around discipline and behavior to districtwide changes. We have seen district PBIS Leadership Teams work to adopt a uniform referral form and policy across all schools, integrating PBIS with other systems such as RTI (response to intervention) or multi-tiered system of supports (MTSS) and maintaining core features for sustainability.

The bottom set of boxes in Figure 1.3 refer to the components that must be developed and maintained at all levels, and particularly at the school level:

- **Training** includes the installation of the framework initially, as well as the development of internal capacity to train new staff and students.

Figure 1.3

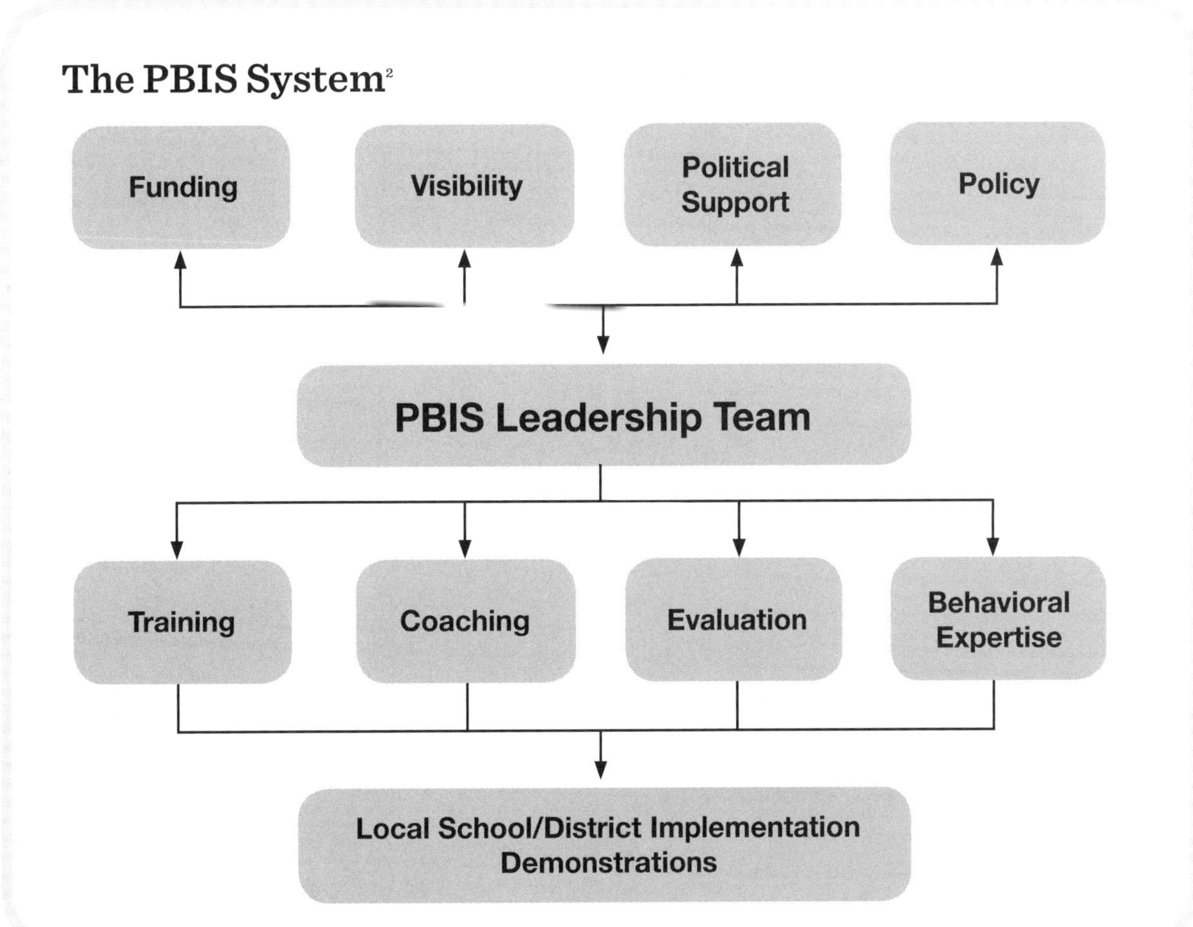

[2]From *Implementation Blueprint and Self-Assessment* developed by the National Technical Assistance Center on PBIS, 2010.

- **Coaching** is essential to ensure that the knowledge acquired through training is applied accurately. We know from research that transfer of knowledge to the classroom level is accomplished most effectively when coaching is part of the process. Administrators need to focus on ensuring that PBIS coaches or those who provide the essential coaching functions are allocated the time, FTE, to accomplish the work, including training and development.
- **Evaluation** is a core feature of PBIS implementation and sustainability. Each school must ensure that routines for collecting and using data accurately in decision making are established and that they become a permanent feature.
- **Behavioral expertise** is necessary; schools and PBIS Leadership Teams must have staff with the specialist knowledge and skill to apply to all tiers of intervention.

All parts of this system are needed to ensure that PBIS is completely functional and sustainable. At the end of implementation, your school may be the "model of demonstration" site for your district. Keep this graphic in mind as you begin the early stages of implementation, when it is easy to lose sight of the big picture and be consumed by the initial steps.

What Type of Training Is Involved?

Most states have PBIS training sites, mostly housed in departments of education or large universities. Some states use the "cohort method," in which districts apply to the cohort and are trained over a one- or two-year period. Some states primarily train coaches, or coaches and administrators. Other states offer a variety of training opportunities for coaches to continue the process of implementing and sustaining PBIS. Still other districts conduct trainings on their own without the benefit of a large organization to turn to for PBIS training knowledge and experience. If you are interested in formal PBIS training (which we recommend), start with your state department of education or do an Internet search for PBIS and your state.

What Type of Funding Is Required?

Funding needs vary from district to district. When your school or district makes a decision to implement the PBIS framework, contact the PBIS centers in your state to learn about funding requirements. Some expenses might include the cost of training as well as manuals, guest teachers for the PBIS Leadership Team attending training, planning time for the Leadership Team, release time to prepare lesson plans for teaching schoolwide expectations, incentives for a reinforcement or reward program, and general office supplies. Some schools also purchase a curriculum for Tier 1 interventions, such as Second Step or Responsive Classroom (Developmental Designs for middle school students), to integrate within the framework. In addition, your school may decide to use a Web-based data collection system, such as SWIS (see page 74), that requires a subscription fee.

What Are the Expected Outcomes of PBIS?

Having good behavioral *systems* and disciplinary *practices* in place, and using *data* to confirm or deny your hunches will create outcomes that every school wants to see: improved social and behavioral competence and improved academic achievement. Schools that use the PBIS framework see a decrease in the number of office discipline referrals (ODRs) and suspensions and an increase in academic achievement. Teachers have more time to teach, students have more time to learn, and administrators have more time to run the school rather than spending their days dealing with behaviors. All of this improves favorability with stakeholders and the surrounding community.

Teachers and staff also may experience their schools and their students in a different way. Beth recalls talking with a middle school teacher whose school was in its second year of PBIS implementation. She had been ready to resign her position and leave the field of teaching altogether when her school adopted PBIS. But using PBIS completely changed her experience in the classroom and her view of her career because she was given the tools to work with disruptive students. Now she is recommitted to her profession and reenergized in her work with students. Stories like this from teachers and administrators are common and, though anecdotal, they represent the powerful potential of PBIS in preventing or slowing staff turnover, which remains a huge challenge for schools.

Resource

The website www.pbis.org, developed and maintained by the OSEP Technical Assistance Center on PBIS, offers PowerPoints and training videos you can use for personal and professional development in PBIS.

Chapter 2
The PBIS Leadership Team

Implementing and sustaining PBIS schoolwide occurs through the guidance and actions of a leadership team dedicated to this purpose. It is therefore critical to develop a strong team in which members are knowledgeable in PBIS practices; are enthusiastic, motivated advocates of this behavioral approach; and possess a variety of skills and attributes that will contribute to the team's effective function. You can find a wealth of information on general leadership team functioning from the literature in the fields of education, business, and health care. All agree that well-functioning teams are imperative for success.

Successful implementation requires a hands-on PBIS Leadership Team that is dedicated to doing the work involved with PBIS.

When a building's PBIS Leadership Team is well developed and well coached, the tasks associated with initial implementation are divided among team members. In many cases, someone on the building's staff performs the PBIS Leadership Team coaching function; however, this does not mean that the coach becomes the only face of PBIS in the school—nor does he or she do all of the work involved. We have seen coaches become experts in PBIS, and, when their leadership team meets, members remain somewhat dependent on the coach and hesitant to take responsibility for tasks, while the coach's to-do list becomes unmanageable. Then, if the coach leaves the building or burns out from shouldering so much of the responsibility for PBIS, the team flounders. For this reason, successful implementation requires a hands-on PBIS Leadership Team that is dedicated to doing the work involved with PBIS.

This chapter provides information on setting up a PBIS Leadership Team in your school. We describe how the team operates to guide the implementation process, and we detail the specific role that administrators play in PBIS implementation. Because the PBIS coach is so critical to success, we devote another whole chapter to this role; see Chapter 3 for more information about PBIS coaching.

Role of the PBIS Leadership Team

The PBIS Leadership Team is responsible for implementing PBIS throughout the school. This group tackles many of the foundational, behind-the-scenes tasks and decisions that determine how PBIS will function in a specific school building. For example, the leadership team works to create a list of behavioral expectations for all students and sets the pace of implementation.

The team ensures that school staff are trained to teach behavioral expectations to students and that staff are successfully using PBIS. Team members continually evaluate and improve PBIS practices, and they inform others about their work. At least once a month, the team holds a staff presentation to share data and give a general update on PBIS implementation. The team may also communicate outcomes to the school board, the district administration, and the wider school community, including families. In short, the leadership team serves as the public face of PBIS and provides the momentum to sustain its practices over the long term.

Figure 2.1 illustrates the main goals and tasks of the PBIS Leadership Team. (This graphic is included in the Implementation Blueprint as well as in other resources on the PBIS website, www.pbis.org.) Note the team's primary functions: making agreements; creating a data-based action plan; implementing the plan; and evaluating implementation, fidelity, and outcomes. **Figure 2.2** summarizes the key responsibilities of the administrator, the coach, and the other members of the PBIS Leadership Team.

Figure 2.1

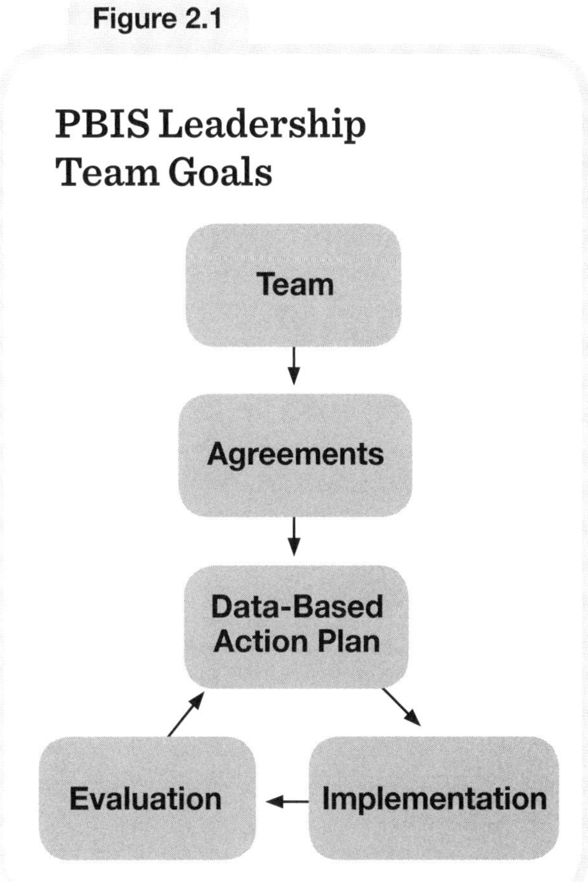

Figure 2.2

Key Responsibilities and Tasks for PBIS Leadership Team Members

Role	Key Responsibilities	Tasks Involved
Administrator	Actively supports PBIS	• Publically states support for PBIS with stakeholders: entire staff, district, families, and community • Dedicates financial and practical resources to implementing and sustaining PBIS
	Supports PBIS as a priority	• Identifies PBIS within the top three priorities for school improvement • Documents this priority in the written plan, newsletters, etc.

continued →

Figure 2.2

Key Responsibilities and Tasks for PBIS Leadership Team Members, continued

Role	Key Responsibilities	Tasks Involved
Administrator (continued)	Attends PBIS Leadership Team meetings regularly	• Attends most meetings • Shares leadership • Supports coach and others • Implements decisions • Funds startup costs
	Ensures that the PBIS Leadership Team meets regularly	• Provides resources (release time, paid time, space, and materials) • Encourages team to schedule meetings to present progress to others
Coach	Assists the team's implementation of the elements of PBIS	• Recognizes missteps taken by the team and works to get back on course • Collects, understands, and uses data • Assesses fidelity
Rest of the team	Is organized and meets regularly	• Identifies essential roles: team lead, note-taker, time-keeper, data resource person, etc. • Sets calendar dates and times for a full year's worth of meetings • Uses an action plan and determines accountabilities for who, what, how, and when tasks will be completed • Documents decisions (in meeting minutes)
	Uses data to make decisions	• Accesses and uses data that measure progress toward implementation • Reviews data at the beginning of each meeting • Uses student data (office discipline referrals, or ODRs) to identify school needs, to guide problem solving and action planning, and to reevaluate actions and outcomes • Adopts a routine for reviewing implementation and outcomes regularly throughout the year
	Presents data to staff and community	• Plans frequent opportunities to demonstrate progress and outcomes • Frequently solicits staff and parent input • Sets up regular presentations to school board, PTO, and other essential groups

Role of Building Administrators in PBIS Implementation

Building administrators are key to successful implementation of PBIS. Research clearly demonstrates how important administrative support is for implementing and sustaining PBIS.[3] What's more, new research on staff investment in PBIS tells us that administrator influence is essential if we want staff to adopt PBIS initiatives.[4] Schools trying to implement PBIS without administrative leadership often struggle to get staff members on board. Principals who communicate the need for PBIS and the value of PBIS to their school community will have a grateful PBIS Leadership Team.

Commitment and Support

Having the administration on board provides the backbone needed to rally the staff in using positive behavioral procedures. For some teachers, moving to a proactive behavioral strategy from a reactive strategy represents a huge shift in the way that they manage challenging behaviors. According to Kevin Filter's research, the level of staff buy-in is directly related to the way in which each staff member perceives the administrator's ability to successfully create and support change.[5]

Administrators can show their commitment to change by identifying PBIS as one of the top three priorities for school improvement (in written plans, newsletters, and so on) and by acknowledging that it takes three to five years to fully implement the first tier of PBIS. In addition, budgetary support is essential for success. Administrators must secure adequate full-time equivalent (FTE) staff allocations for a coach and leadership team members. In our experience, many coaches are recruited or assigned responsibilities but nothing is removed from their other assignments. Coaches and team members need their workloads rebalanced in order to successfully carry out their PBIS responsibilities.

One thing that we appreciate about supportive administrators is how their involvement keeps the momentum of implementation rolling. When Beth was working as a coach, decisions could be made easily at her school because the principal was an active participant in PBIS meetings and played a role in the decision making. Beth knew that PBIS would be in the school for the long haul when the principal took responsibility for announcing to the staff the new practices that were being implemented. Staff could voice their discontent and they would have discussions, but the principal always made the final decision based on what she thought was best for the school.

Support for Coaches

If a coach is a building-based coach, the role and functions will take more time in the early stages of implementation than later, depending on how stable the process is and how well responsibilities are being shared among team members. Though it's difficult to estimate, some coaches have told us they need anywhere from one-third to a full day per week to carry out their PBIS assigned tasks and responsibilities.

District-level coaches (sometimes called external coaches) are often half- to full time, and they usually manage PBIS implementation in several schools. District-level staffing decisions should be based on the stages of implementation at various schools. Early stages require much more time and energy. Schools that have used PBIS for many years may have had significant turnover and dropped off course; consequently, they can often be thought of as new and emerging schools. Administrators should ensure that district-level coaches have a "mixed caseload" of schools representing a spectrum of needs and intensity.

As a coordinator and regional coach, Char worked with new coaches and planned coach trainings each year. One of the biggest obstacles she saw for coaches was the lack of time allocated to learn about PBIS, to develop skills, and to complete their tasks. See Chapter 3 for more details about the role of coaches.

[3]Coffrey and Horner, 2012.
[4]Filter and Sytsma, 2013.
[5]Ibid.

Staff Development, Training, and Resources

Another way for the administration to show commitment to PBIS is to provide staff development time for the PBIS Leadership Team to attend trainings. Building administrators should also explain to all staff why preventing negative behavior is good for the school in the long run and educate all staff about the need for universal (schoolwide) intervention—PBIS Tier 1. Administrators must then be committed to training the whole staff on Tier 1 universal interventions. When resources are required—such as release time, paid time, space, and materials—administrators must take the lead to fulfill these needs.

Presenting Team's Progress to the School

As implementation continues, administrators encourage the PBIS Leadership Team to present progress to the school faculty. For example, the team could do a presentation on data findings for office discipline referrals (ODRs). Or team members might present progress to district administration.

Communication

In the first stages of implementation, the administrator should support the PBIS initiative publically with verbal, written, and visual statements. This support for PBIS should be evident to the entire staff, to the district, to families, and to the community. As implementation continues, the building administrator also plays a key role in communicating success with PBIS to the district as well as the community. This might mean speaking at school board meetings and open houses where the outside community is invited in. It also includes written statements in newsletters and on the school or district website.

Participation

Building administrators may want to create an action plan for their participation in the PBIS implementation process. The plan can serve not only to guide their own actions but also to support future administrators who may replace them. Active participation is a key way for administrators to demonstrate their commitment and support to the team.

The building administrator actively participates in PBIS training and leadership meetings, attending as often as possible. In addition, administrators can help by visiting classrooms and observing the practices of PBIS in action. These visits enable administrators to identify which teachers may be struggling with classroom management and may be in need of coaching.

Leadership

Successful implementation of PBIS relies on influence from the building administration, mainly the principal. The principal guides the school in meeting yearly improvement plans and district-level initiatives. Sometimes principals make choices that are not popular with many staff but are good for the school as a whole. One school social worker told us of a time when her principal freed up a teacher from her daily advisory to do PBIS duties (managing the weekly "Caught You Doing Good" tickets and operating the school reward store). Other teachers thought this was unfair—they had to take on the other teacher's advisory students—but the principal felt this was important to keep PBIS on track. In the end, others could see the value of this decision, and, to help them feel appreciated, the principal thanked the other teachers for their understanding and their help in taking on the additional work.

Principals inevitably face teachers and other staff members who have philosophical objections to PBIS or who wonder if PBIS is even necessary. Schools that have not successfully implemented PBIS may cite a lack of leadership from building administration, and even district administration, as a reason for its failing. Academic success and test scores often take precedence over other initiatives, such as reducing suspensions and decreasing challenging behaviors. All of these challenges point to the need for administrators to take an active leadership role in PBIS implementation.

Staff need to feel secure when asked to make a major systems change, going from a punitive discipline structure to one where we teach students not just reading and math skills, but also behavioral skills as a way to prevent disruptions to academic learning. According to researcher Sharon Lohrmann, when principals have difficulty leading a school through changes to the system, staff members often react with defensiveness, passivity, negativity, and unwillingness to collaborate.[6]

Building principals need to be openly committed to PBIS. Staff members need to see the principal as an active participant on the PBIS team. They also need to see the principal hold all staff members accountable for implementing Tier 1 interventions. In all these ways, principals set the stage for successful PBIS implementation by being leaders.

Forming the Rest of the PBIS Leadership Team

Once the administrator is on board with PBIS, the next step is to complete an audit of the other teams in your building. This is one way to work smarter, not harder. Consider all of the committees and groups currently meeting in your school to ensure that the PBIS Leadership Team will integrate efficiently with the other teams and not duplicate what they are trying to achieve. For example, take a close look at committees such as the Sunshine Club, Professional Learning Committee, and Character Education Committee, if you have these. Perhaps the goals or makeup of some of these groups could be changed up a bit, or eliminated altogether, to free up staff to join the PBIS Leadership Team.

To help assess the other teams in your building, complete the **Audit of Existing School Committees and Initiatives** matrix on page 22. List all of your school's committees and groups, and the purpose of each. Consider eliminating committees that do not support your school improvement plan or combining committees with similar functions to free up staff time and increase participation on the PBIS Leadership Team. A word of caution: This process, though logical, takes time to complete in a thoughtful way; be sure to gather staff buy-in and support for changes to existing committees

What Is the Ideal Team Size and Length of Service?

We are often asked how big the PBIS Leadership Team should be. Sometimes the team size is dictated by the training organization. Keep in mind that as group size increases, so do group dynamics and complexity. Here are a few findings from research on group size:[7]

1. Larger groups require more structure.
2. Ideal group size is five to seven.
3. Groups that are too small (fewer than five) may have limited viewpoints and lack the critical mass to achieve the best outcome.
4. Ideal size for decision making and problem solving may be groups of seven to fifteen.
5. Other research argues in favor of small groups (three to five or two to three) rather than individual problem solving.

However large or small you decide to make your PBIS Leadership Team, understand the advantages and disadvantages of various group sizes. If you have a larger team, provide the structure and facilitation needed and consider forming subgroups for specific purposes.

Generally, team members agree to be part of the team for at least three years—long enough to become fluent and effective. You may want to consider a staggered rotation so that the entire team does not turn over at once. Expect, however, that there will be turnover that is not planned, as well. Be proactive in establishing a plan for who, how, and when new team members will receive essential training to assume new roles.

[6] Lohrmann, et al., 2008.
[7] Romano and Nunamaker, 2001.

Audit of Existing School Committees and Initiatives

List *all* of your current building committees and initiatives and fill in the columns for each. Then review the results and answer the questions that follow the chart.

Committee or Initiative Name	Research- or Evidence-Based?	Purpose?	Promotes Safe Schools or Academic Achievement?	Possible to Combine, Tweak, or Eliminate?
	Yes No		Yes No	Yes No
	Yes No		Yes No	Yes No
	Yes No		Yes No	Yes No
	Yes No		Yes No	Yes No
	Yes No		Yes No	Yes No
	Yes No		Yes No	Yes No

What committees or initiatives duplicate efforts?

What committees could be combined, refocused, or eliminated?

Make an action plan page to track your next steps.

Who Should Be on the Team?

The PBIS Leadership Team typically includes the building administrator, a designated PBIS coach, and other team members. The administrator takes on the task of inviting staff to be on the PBIS team, identifying an effective, representative group of individuals who will work well together. He or she identifies who will be the building's PBIS coach and carefully chooses staff from a wide spectrum of individuals. Because PBIS is a true schoolwide initiative, the team should be made up of a cross-section of school personnel and community members, including:

- general and special education teachers
- behavior specialists
- paraprofessionals
- school psychologists and social workers
- counselors
- office staff
- hall monitors
- librarians and media specialists
- athletic coaches and directors
- custodians
- food service staff
- bus drivers
- students
- parents and guardians*

Ideally, your PBIS Leadership Team will reflect the race and ethnicity of students in your building. In addition to representing a cross-section of staff and community, consider individuals based on their skill set, their ability to work together as a group, and their motivation level. Potential team members may volunteer, or the administrator may recruit people according to what and how they will contribute to the purpose and desired outcomes of PBIS. For example, someone might be good with numbers, be loyal to the school, possess excellent classroom

The administrator takes on the task of inviting staff to be on the PBIS team, identifying an effective, representative group of individuals who will work well together.

management skills, have knowledge of behavioral programs, or be well-connected to the students. One administrator invited the teacher who wrote the most office discipline referrals to serve on the PBIS team, and he ended up loving the experience. While the staff was initially surprised to see him on the team, they eagerly welcomed him and he proved to be an invaluable team member. What's more, his response to behavioral disruptions in his classroom became more proactive as a result of his time on the leadership team.

One benefit of having team members from across your school setting is that it increases the buy-in from all areas of the building and ensures that voices from all disciplines will be heard. This is important because the needs of physical education teachers may be different from the needs of language arts teachers, which may be different from the needs of people who work in the office. Never assume that you know the needs of all areas of the school. When having discussions about handling voice levels in the classroom, for example, we may discover that the math teachers want more quiet, while the science teachers allow kids to be louder.

As you build your PBIS Leadership Team, its membership may change as the school year progresses and certainly from year to year. Building the team is a process that takes time; these teams develop into effective working groups through a series of phases. (For more on these phases, see "Getting Started as a Team" on page 24.)

Key Expertise Needed

Be sure someone on your PBIS team can provide *behavioral expertise*, especially as the team considers interventions that move from Tier 1 to

*Due to confidentiality, when student or staff names are going to be discussed at a PBIS Leadership Team meeting, parents and guardians should not be in attendance.

Tiers 2 and 3. This could be the school psychologist, school social worker or counselor, or an experienced special education teacher. The team will benefit from this expertise during discussions of behaviors, such as determining the function of a student's behavior or designing interventions to decrease disruptive behaviors and improve a student's repertoire of acceptable behaviors.

Allow all voices to be heard, share options and opinions, and resolve to make a decision.

Your team should also identify someone who will take responsibility for *handling data tasks related to PBIS surveys and other assessments.* Currently, districts are encouraged to identify a person who can fulfill this role and serve as the PBIS assessment coordinator for all schools in the district. Schools interested in using the PBIS assessment tools should contact their state PBIS Leadership Team to identify the local assessment coordinator. The local coordinator provides schools with an individual school identification number, which enables any team member to log into the PBIS website (www.pbisapps.org) and review the school's data for all PBIS assessment tools.

In addition, designate one PBIS Leadership Team member—often the coach—who is willing to take responsibility for *assisting your school in using PBIS assessment tools and data* for active problem solving, measuring progress, assessing fidelity, and identifying supports needed for sustaining PBIS. We encourage coaches to infect their colleagues with an insatiable curiosity about the data on progress, fidelity, and outcomes so that multiple members of the team become data experts and use it frequently to track their school's implementation.

Getting Started as a Team

Once the PBIS Leadership Team members have been identified and have made a commitment to the process, it's time to build a cohesive group by creating shared agreements, particularly when it comes to running meetings and making decisions. The following ten tasks should be decided at your first meeting.

1. Develop Norms and Decision-Making Procedures

It is helpful for teams to begin with a discussion of the norms that will guide their work together. Set a regular date, time, and place for your meetings (such as every other Monday at 7:00 in Ms. Nelson's room). The facilitator should set the agenda and send it out ahead of time so members can come prepared. Besides these logistics, decide how you will run your meetings (for example, how to deal with disagreements, keep the workload equitable, and celebrate progress together).

You'll also want to determine how you will make decisions. There are many ways to do this, so be sure to discuss the options as a team. Establish whether you will use full consensus (everyone agrees wholeheartedly), working consensus (everyone agrees but some members may have reservations), majority vote, fist-to-five consensus building, or something else. Each method has pros and cons, but defining how decisions will be made from the start will likely help move your team along when it is faced with making a controversial decision for your school. Allow all voices to be heard, share options and opinions, and resolve to make a decision. To record the norms you establish, see page 32 for a reproducible sample form titled **Routines for Conducting Effective and Efficient Meetings.**

At your first PBIS team meeting, you might establish ground rules such as the following:

- Meetings will start and stop on time.
- Facilitator will run the meeting.

- Notes will be taken on action items, not on people.
- Use "I statements."
- Everyone gets a turn to speak.
- Be open to new ideas.
- It's okay to disagree.
- Maintain meeting confidentiality—be careful about sharing staff or student names outside of the meeting.

Some teams create a matrix for detailing members' behavior, which is another way of establishing operating norms and behavioral expectations. Imagine practicing in words and actions what you may be doing with students, as shown in **Figure 2.3**.

Resource

The Florida PBIS network has a whole set of resources to help leadership teams and coaches handle the common challenges that arise in group work. See flpbs.fmhi.usf.edu.

Figure 2.3

Sample PBIS Leadership Team Behavior Matrix

Respect, Learning, and Responsibility

PBIS team members model respect.	• Smile, be friendly, and greet each other. • Listen to others' ideas, saving questions and comments until they have finished speaking. • Stay on task. • Be on time and attend at least 80 percent of team meetings.
PBIS team members model learning.	• Be open to new ideas. • Participate in professional development opportunities. • Share articles pertinent to team discussions.
PBIS team members model responsibility.	• Be an active participant—volunteer, offer to help others. • Meet action plan deadlines.

PBIS Leadership Teams and the TIPS Model

As you form your PBIS Leadership Team, consider adopting Team-Initiated Problem Solving (TIPS). This research-based approach to problem solving at the team level includes a model for establishing effective teams, which you can integrate into the development of your PBIS team. A school using TIPS receives additional training on how to follow prescribed meeting foundations, which outline the roles, responsibilities, procedures, and follow-up for effective, efficient meetings. The goal is to ensure that meetings have predictability, participation, accountability, and communication. TIPS also includes an electronic system for recording meeting minutes. For a more detailed discussion of TIPS, see Chapter 5.

2. Establish Team Roles and Responsibilities

Team meetings are more effective, efficient, and organized when roles and responsibilities are clearly defined and shared. Begin with identifying team members to take on the following roles:

- **Team leader or facilitator:** someone skilled in running meetings and handling issues that are common in group work.
- **Note-Taker** (or at least decision-recorder): someone skilled at taking thorough, accurate notes and who will follow through with sending the notes to all team members in a timely manner—no more than two days after the meeting. These can be shared in a variety of ways, including Dropbox, wikis, or Google Drive.
- **Timekeeper:** a team member who ensures that meetings start and stop on schedule.
- **Data manager:** a person with data expertise who is responsible for verifying that data are being collected and recorded consistently and accurately. This person should bring current referral data to the meetings. (Alternatively, you might opt to create a subteam to handle the task of managing data.)
- **Archivist:** someone who collects and stores meeting notes and photos to tell the school's PBIS story.

3. Schedule Regular Meetings

Try to schedule meetings for the whole year up front. It's easier to reschedule than to find time once the school year has begun. In our experience, new teams frequently meet biweekly. Whatever meeting schedule you choose, try to make the process predictable and productive. You are creating the structural support for ongoing action. Start and end on time and take attendance.

4. Establish a Meeting Agenda

Many teams create a standing agenda, which reflects regular topics that are pertinent to early phases of implementation. (For a template, see the reproducible **PBIS Leadership Team Meeting Agenda** on pages 28–29.) Well in advance of each meeting, share the specific agenda with team members and solicit their input. This allows time to modify the agenda as needed. It may be helpful to differentiate topics on the agenda; for example, some items might be purely informational while others need to be discussed or a decision might be required on the topic. Also consider setting timelines or limits for each topic.

Note to Administrators

Consider adding a PBIS implementation update as a regular agenda item for full staff meetings each month. This is a good way to inform your colleagues and staff about the progress of PBIS. You may use this time to celebrate successes or to gather new ideas for preventing disruptive classroom behaviors. The PBIS Leadership Team can speak at staff meetings, letting staff know about upcoming new systems or practices. For example, if the PBIS Leadership Team would like to implement a monthly honoring ceremony for the whole school, use this meeting time to gauge the interest of staff and get their input to work out some of the details about how to select students.

Coach's Tip from Beth

Be proactive in prompting team members about upcoming topics by sending out the meeting agenda well ahead of time. This helps develop continuity and accountability. When team members know that one of the tasks they are responsible for will be discussed at a meeting, they are more likely to come to the meeting prepared to give an update on the item delegated to them.

5. Effectively Facilitate Meetings

Ensure that whoever leads or facilitates PBIS Leadership Team meetings has skills in running meetings and handling common issues in group work. We all know what it's like to be in a meeting that fails to cover the agenda or achieve actions items, gets hijacked by off-topic items, or otherwise gets derailed. The leadership team norms you establish should emphasize a shared approach with group accountability. For a sample procedural checklist for conducting meetings, see the reproducible **PBIS Leadership Team Meeting Checklist** on pages 30–31. This checklist has been developed to help you prepare for, conduct, and evaluate meetings. In addition, the reproducible **Routines for Conducting Effective and Efficient Meetings** on page 32 helps ensure that meetings are successful.

6. Use Data-Based Problem Solving at Each Meeting

Using data should be an active part of your PBIS Leadership Team meetings and the team's work in general. As noted on page 26, we recommend that you designate a team member to serve as your data manager or assign a subteam to take on this role. However, as a group, you will still be interacting with data and building a decision system that relies on data. Indeed, data should inform *all* of your PBIS decisions and practices. The team, with help from the coach and data manager, has the challenge of becoming fluent in understanding the various classes of data and the tools that measure effort, fidelity, and outcomes. At all times, team members need to feel that they have ready access to this information.

Effective use of data is a large part of the team's responsibilities from the very beginning, when you collect baseline data to garner buy-in from other school staff. As the process of implementation moves forward, the team continues to collect, analyze, and use data to determine next steps and to communicate progress to other staff, to administrators, and to the larger community. See Chapter 4 to learn about specific data tools and resources.

As you work to improve the behavioral climate in your building, staff will need to have bold conversations about school—the environment, student and staff demographics and relationships, and schoolwide systems and practices. Looking at data can open some wounds, but it can also eventually heal them. See Chapter 5 to learn more about effective data-based decision making.

7. Develop an Action Plan and Meeting Summary

Be sure to document the decisions and tasks that are generated in team meetings, as well as the tasks that have been completed. Having all of the activities of your PBIS Leadership Team in one document keeps key players responsible and provides an easy way to monitor and manage the implementation activities. **Figure 2.4** on page 33 shows a sample action plan; notice that the first action item lists department chairs as well as PBIS team members as being responsible for establishing professional learning communities (PLCs). Sharing responsibility in this way invests your whole school in PBIS implementation. Also, note how this action plan is rooted in the eight key features of the PBIS framework listed on page 9 in Chapter 1. This keeps the team focused on PBIS and avoids taking on action items that are not part of that mission.

PBIS Leadership Team Meeting Agenda

Date:______________________________

Meeting facilitator: ______________________________

Note-taker: ______________________________

Time keeper: ______________________________

Attendees: ______________________________

Review Time Allotted: __________

Things Going Well		**Critical Issues and Concerns**	
Topic	Data	Topic	Data

continued →

PBIS Leadership Team Meeting Agenda, continued

Action Items Time Allotted: __________

Item	Action Plan/Responsible Person/Due Date
Data review (ODRs, suspensions)	
Progress toward meeting previous action items	
Follow-up from previous action items	
Additional items	

Next meeting date and time: ______________________________

Next meeting facilitator: ______________________________

PBIS Leadership Team Meeting Checklist

Preparing for the Meeting	
Person Responsible:	
	Review agreements and tasks from previous minutes.
	Identify/review/develop agenda items.
	Invite/remind/prepare participants.
	Prepare/review materials.
	Check/confirm logistics (e.g., room, location, time).
Opening the Meeting	
Person Responsible:	
	Acknowledge/introduce participants.
	Review meeting purpose.
	Review/assign roles.
	Review/modify agenda items (e.g., discussion, decision, information).
	Assign number of minutes for each agenda item.
	Set/review meeting rules and routines.
	Other:
Conducting Business	
Person Responsible:	
	Follow agenda items.
	Stay within timelines.
	Follow/review rules and routines.
	Restate/review/remind others of each agenda item's purpose or outcome.
	Other:

continued →

PBIS Leadership Team Meeting Checklist, continued

Concluding the Meeting	
Person Responsible:	
	Review meeting purpose.
	Review/summarize agreements and tasks.
	Evaluate extent to which agenda items were addressed.
	Review new agenda items.
	Review compliance with rules and routines.
	Acknowledge/reinforce participation, actions, and outcomes.
	Indicate next meeting date, time, and place.
	Other:

Following Up	
Person Responsible:	
	Distribute minutes.
	Complete agreements and tasks.
	Contact/remind participants.
	Prepare for next agenda.
	Other:

Other Notes/Observations

Routines for Conducting Effective and Efficient Meetings

As you establish group norms, use the following chart to record your team's decisions about how meetings will be conducted and problems solved.

1. How are decisions made?
2. How are problems, conflicts, and disagreements to be resolved or processed?
3. How are roles and responsibilities (such as leadership/facilitation, recording minutes, reporting) assigned and conducted?
4. How is participation encouraged and reinforced?

Coach's Tip from Beth

When I started with PBIS, I tried to implement everything that our school was missing from the list of critical elements all at the same time. Many projects got started, memos were written, promises were made . . . and not much was implemented well. Overloading your team with too many things creates chaos and frustration. Start simple with a couple of items that can be easily accomplished, such as developing the three to five schoolwide positive behavioral expectations or creating the criteria for student of the month, and then slowly start adding other items.

8. Evaluate Team Meetings and Functioning

Build in a simple process for checking in with team members about meetings, including how efficient they think meetings are being conducted and how they think the team is functioning in general. This can be as simple as a "thumbs up–thumbs down" voting system. Also be sure to have a process for ensuring the accomplishment of action steps. See the Appendix on page 155 for more examples of how to evaluate meetings and functioning. Be open to making adaptations to improve the process. Part of this process will undoubtedly include addressing team turnover. Assume turnover will happen on the leadership team and have a plan for preparing and engaging new team members.

Figure 2.4

Sample PBIS Action Plan

Key PBIS Feature	Action/Activity	Who is responsible?	When will it be started?	When will it be completed?	When will we evaluate it?
#3	Create 3–5 schoolwide positive behavioral expectations	PBIS team Dept. chairs Admin.	ASAP	ASAP	Spring—SET evaluation
#6	Acknowledge student behavior in monthly recognition program	PBIS team Admin.	October	End of the year	Each faculty and PBIS meeting
#8	Establish data systems to monitor implementation of PBIS	Coach/data manager PBIS team Admin.	September	Ongoing—end of the year	Monthly PBIS team meetings

9. Follow-up and Next Steps

At the close of every meeting, review and summarize decisions and next steps, including assignments, due dates, and future meeting dates.

10. Celebrate and Share Successes

Though gratifying, implementing the PBIS framework is a lot of work for everyone involved. It's critical for the PBIS Leadership Team to acknowledge and celebrate the successes achieved as you advance toward full implementation. Plan celebrations to share these successes with the whole school—both staff and students.

Chapter 3
The PBIS Coach

In the world of PBIS, "coaching" refers to a set of functions that are needed to support and guide the PBIS Leadership Team and school as they work to implement and sustain the key features of PBIS. The research literature indicates that real change in classrooms is related more to "coaching" than to training alone.[8] Experts Kathy Froelich and Enrique Puig say that both the art and science of coaching are necessary for successful professional learning experiences.[9] The key functions of coaching are described in the Implementation Blueprint (see www.pbis.org) and include the skills and knowledge needed to assist PBIS Leadership Teams during initial training, implementation, and sustaining and continuous improvement phases. Coaches assist teams in adapting the PBIS framework to their particular school and in using data regularly to ensure fidelity in implementation and in achievement of outcomes.

The tasks and responsibilities of a PBIS coach may be built into existing staff positions, such as a general or special education teacher, behavior specialist, school psychologist, social worker, counselor, or administrator. This is especially true if the coach works with only one school, with time allocated to the individual who assumes those responsibilities. In other cases, these responsibilities may be assigned to a district-level coach who serves multiple buildings.

As Char describes: When I meet new coaches who are with their teams at the beginning of a two-year training process, I recognize in them both enthusiasm and a sense of anxiety. Nine years ago, when I started as a PBIS state coordinator, I had to hit the ground running. I knew a lot about PBIS for individual students and as a schoolwide system of practice, but I had a lot to do to pull that together in a meaningful way for coaches and their teams. Early on my team and I struggled to define what it meant to be a coach: *What did coaches do? Who should be a coach? What was the difference between a coach and a team leader?* In those early days, we offered meetings and networking opportunities for both coaches and team leaders. Today, we put role descriptions on our website, explain these roles at administrator meetings before schools apply, and define them again once schools have been accepted into a cohort. We urge administrators to recruit people whose skills match and strongly advocate for assignment of FTE so that coaches can be successful. Still, coaches often report that they are struggling to understand the scope of their job and what they need to be successful. So we build in ongoing training and support the entire system so that no component is standing on one leg.

In this chapter, we discuss coaching as a set of PBIS functions performed within the context of the schoolwide system.

In this chapter, we discuss coaching as a set of PBIS functions performed within the context of the schoolwide system. We describe the role and associated responsibilities, explaining

[8] Joyce and Showers, 1995.
[9] Froelich and Puig, 2007.

What a Coach Is *Not*

As we clarify the role and responsibilities of a PBIS coach, we believe it is important to identify what is *not* part of the role. First, coaches are not administrators. They do not have responsibility for personnel decisions or staff evaluations. This can get a little murky because sometimes coaches conduct various observations within the school around PBIS implementation, but this is not for purposes of evaluating staff. PBIS coaches gather and report data, and sometimes data can be associated with the school staff in sensitive ways that require thoughtfulness. While PBIS coaches do not handle personnel conflicts or performance issues, they sometimes serve as team leaders or facilitators and it is helpful if they can facilitate compromise, conflict resolution, and consensus building.

the significance of coaching for and within the schoolwide system. We also talk about what knowledge coaches need, how to continually develop as a coach, and where to find resources.

Role of the PBIS Coach

The role of the PBIS coach is interesting and challenging—an exciting career opportunity for any educator. Most of us know a little bit about coaching as it relates to sports and perhaps academic or instructional coaching or teacher mentoring. While some of the same skills apply, the PBIS coaching role is quite broad. Recall that the PBIS framework is defined as a set of practices that are applied throughout the schoolwide system. The coach thus serves not only the PBIS Leadership Team, but the entire system of the school as well. Because PBIS aims to change the system, PBIS coaches are considered change agents. Consequently, coaches benefit from a broad understanding of how systems change; from the big picture of PBIS; and from the details of process steps (such as team and action planning), practices, problem solving with data, and communication.

Basic Knowledge That Coaches Need to Be Successful

There are several possible levels of coaching in PBIS. These include a local, or Leadership Team coach, also known as an internal coach, and coaches who work at the district, regional, or state level. We will focus our discussion on the internal or school-based coaching role.

One of the main goals for a new coach is to develop a thorough knowledge of PBIS. Coaches must be able to describe to others exactly what the PBIS framework is and what it isn't. Do this by finding your own words to explain the features and implementation process of PBIS. Look at the key visuals and practice with others. You will need to relay this information again and again.

Coaches are a primary support to the PBIS Leadership Team in achieving and sustaining the major features of PBIS implementation. To educate others about PBIS, coaches should explain the features and use examples of what they look like in action. Examples can be collected either from other schools in the area that have already implemented PBIS or from websites. We have found that many coaches underutilize state and national websites as resources for their schools; numerous helpful websites are available (such as PBIS Maryland at www.pbismaryland.org).

Coach's Tip from Beth

Do not get caught up in doing too much too fast or comparing your school to another. Make sure you are monitoring your progress and ensure that your team reviews progress data when action planning and problem solving. You want to understand what your data mean and distinguish between moving slowly and being stalled.

When I was a PBIS coach, I made sure every form was filled out, every checklist completed in a timely manner; I collected surveys from staff and students to get their opinions; I sorted behavior data eight different ways and still I wasn't sure what the next step should be. I remember talking with Char about this. Char's suggestions were simple—focus only on a couple of things rather than trying to tackle everything at once.

Coaches benefit from developing confidence and gentle assertiveness to nudge team or staff members to follow through with surveys or to redirect a team that gets off course.

One key area of knowledge coaches need to cultivate and to pass onto the team relates to data resources. The PBIS initiative provides all the evaluation tools needed for successful implementation at www.pbisapps.org. Chapter 4 discusses these tools and how to use them. As you get started in your new coaching role, take time to learn about these tools and get familiar with their acronyms and abbreviations: TIC (Team Implementation Checklist), SAS (Self-Assessment Survey), SET (School-wide Evaluation Tool), BoQ (Benchmarks of Quality), ODR (Office Discipline Referral), and more. Becoming very fluent with acronyms and terminology will help you be a more effective coach who can also help team members develop a deeper understanding of the data and really use it.

Role of Administrators in Selecting and Supporting Coaches

Of course, prospective coaches need to understand the role, function, and responsibilities of the PBIS coach during the implementation process. Equally important, administrators need to understand the role, responsibilities, knowledge, skills, and competencies of a PBIS coach. Whenever possible, administrators should recruit a staff member who already possesses the knowledge and skills required for this coaching role. It is essential that administrators explain this role and function to the PBIS Leadership Team and staff at the very beginning of implementation. This paves the way for the coach to successfully lead implementation efforts.

Every school and district should ensure that it has a strong PBIS coaching system. If that sounds daunting or unfamiliar, one of the main reasons for this book is to help dispel those obstacles. Creating and supporting a strong working system at the district level is the responsibility of the district PBIS Leadership Team. (For more information, see the Implementation Blueprint at www.pbis.org).

In short, when it comes to PBIS, you need to be able to explain it, present it, teach it, model it, discuss it, and pass it on.

Skills

PBIS coaching skills include those behaviors necessary to put knowledge into action, which means you will use all of the skills you have acquired thus far working in education. In addition, since your coaching role involves coaching a system and a team rather than individuals, it would be helpful to develop or hone skills in the following areas:

1. Group facilitation (effective meetings, planning, and follow-through; knowledge of group development)
2. Conflict resolution
3. Consensus building
4. Communication (written and oral)
5. System change practices

Attributes or Personal Characteristics

Personal attributes include not only inherited traits but also learned behaviors. Being a good coach is easier if you know your strengths and are willing to build from your needs. Remember that you don't have to be born with the characteristics of a successful leader and change agent—you can actively develop them as well. As you begin, consider identifying someone in your professional life who you can count on to be honest with you. Then enroll that person as your personal mentor.

Think about the following characteristics. Which ones best describe you? Which ones do you need to develop? Ask your personal mentor to do this as well and then discuss them together.

- sociable
- patient
- flexible
- able to handle complex and ambiguous tasks
- resilient
- approachable
- trustworthy

Self-Direction

It's important for PBIS coaches to have the ability to be self-directing or self-led. In an emerging field where knowledge and application are changing, professionals such as coaches need to be able to accommodate this change. Adopt the mindset of personal continuous improvement, if you don't already possess this trait. While your environment may be resource rich, it also may not be. Even available resources may not match your particular need. The following list will help you discern where you are at as a PBIS coach and where you would like to go.

- Develop a personal mission with respect to PBIS coaching.
- Assess your knowledge, skills, and attributes (see page 43 for self-assessments).
- Develop a tangible self-improvement action plan, with goals that are achievable and measurable and with timelines that include benchmarks of achievement.
- Develop resources for your self-improvement (personal, professional, tangible, and sharable).

Responsibilities of Coaches

Guide the Team

Guiding is a key aspect of what coaches do. You will be the one who teaches and prompts the PBIS Leadership Team about all aspects of PBIS at each stage of implementation. Guiding a team while you are still learning about PBIS yourself can be a challenge; however, if you participate in an organized training program you will receive a solid foundation from experienced guides.

Clarify Concepts

As you learn the meaning of the basic PBIS concepts and terms, you will be one step ahead of your colleagues and can help them learn and integrate these terms, as well. Try to describe the concepts in your own words, but know where to find resources that can help you explain difficult concepts and that can serve as resources for your colleagues, as well.

Coach's Tip from Beth

Don't be alarmed if you do not understand every concept at the onset. Some of the concepts that confused me in the beginning were implementation with fidelity, data-based decision making, and how to get the staff involved. Focusing on one aspect of the program at a time from which to build your knowledge base will help you avoid feeling overwhelmed with confusion.

Find Examples

Using examples of PBIS implementation will help bring otherwise dry concepts to life as you convey these new ideas to your team. From the myriad of possible examples, select those that best match your school's unique characteristics. For instance, many states have PBIS websites that can help you explain and define the concepts of PBIS. The website www.pbis.org has vast resources including videos and PowerPoint presentations, and the digital download of this book includes a PDF presentation. See page x for how to download.

Model Data-Based Problem Solving

With your PBIS Leadership Team, select a decision-making model that uses data to guide problem solving. (See Chapter 5 for more on data-based models.) As you learn about various tools and data sources, make sure you understand how to:

- use and interpret the multiple sources of data and tools
- implement and use the school's data system
- support and encourage the data manager or team in data collection
- ensure that behavioral referrals are completed and done with fidelity
- monitor that data are being entered into the data system in a timely manner
- report the data to the team and staff
- show the team how to use the data to make decisions and evaluate progress

Once you understand these tools and data, you can gradually pass this knowledge to your team members. Help them build their own understanding and capacity. Teach team members how to access, retrieve, report, and use the various sources of data.

Pace the Implementation

This is an important part of your role. Sometimes new teams are so enthusiastic that they try to do too much too fast. It's hard to recognize that while you are in the process. Remember that, as you implement each feature, you need to be sure that you have buy-in from the school staff and that you have thought about how each of those pieces will be sustained in the face of any changes. Most teams with whom we have worked realize they need to slow down and make sure these elements are solidly in place. You may need to remind the PBIS Leadership Team that implementation occurs over time and is a long-term commitment.

Check Fidelity

A key part of your work will be using formal data tools to measure fidelity. In addition, informal measures will help ensure that the implementation process is moving along as it should. From the beginning, you can do some casual checks to see if staff (all staff, not just teachers) can say what the school behavioral expectations are. Ask other leadership team members to help with this. When the teaching is in place, you can also observe and ask if teachers and others are actually teaching the behavioral expectations using the behavioral matrix the PBIS Leadership Team has developed and the school has adopted. For each of the eight key PBIS features, you can conduct simple interviews, observations, and other means for checking whether these aspects of the PBIS framework are actually being used. While the formal PBIS assessment tools provide a critical snapshot of fidelity, don't be bashful about creating some easier, more frequent checks on the fidelity of staff actions.

Seek Ongoing Buy-In on Each Feature

This is similar to checking fidelity in many respects. For example, if staff members buy in to the behavioral expectations, we assume that they follow through with the changes that the school adopts. Frequent discussions at staff and department meetings can help bring forth staff members' thoughts and reactions. Some schools develop simple surveys to check on fidelity. **Figure 3.1** on page 40 shows a sample report on fidelity. It is followed by a **Fidelity Report** template on page 41 that you can use in your school.

> Remember, as you implement each feature, you need to be sure that you have buy-in from the school staff.

Communicate

Prompt your PBIS Leadership Team to develop a strategy and plan for communicating PBIS progress and other related news with key stakeholders—the school board, the district administration, and the wider school community, including families. The following questions may help inspire your process of guiding the team's communications:

- What is the message? (key message, right message to right person, right time)
- Who is the audience? (internal, external, community)
- What is the purpose? (increase awareness, inform, engage, promote, foster buy-in)
- How will you do it? (newsletter, posters, workshops, case studies, presentations, videos)
- When will you do it? (beginning: awareness; middle: progress; end: selling achievements)

System Coaching

One unique aspect of PBIS coaching is your role as a system coach. PBIS is a systems approach to changing the school climate. Some other coaching models describe the role as working with

Figure 3.1

Sample PBIS Fidelity Report

PBIS Component	Classrooms	Areas	Comments
Expectations are posted and visible (include non-classroom areas).	Ms. Garcia Mrs. Johnson Ms. Pitt	Hallway 2nd floor bathroom areas	Missing in media center and cafeteria
ODRs are filled out completely.	70% of random classroom ODR checks	N/A	Missing location and motivation
Teachers are using at least 3 interventions before ODR.	82% of random classroom ODR checks	N/A	Redirection seems to be used without success.
Teachers are actively supervising areas (hallways, entry, cafeteria).	Observed Ms. Olson, Mr. Lang	Morning hallway duty	They engaged with students and walked around the entry area.
4:1 positive to negative comments are used by all staff.	Observed Ms. Garcia and Ms. Pitt for 20 minutes during morning meeting	N/A	Ms. Garcia—15 positive, no negative comments; Ms. Pitt—12 positive, 2 negative comments
Staff reinforces positive behaviors in non-classroom areas.	N/A	Morning duty	Staff greet students and say, "Thanks for taking your hat off."
Non-teaching staff (cafeteria staff, custodians, office staff) are using positive language with students.	N/A	Cafeteria	At breakfast, food service staff says "good morning" and "thank you."
5–8 students chosen at random can say the expectations.	N/A	Various	Yes—asked 6 students
Posters in the school reflect our student makeup.	Various	Various	Need more posters of Hispanic leaders; add to action plan at next meeting.
Behavior management staff follows school behavioral expectations and continuum for misbehaviors.	N/A	Various	Yes—used processing sheet, reminded students of expectations, referred 2 students who were fighting to administrator. Remind them to say "expectations," not "rules."

PBIS team member: ______________________

Date: ______________________

Fidelity Report

PBIS Component	Classrooms	Areas	Comments
Expectations are posted and visible (include non-classroom areas).			
ODRs are filled out completely.			
Teachers are using at least 3 interventions before ODR.			
Teachers are actively supervising areas (hallways, entry, cafeteria).			
4:1 positive to negative comments are used by all staff.			
Staff reinforces positive behaviors in non-classroom areas.			
Non-teaching staff (cafeteria staff, custodians, office staff) are using positive language with students.			
5–8 students chosen at random can say the expectations.			
Posters in the school reflect our student makeup.			
Behavior management staff follows school behavioral expectations and continuum for misbehaviors.			

PBIS team member: ________________________________

Date: ________________________________

individuals, providing guidance, performance feedback, and so on. In contrast, a system coach works with the leadership team and the school as an entire system. Therefore, as the coach you are supporting the system.

System thinking: let's try a simple description. Think about the system as the "whole," in this case the whole school. Then think about it as made up of interdependent groups of individuals, structures, and procedures. System theory predicts that a change in one part of the system will lead to changes in other parts. This approach moves us away from isolated departmental or individual approaches.

System theory predicts that a change in one part of the system will lead to changes in other parts.

In our experience, education continues to be very hierarchical in structure. Initiatives often become associated with a certain branch, department, or administrator. When we visit schools, we sometimes hear staff refer to the PBIS Leadership Team as "those people," or we hear team members talk about feeling as if PBIS is in competition with Responsive Classroom initiatives. These examples suggest that the "whole" has not yet been developed in these schools. The priorities of various initiatives have not yet been integrated. If PBIS is to become truly incorporated into the culture of a school, the PBIS team cannot work in isolation.

Developing as a Coach

Few people would argue with the need for education professionals to be on a continuous improvement plan. Education is, after all, our very business and *raison d'être.* We teach and we are lifelong learners. What may have changed over the last decade is our deeper understanding of how to best foster continuous and deep learning. We laugh often during PBIS team training that we have abandoned the "train and hope" model (in which administration assigns the building staff to sit through a one-day training and hopes that staff will buy in and implement it on Monday morning). Instead, administrators have restructured staff training based on a team approach that uses frequent teaching and coaching. We know, for example, that the "sit and get" model translates to about 1 percent of change in a classroom, while training combined with ongoing coaching leads to 95 percent change in classroom practices.[10] That's terrific! But how does it work for you? *You* are the coach.

Some of us in the PBIS initiative began our work with little guidance for our coaching roles. When Char began, she stumbled a lot and had several trial-and-error learning experiences. She was lucky to find some of the pioneers around the country from whose experience she learned many lessons, not the least of which was to be patient and accept that everything was not going to unfold according to her wishes. She heard Susan Barrett and her colleagues in Maryland speak at a national conference on PBIS, in which Susan said, "We are building the plane as we fly it." Aptly stated and oh-so-true. Through our collective experience, we have developed the following list of important lessons for those of you taking on the role of a PBIS coach:

1. You have to be comfortable with ambiguity and recognize that it is not necessarily bad.
2. It's important to network with others in similar positions, especially with those who have more experience than you do.
3. As a coach, you need to be self-directed, empowered to seek out information, and comfortable with creating some of your own answers and clarity.

This section will provide some shortcuts, tips, and voices of experience to help you move along a continuum of growth.

[10] Joyce and Showers, 1995.

Training and Resources

As an educator, you already have a rich base of knowledge, skills, and attributes. To that, we add means and resources of enhancing this base. As self-led, lifelong learners who are hungry to master their craft, coaches have several means by which to increase knowledge and skills in PBIS coaching. As we mentioned earlier, the majority of states are involved in some level of statewide implementation of PBIS. Some states have been using PBIS for more than fifteen years. This means that states frequently have a statewide system in place to support coaches. These coaching resources may include special Web-based information, coach training, webinars, coaching conferences, and much more. Coaches can:

1. Participate in a formal team training that introduces a rigorous scope and sequence for PBIS implementation. We highly recommend these formal training processes, which include ongoing coaching to both coaches and leadership teams. Team trainings provide a very important source of understanding and team capacity building.
2. Attend specialized training and networking opportunities for PBIS coaches. Often, these are offered by state departments of education. Some states even sponsor statewide conferences for coaches. These events provide opportunities for applied learning and practice.
3. Find and utilize resources.
   a. Contact your district office to see if it has a support system for PBIS and PBIS coaching, including formal team training and coaching support.
   b. Contact your state or regional PBIS office for coaching resources. (For a list of these offices, go to www.pbis.org/links/pbis_network/default.aspx.)
   c. Visit www.pbis.org. It is full of information on PBIS in general; national presentations, evaluation tools, and blueprints for evaluation, implementation, and training; and state, regional, and national conferences. These resources offer readily available online material as well as webinars and other forms of technical assistance.
   d. Access other national websites that focus on PBIS and the role of coaches.
   e. Use Web-based resources for coaches, which include practice examples, forms, and contact information. These, too, are offered by many state departments of education. Some offer specific "coaches' corners" that focus on issues specific to PBIS coaches.
4. Identify a mentor or coach with whom you can work.
5. Take coach self-assessments to gauge how you are doing. These simple tools will help guide your knowledge search. See the following section for details.

The References and Resources (page 188) lists state PBIS websites, as well as team trainings and coaching resources.

Self-Assessments

You can find several coach self-assessments at www.pbis.org and state websites. The Appendix also offers three examples; see pages 156–162. These quick and easy checklists will help you gauge how you are doing by identifying areas of knowledge, skills, and attributes for further development. Choose one assessment and try it. While the assessments provide a numerical score, what's more important is that the process leads you to self-reflection and action planning.

We have also created a one-page **Coach Action Plan** (see page 45) that you can easily modify to suit your own preferences and needs. Again, the form isn't as important as taking decisive action and following through on your plans. The action plan provides a structure to encourage you to develop objectives, find appropriate resources, and begin the process of meeting your goals. For coach development, like all other aspects of PBIS implementation, we discourage the "sit and get" method in favor of learning that relies on frequent modeling, practice, and feedback.

Coaching an Evolving Process: The Wisdom of Situational Leadership

Many years ago, Char participated in a year-long leadership fellowship called ARISE. The fellowship was designed to help participants become aware of themselves as instruments of change. Educators serving in leadership roles rarely get systematic training for some of these roles, and all were grateful for this opportunity. The fellowship focused on self-development as well as leadership and organizational skills. The focus was powerful; the learning priceless. PBIS coaches are in a similar situation—as leaders, coaches, and change agents who need personal, process, and content knowledge to succeed.

As a change agent, you will also benefit from understanding how change occurs within systems and with groups of people. The science and practice of organizational development offers some great resources. For example, Paul Hersey's Situational Leadership model aptly demonstrates how the coaching role must evolve to meet the shifting needs of a PBIS group during the implementation process. The basic idea is that effective leaders (coaches) can and should adapt their leadership style to the Performance Readiness of the group they're working with. Leadership style relates to both task direction and relationship between leader and followers. This developmental approach to coaching can be integrated into the various stages of PBIS implementation.

Hersey defines four Performance Readiness levels of teams on the basis of their ability and willingness to complete a job, task, or activity. These correlate with four corresponding leadership styles that have the highest probability of successfully and effectively influencing the team to perform. Each of these styles is described here. As you read through the styles, consider both your past and current experiences in leadership roles.

Hersey illustrates his concept in a matrix of four quadrants (see **Figure 3.2** on page 46). Basically, leadership starts with matching your leadership behaviors with the performance needs of the team or group you are trying to influence. It is not necessarily a linear progression. The ability and willingness of the team can vary with different jobs, tasks, or activities. For instance, the members of a new team will likely bring some applicable knowledge and experience to the table and will most likely want to be there contributing to the success of the task you are hoping to have them do. You wouldn't treat them the same as a team comprised of individuals who don't want to be there. Your attempts to influence should meet them where they are at. Let's discuss the leadership styles labeled Style 1 (S1), Style 2 (S2), Style 3 (S3), and Style 4 (S4):

- S1 refers to leadership that is heavily task-oriented, where the leader defines the what (task), how, when, and where of the task. This is an appropriate response to a team that is not yet able to successfully perform the task at a sustained and acceptable level and may lack the confidence, commitment, or motivation to do so.
- In S2, the leader provides direction and relationship behavior as an appropriate response to a team that is confident, committed, and motivated to complete the task but isn't necessarily ready to do it on its own.
- In S3, the leader increases shared decision-making and relationship support and decrease directive behaviors. This is in response to a team that can perform the task successfully and effectively at a sustained and acceptable level, but is feeling a little insecure about doing so on its own.
- In S4, the leader delegates the process and responsibility to team members who demonstrate their ability and willingness to do the job. The leader still monitors the team's activities but can trust the team to keep him or her informed.

Coach Action Plan for Professional Development and Support

Within each area (Data, Practices, Systems) investigate professional growth goals, resources, and support needed to accomplish each goal and a timeline for completion.

Area	Goal/Outcome Statement: WHAT needs to be accomplished?	Resources/Support Needed: HOW will this goal be accomplished?	Timeline: WHEN will this goal be accomplished?
Data			
Practices			
Systems			

Adapted from the work of Timothy J. Lewis and Susan Barrett for the OSEP Technical Assistance Center on PBIS. Copyright © 2004. Reprinted with permission from the authors.

Although all team members are highly qualified, credentialed professionals, they may vary greatly in terms of experience, knowledge, and even willingness to participate in PBIS specifically.

The leader's role is a fluid thing. Groups of people come together with various levels of readiness. While the individuals within the group may be experienced and knowledgeable in their professions, the skill sets they possess may be different from what is needed in a new group organized for new purposes. The continuum of groups ranges from those who are unable or unprepared to take responsibility for the task, to those who are willing but lack confidence, and finally to those who are able, confident, and willing to complete a task and take responsibility.

The same is true when we consider a new PBIS team. Although all team members are highly qualified, credentialed professionals, they may vary greatly in terms of experience, knowledge, and even willingness to participate in PBIS specifically. Frequently, members are willing but do not have a clear idea of how or where to start. In our experience, teams often report those first few months or longer as a "maze" where they experience a lot of stimulation and so much information that they sometimes lose track of the roadmap. In these early stages, coaches can offer more task direction. Figure 3.2 illustrates the combination of group readiness and leadership style.

Figure 3.2

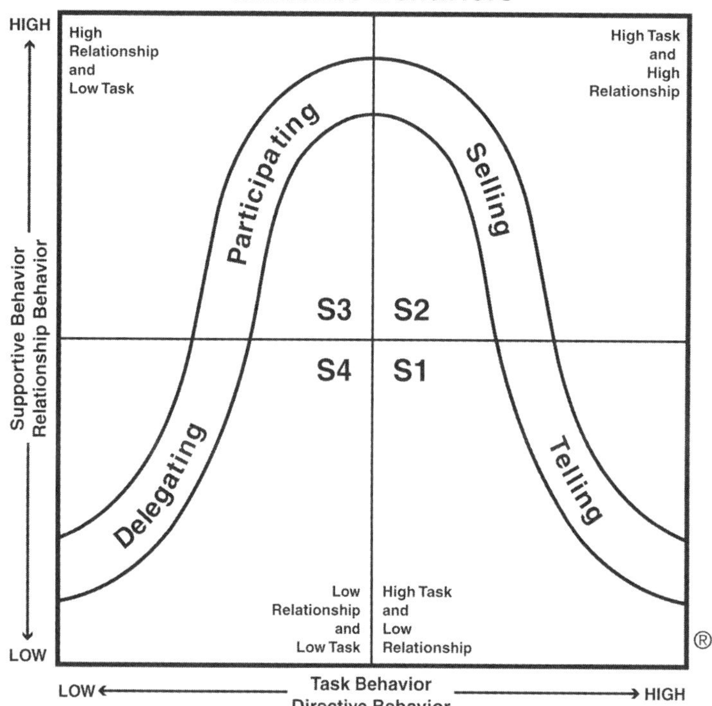

Performance Readiness®

HIGH	MODERATE		LOW
R4	R3	R2	R1
Able and Confident and Willing	Able but Insecure or Unwilling	Unable but Confident or Willing	Unable and Insecure or Unwilling

Chapter 4
Data and Assessment

PBIS implementation involves changing the practices for behavioral interventions at school. This effort takes some staff members out of their comfort zone for handling student disruptions and asks them to try something else instead. Some staff members rely on turning students over to someone else to deal with the problem and the solution. Other staff members fear that, because you are looking at behavioral data and talking about the data of their students, you are tracking whether or not they are good teachers. In reality, you collect and interpret the data to determine progress toward meeting school goals. Are office discipline referrals (ODRs) going down? Where in the building do most of these behavioral referrals come from? Are your actions helping improve the school climate? By documenting the current situation and then tracking the changes, you will know whether your efforts are making a difference. Assessments and surveys help you gather staff input in the design and implementation of ideas for change.

PBIS is a framework, not a program. This means every school will implement plans that work for their own building and community. There is nothing scripted and no curriculum to buy. Most assessments are online and free. The one tool that is not free is the online Schoolwide Information System (SWIS), which helps schools track their ODR data; schools are charged development and maintenance costs for this tool. Good implementation of PBIS practices requires the commitment and hard work of school and district personnel. But without good data and assessment reports, we are simply throwing the spaghetti at the wall, seeing what sticks, then trying something else. This chapter introduces leadership teams to the various types of data and describes their uses in implementing and sustaining PBIS.

Without good data and assessment reports, we are simply throwing the spaghetti at the wall, seeing what sticks, then trying something else.

Role of Data in PBIS

Defining Data

What are data? Here are four viable answers:

A: Data are numbers.

A: Data are bits of information.

A: Data are detailed collections of information that can be queried, used, and grouped to provide answers to various questions.

A: Data are information you collect to learn something. (This is from a group of second graders. I think I like this definition best!)

Simply put: Data help you know where you are. If you don't know where you are, you won't have any idea where to go.

School Data

Data collection is the science behind the art of teaching. If you don't review the data collected by your school, you make decisions based on hunches or beliefs. Someone at one school said to me, "We don't want to change our system this year because we have always done it this way and aren't ready to change it." Tradition. The staff at this school also couldn't say what was working well and what needed more work. Consider the assumptions you make about your school or what the community perceives to be true about your school. Data are used to evaluate progress, to determine trends, and to measure outcomes.

Fortunately, you have easy access to much of the information you'll need. Here are the types of data that are generally already tracked at schools, along with descriptions and some ways to analyze them:

- office discipline referrals (ODRs; sometimes referred to as office behavioral referrals)
- suspension rates (What are the problem behaviors and who is getting suspended?)
- grades—midterm and final (Improved behavior generally improves grades.)
- curriculum-based measures of student learning (Are reading and math scores improving?)
- classroom observations (Are classrooms using similar language for behavioral expectations?)
- attendance and tardy rates (Look for patterns regarding classes and individual students.)
- after-school program attendance (Kids who attend these programs are usually more connected to their schools.)
- meeting minutes (e.g., faculty, grade-level, team, other groups and committees that meet on a regular basis)
- nurse log books (Are students leaving the same class on a daily basis?)
- school facility repair reports (Look for vandalism.)
- summative data (collected once per year, usually at the end of a school year)
- number of students receiving free and reduced lunches
- survey results (e.g., staff and student climate surveys, parent surveys)
- student demographics (How does your school embrace the diversity of the students and staff?)
- student enrollment and unenrollment rates (Why are students coming or leaving your school?)
- staff turnover rates (Why are staff leaving your school?)
- staff member sick days used
- summer school attendance (Improved academic skills generally lead to reduced problem behaviors.)
- district testing and year-end, statewide testing results (Where is your school doing well and where is it struggling?)

This list illustrates how many data sources you may already have available, while also pointing out that you need to know which data are relevant for which decisions in order to develop effective solutions. Once you gather this data, make summary lists, charts, or graphs to post so that staff can analyze, draw conclusions, and ask questions. From these charts you can start to cross-reference ideas and hunches. How do attendance rates affect grades? How do grades affect suspension rates? Is there a correlation between ODRs in the morning and staff supervision assignments?

In this way, you can use data when communicating with stakeholders about what is going well in your school and what may need some work. This allows them to make their own decisions based on facts. Presenting behavioral data along with academic data offers a complete picture of your school. It can help families decide if your school is a good fit for their child. Behavioral data can also be used by district personnel to address staffing needs, helping them determine, for example, whether more behavior specialists or social workers are needed. If your community senses that there are too many fights in your school, see what the data say. Your data may show fights were not nearly as common as the community thought, and sharing that data with the community could help them see your school in a better light.

Types of Data in PBIS

One of the remarkable aspects of PBIS implementation is the emphasis on data as a key foundation. Remember in Chapter 1 we introduced the three PBIS elements—data, systems, and practices—needed to support outcomes (see Figure 1.2 on page 11). Not only are the data foundational to PBIS, but also, PBIS has developed the tools and the guidance to use them correctly so that you can implement the framework with fidelity. The tools are free (except for the SWIS suite), online, and readily available to the team 24/7. This section focuses on three types of data and the tools that measure them:

- progress data
- program fidelity data
- student outcome data

What makes PBIS stand out from other frameworks is the data infrastructure, which includes clear descriptions of the data, specific tools for measuring each data point, clear guidance for using the tools, and easy and effective online access to results. Everything you need is ready and accessible from the beginning.

Progress Data

During PBIS implementation you create data-driven action plans to guide your work. You track the progress of your action plans by using implementation data that come from surveys and PBIS assessment tools. Getting all the data features in place is essential, and the results from these tools guide the next steps in your action plans. In addition, monitor behavioral data such as ODRs. Assuming that all the features of PBIS are implemented with fidelity, the number of behavioral referrals should decrease. And while ODRs are also considered outcome data, they are definitely something that should be monitored quite closely as you progress.

Fidelity Data

Fidelity refers to the extent and accuracy with which you are following the PBIS framework, how well your plans are being consistently followed by staff and students, and how well the model is being used with integrity. Fidelity measures, then, are tools used to answer the questions about accuracy, completeness, and integrity of implementation. As noted previously, some of these measures have already been created and tested and are available online for free. You may also need to develop or use some additional informal measures, such as observations, staff ratings, and surveys.

Of the eight features in the Tier 1 PBIS framework, if you implement only two or three out of the eight, you cannot say you are implementing PBIS with fidelity. More specifically, you might have partial implementation of all features and still not have met fidelity. The criteria for fidelity are based on certain cutoff scores on different instruments. With the School-Wide Evaluation Tool (SET), for example, the criterion is 80 percent on overall implementation. Fidelity criterion on the Benchmark of Quality (BoQ) is 70 percent. If you have 60 percent, it means you have bits and pieces in place but not enough to claim full fidelity. The extent of fidelity relates directly to outcomes and sustainability. Research has shown that schools that achieve at least 80 percent on the SET will demonstrate changes in student behavior measured by ODRs.[11]

Outcome Data

What are outcome data and how do we measure them? Rob Horner, George Sugai, and other PBIS leaders note that at the end of the day, all of the time, money, and investments related to PBIS are about changing the school culture—and

[11]Horner, et al., 2009.

this is reflected by changes in student behavior. Outcome data, then, tells you how well your efforts are paying off toward meeting your desired results. The most commonly used measure of student behavior across the nation is the office discipline referral, or ODR. When PBIS was developed, there was no need to reinvent the ODR model because ODRs tell you how many students are leaving the classroom due to behavior problems and, therefore, missing out on learning. (See pages 73–80 for a detailed discussion of ODR data.)

Assessment Tools

This section provides both an overview and a deeper understanding of each of the PBIS assessment tools. We discuss how to use and interpret them and ways to triangulate or integrate these multiple data sources. Developed by the University of Oregon more than a decade ago, PBIS assessment tools help schools through the PBIS implementation process. These tools are available at www.pbisapps.org and are free of charge to schools. To access the tools, you just need to obtain what's called a PBIS assessment coordinator account for your district (also free). This coordinator account is a one-time application, unless you have staff turnover and someone new steps into that role. By logging into this website, your team can take advantage of the terrific range of support in using these tools, including user manuals, video tutorials, and other resources. **Figure 4.1** compares the various tools.

This book focuses on Tier 1 assessment tools, but the PBIS website includes assessment tools for each of the three tiers. All the tools include three types of graphic and tabular reports, and all are easily and instantly accessible at the website through your school PBIS account. You can implement the assessment tools gradually, based on the following advice:

- The PBIS Leadership Team should start by completing the Team Implementation Checklist (TIC), which provides a snapshot of where the team thinks they are in the

Figure 4.1

PBIS Assessment Tools and Purpose

Tool	Who uses it?	Method	What does it track?
Team Implementation Checklist (TIC)	PBIS Leadership Team	Self-report	Progress Action planning Implementation fidelity
Self-Assessment Survey (SAS)	School staff	Survey	Fidelity of staff needs
School-Wide Evaluation Tool (SET)	Outside evaluator School staff	Interviews Observations Products	Implementation fidelity
Benchmarks of Quality (BoQ)	PBIS Leadership Team	Self-report Survey	Implementation fidelity Action planning

implementation process. The TIC monitors the progress of implementation and outlines who is responsible for what.

- Next, everyone on the school's staff completes the Self-Assessment Survey (SAS) to identify areas they perceive as needing the most attention.
- The School-Wide Evaluation Tool (SET) is a research-based tool used to measure PBIS fidelity. Conducted by a trained SET evaluator who is not associated with the school.
- Some PBIS teams use the Benchmarks of Quality (BoQ) scale as another self-assessment tool. The BoQ is completed by the PBIS Leadership Team and coordinated by the coach. It provides another measure of fidelity of implementation. Usually, schools would use either the SET or the BoQ in a single year, not both.

As you achieve implementation fidelity, your PBIS Leadership Team will look at outcome data. All of the previous tools mentioned above are checks and balances to ensure that the various pieces of PBIS are firmly in place. Remember, the research tells us that schools that demonstrate fidelity with all core features of PBIS reflect measurable changes in student behavior through reduced ODRs.

The following sections provide more detail about these four tools.

Team Implementation Checklist

The Team Implementation Checklist (TIC) is completed by the school PBIS Leadership Team and represents the team's perception of progress at any given time. Some teams review the TIC monthly and some quarterly or annually, depending on what stage of implementation they are in. New schools tend to use the TIC more frequently. The TIC measures progress and provides a historical or chronological record of the school's implementation. It comes with an optional action plan format and is a convenient way to keep activity on track. This tool measures progress and achievement in each area by marking as completed, in progress, or not started. (See the Appendix or www.pbisapps.org for an example of the TIC.)

Self-Assessment Survey

One of the PBIS Leadership Team's first actions should be to have staff complete the Self-Assessment Survey (SAS) to identify areas they perceive as needing the most attention. Remember, staff members include office support personnel, paraprofessionals, media center specialists, custodians, food service workers, and bus drivers—and all should be surveyed. In this way, SAS represents a broader staff view of both implementation progress and priorities for change. A very useful way to take the temperature of your school, the SAS measures staff perceptions of the four systems in your building:

1. Schoolwide
2. Classroom
3. Non-classroom
4. Individual student

The schoolwide component provides a good comparison with the TIC, which enables your leadership team to examine whether the staff and the team have similar perceptions about what features are in place. It can be quite informative to compare these views. The PBIS Leadership Team, so deeply immersed in PBIS, monitors the implementation of the action plan using the TIC, while the staff monitors the success of the implementation via the SAS.

The SAS is an online survey that takes about twenty minutes to complete. Staff members rate a number of items according to its implementation phase (complete, in progress, or not started) and then also rate its importance (high, medium, or low). We heartily recommend that your leadership team take the SAS before asking staff to take it. Familiarize yourself with the wording to clarify what items mean and with the rating system to understand how to rate items.

Many schools conduct the SAS during a staff meeting using the computers in the media center.

You will have to be more creative to get other staff such as kitchen personnel and bus drivers to participate. (We hear that food reinforcements go a long way!) We also encourage you to find the SAS guide on the www.pbisapps.org website under "Resources"; give this one-page handout to staff to instruct them on completing the SAS.

A word of caution: Be careful about creating online shortcut links to the SAS. We have known several schools that did this only to find later that all their data was lost. While it is possible to do the SAS with paper and pencil, why do so when it is free online and you can then track the ongoing history of your school's implementation progress?

The district staff person who is the PBIS assessment coordinator can log into the school's assessment account, open the survey, and set a timeframe for staff to complete it. One day after the window closes, the results are available. You can review different report formats. The Item Report lists the questions staff responded to and is color-coded according to staff perception of importance. Items and tasks that have been determined by staff as critical for attention are displayed in red; items needing moderate attention are shown in yellow. Compare these SAS results with the TIC as an aid in developing an action plan. (See the Appendix or www.pbisapps.org for a copy of the SAS.)

School-Wide Evaluation Tool

A useful addition to the other sources of data (TIC, SAS), the School-Wide Evaluation Tool (SET) is a research-based evaluation tool used to measure fidelity of implementation for Tier 1. This tool has seven subscales that correlate with the subscales of the TIC. The SET is conducted by a trained evaluator who is not part of the school or district. Some states use the SET as part of an overall statewide evaluation of PBIS implementation. The generally accepted criterion for fidelity in initial implementation of PBIS is the "80/80 Rule"—scores of 80 percent on the Teaching Expectations Subscale and 80 percent on Overall Implementation. (See the Appendix or www.pbisapps.org for a copy of the SET.)

Coach's Tip from Beth

I remember the first time our team completed the TIC and staff completed the SAS. I tried to create action plans to implement everything that our staff thought was missing from our PBIS plan. Don't try this. Choose a few things that can be easily implemented along with one item that may take a longer time. Consider starting with items that your staff rated as high priority on the SAS.

Benchmarks of Quality

The Benchmarks of Quality (BoQ) was developed in the Florida PBIS initiative as a means to evaluate PBIS implementation at Tier 1. This self-assessment tool is completed by the PBIS coach and the leadership team. Online training and resources are available at the PBIS website.

The BoQ has ten subscales that measure fidelity and that also correlate with the TIC and the SET. A score of 70 or greater on overall implementation is the criterion for fidelity. (See the Appendix or www.pbisapps.org for an example.)

BoQ or SET?

Whether you use the BoQ or the SET may depend on the particular state in which you reside. When the SET is used, it is typically done twice in the first year and once each year thereafter. Different states have different practices and policies around this. SETs are very labor intensive and costly, and thus challenging to sustain on a statewide basis. Many states opt for the BoQ. Unlike the SET, which requires an outside evaluator, the BoQ is a self-assessment that involves the PBIS Leadership Team and is coordinated by the PBIS coach. Some schools find the BoQ more detailed than the SET and therefore more helpful for planning. Other schools use a combination of both tools.

Integrating Multiple Sources of Data

In addition to thoroughly understanding the purpose and method of each PBIS assessment tool, leadership teams also must adopt the essential practice of integrating these multiple data sources, or "triangulating data." Triangulation uses at least two different data sources to corroborate the results and, therefore, increase your confidence in their validity. For example, when you look at the results for your school from both the TIC and the SET, you will gain some insight into whether there are discrepancies between the two instruments. What you as a PBIS Leadership Team perceive to be in place may not be perceived that way by the rest of the staff. Char has known administrators who, upon comparing the results of their spring SAS with the TIC, have revised their implementation action plan based on where staff perceived progress to be. This is a great example of using multiple data sources in planning.

Multiple assessment tools should be part of the implementation process from the beginning. They are all integral to implementation and are designed to measure Tier 1 implementation. They represent different sources of information (team, staff, outside evaluator) and different methods (self-assessment, interview, observations, and permanent products, such as wall posters). They all provide basic evaluation information that, when integrated together, helps you interpret the results—especially when you have discrepancies among those results. When you get the same positive results across multiple tools, this convergence of evidence confirms that you are implementing PBIS with fidelity. As Rob Horner asked, "Did we do what we said we were going to do? Did we implement PBIS with fidelity?" Integrating the data from these tools will help you answer that question with confidence as well as identify areas that need development or tweaking if fidelity weakens over time. **Figure 4.2** on page 54 displays the different tools and their subscales.

Caution: When you can look at multiple tools and see that your school has achieved full fidelity according to the guidelines for the tools, you should also see progress measured by a decrease in the number of ODRs. If you don't see those corresponding positive changes, then the PBIS Leadership Team needs to go back and take a much closer look at the PBIS features and examine whether fidelity was truly met and all features were truly implemented by every staff member, in all settings with all students.

Assessment Reports in Practice

Each PBIS assessment tool produces three downloadable reports that provide various levels of detail:

1. **Total Score Report**—summarizes the overall implementation status. It indicates the overall percentage of items that are "fully implemented" and the overall percentage "partially in place." The goal is 80 percent or more overall.
2. **Subscale Report**—reveals the team's progress on the key features of PBIS implementation. The fidelity criterion score is again 80 percent or above on overall implementation; however, this report also allows you to quickly assess progress in each area.
3. **Item Report**—refers specifically to the score for each question on the assessment. This allows teams to determine specifically what has been achieved and what still needs to be done.

The rest of this section shows examples of how these reports for the various assessment tools might look for schools at different stages of PBIS implementation.

Figure 4.2

PBIS Instruments and Their Subscales[12]

Team Implementation Checklist (TIC)		Self-Assessment Survey (SAS)		School-Wide Evaluation (SET)		Benchmarks of Quality (BoQ)	
Subscale	**Items**	**Subscale**	**Items**	**Subscale**	**Items**	**Subscale**	**Items**
1. Establish commitment	1–2	**1.** Expectations defined	1	**1.** Expectations defined	1–2	**1.** PBIS Leadership Team	1–3
2. Establish team	3–5	**2.** Expectations taught	2	**2.** Expectations taught	3–7	**2.** Faculty commitment	4–6
3. Self-assessment	6–8	**3.** Reward system	3	**3.** Reward system	8–10	**3.** Discipline procedures	7–12
4. Define expectations	9–11	**4.** Violations system	4–8	**4.** Violations system	11–14	**4.** Data entry and analysis	13–16
5. Teach expectations	12	**5.** Monitoring	10–12	**5.** Decision-making system	15–18	**5.** Expectations	17–21
6. Reward expectations	13	**6.** Management	9, 14–16	**6.** Management	19–26	**6.** Recognition	22–28
7. Consequences	14	**7.** District support	17–18	**7.** District support	27–28	**7.** Teaching	29–34
8. Classroom system	15–17					**8.** Implementation plan	35–41
9. Establish info system	18–19					**9.** Classroom systems	42–48
10. Function-based support	20–22					**10.** Evaluation	49–53

Sample Assessment Reports for the Team Implementation Checklist (TIC)

Total Score Report for TIC

Figure 4.3 presents a sample TIC Total Score Report from a school that has been implementing PBIS for two years. Notice the steady, rising slope. Results are displayed in graphic and tabular form. This gives you the big picture and the percentages of PBIS features that are partially or fully in place. A quick glance tells us this school is making good progress.

Subscale Report for TIC

Figure 4.4 on page 56 presents a sample report from a school that has completed two years of implementation and has data from four TICs. The legend defines the darker subscales as the baseline scores and the lighter subscales as the progress after two years. The pattern of scores is not unusual from our experience. It demonstrates

[12]Summaries of the validity and reliability of these tools are available at www.pbisapps.org under "PBIS Assessment Resource Materials," item #30.

Figure 4.3

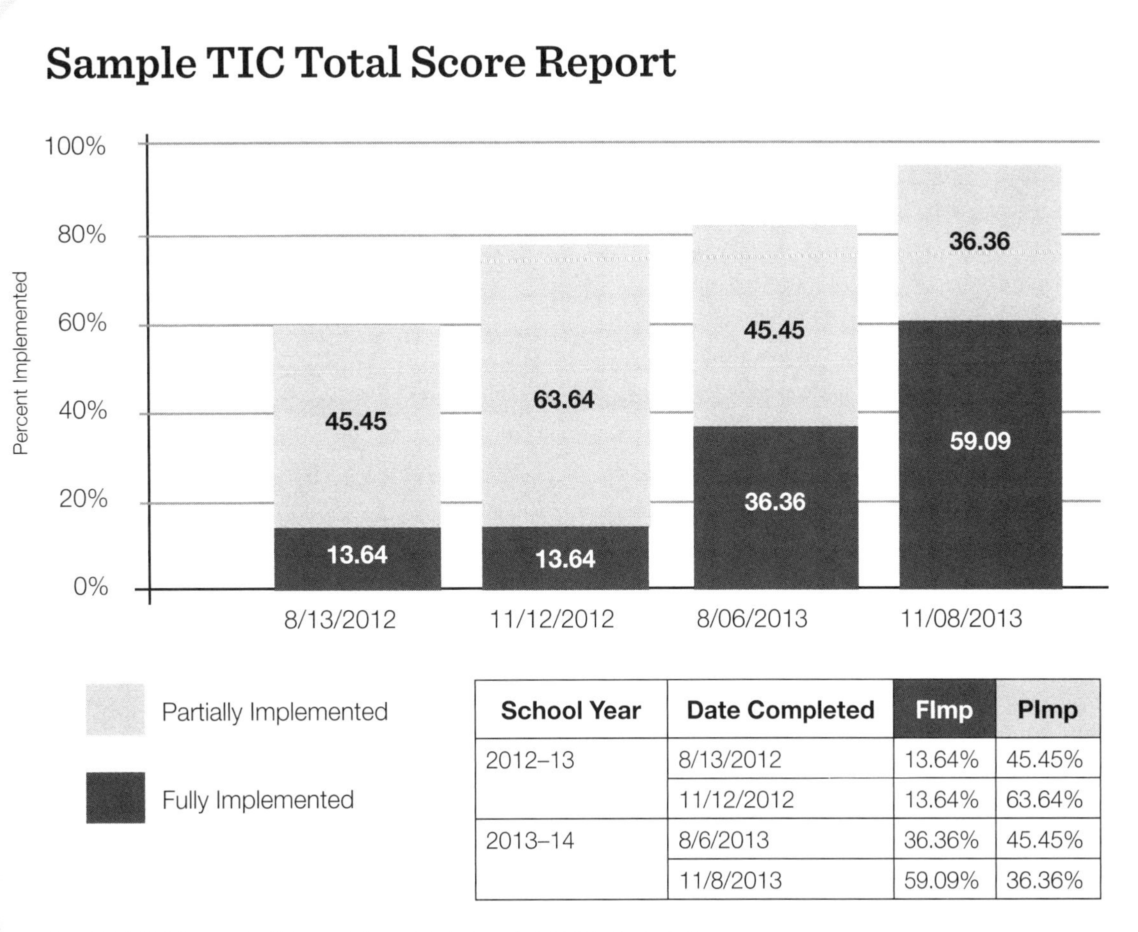

School Year	Date Completed	FImp	PImp
2012–13	8/13/2012	13.64%	45.45%
	11/12/2012	13.64%	63.64%
2013–14	8/6/2013	36.36%	45.45%
	11/8/2013	59.09%	36.36%

some of the fluctuations seen across time. The goal is to achieve scores of 80 percent.

From first glance you can see that commitment was at 100 percent during the first year and dropped below 80 percent in the second year. The leadership team for this school needs to look into that more closely. At the end of year two, the subscales that meet criteria are defining expectations, reward system, and function-based support. Three of the subscales are right at the 50 percent mark—the partially in place status—and reveal that these features still need to be secured into place. This team will want to be sure to examine the Item Report and other sources of data to specifically determine the components that need action. Looking at the items for each of these subscales helps you understand that these tasks are typically not completed or even started at the beginning. You gain more information by understanding the meaning of the subscales and how they fit your school context.

Item Report for TIC

You can get more information about the specifics by looking at this school's Item Report, shown in

Reminder: As a coach and team member, make sure that you are fluent in your understanding of the PBIS assessment tools, what they measure, what subscales mean, the difference between and the value of both different reports and different respondents. This graphic report is available online to any of your school's leadership team members at any time.

Figure 4.5. Items scored 1 or 0 indicate partially in place and not started. When you look at the Commitment item for faculty support, the score of 1 corroborates the trend shown in the Commitment subscale scores in Figure 4.4, which reveal declining commitment. This may indicate some loss of buy-in among staff members. The leadership team for this school will also want to further examine the classroom system at some point. They may not be ready at this time if there are concerns about buy-in from staff. Their Consequence subscale scores in Figure 4.4 suggest that they still need to develop a consistent system for recognizing and responding to behavior. Examining the details and comparing them to other measures will help this leadership team stay on track.

Sample Subscale Reports for the Self-Assessment Survey (SAS)

SAS subscale results from two other schools using PBIS are on pages 59–63.

Figure 4.4

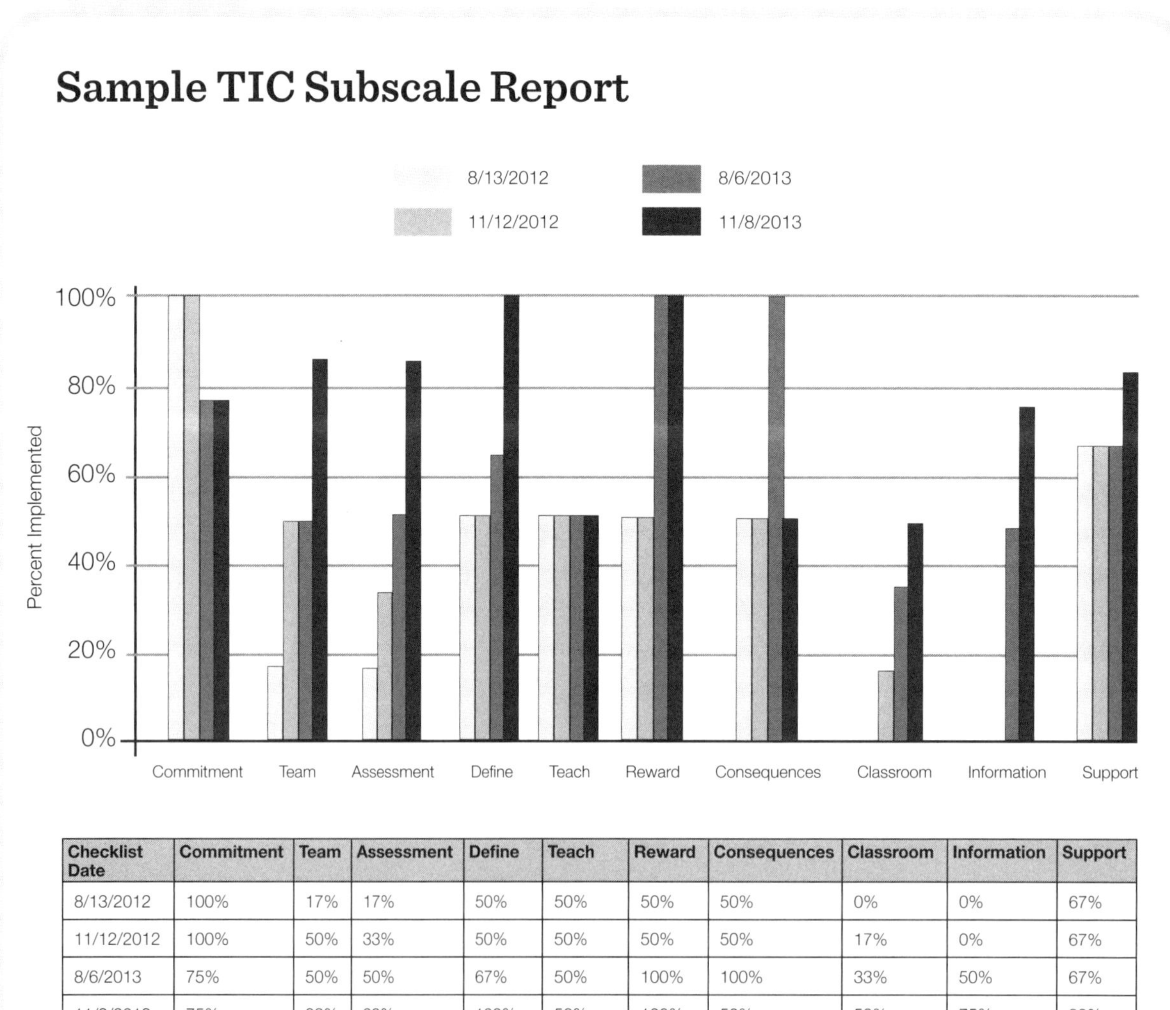

Checklist Date	Commitment	Team	Assessment	Define	Teach	Reward	Consequences	Classroom	Information	Support
8/13/2012	100%	17%	17%	50%	50%	50%	50%	0%	0%	67%
11/12/2012	100%	50%	33%	50%	50%	50%	50%	17%	0%	67%
8/6/2013	75%	50%	50%	67%	50%	100%	100%	33%	50%	67%
11/8/2013	75%	83%	83%	100%	50%	100%	50%	50%	75%	83%

Figure 4.5

Sample TIC Item Report

School Year	Number of Responses	Date Collected
2013–14	**1**	**11/08/2013**
Feature		Score (0, 1, 2)
Establish Commitment		
1. Administrator's support & active involvement.		2
2. Faculty/staff support.		1
Establish & Maintain Team		
3. Team established (representative).		2
4. Team has regular meeting schedule, effective operating procedures.		1
5. Audit is completed for efficient integration of team with other teams/initiatives addressing behavior support.		2
Conduct Self-Assessment		
6. Team completes the Team Implementation Checklist (TIC).		2
7. Team summarizes existing school discipline data.		2
8. Team uses self-assessment information to build implementation action plan (areas of immediate focus).		1
Establish Schoolwide Expectations		
9. 3–5 schoolwide behavior expectations are defined and posted in all areas of building.		2
10. Schoolwide teaching matrix developed.		2
11. Teaching plans for schoolwide expectations are developed.		2
12. Schoolwide behavioral expectations taught directly & formally.		1
13. System in place to acknowledge/reward schoolwide expectations.		2
14. Clearly defined & consistent consequences and procedures for undesirable behaviors are developed.		1
Classroom Behavior Support Systems		
15. School has completed a schoolwide classroom systems summary.		0
16. Action plan in place to address any classroom systems defined as a high priority for change.		1

continued →

Figure 4.5

Sample TIC Item Report, continued

School Year	Number of Responses	Date Collected
2013–14	1	11/08/2013
17. Data system in place to monitor office discipline referral rates that come from classrooms.		2
Establish Information System		
18. Discipline data are gathered, summarized, & reported at least quarterly to whole faculty.		2
19. Discipline data are available to the team at least monthly in a form and depth needed for problem solving.		1
Build Capacity for Function-Based Support		
20. Personnel with behavioral expertise are identified & involved.		2
21. At least one staff member of the school is able to conduct simple functional behavioral assessments.		2
22. Intensive, individual student support team structure in place to use function-based supports.		1

Subscale Report for the SAS—Example 1

The sample SAS Subscale Report in **Figure 4.6** was done after this school's initial team training, and shortly after the beginning of the school year. The school was just starting to use PBIS, so this is a baseline SAS. That's essential to keep in mind.

Again the Subscale Report presents the picture in a table. What do you see? Look at the last column for Implementation Average and notice that this school is at 58 percent—not bad for a baseline. They scored 90 percent for Expectations Defined. Most of their scores are in the 40–60 percent range, which means that some things are partially in place. Now, let's go to the Item Report and see how staff responded to the questions related to the schoolwide system.

Item Report for the SAS—Example 1

This report is one you want to carefully prepare both your team and your staff for so they are not alarmed when they see it. When you receive your Item Report online, it will be color coded. (See the color key at the bottom of **Figure 4.7** on page 60 for color correspondences.) Red/dark gray refers to items and tasks that are not yet in place; yellow/light gray refers to items partially in place; white refers to items fully in place. Those items classified as "partially in place" and "not in place" guide your action planning.

Don't be alarmed by all the dark gray (red when viewed online) in the sample in Figure 4.7. This is a baseline report. Baselines reflect program status before you start. This is a hard concept to understand when you feel blinded by a full page of red. One of the things to remember is what

Figure 4.6

Sample SAS Subscale Report—Example 1

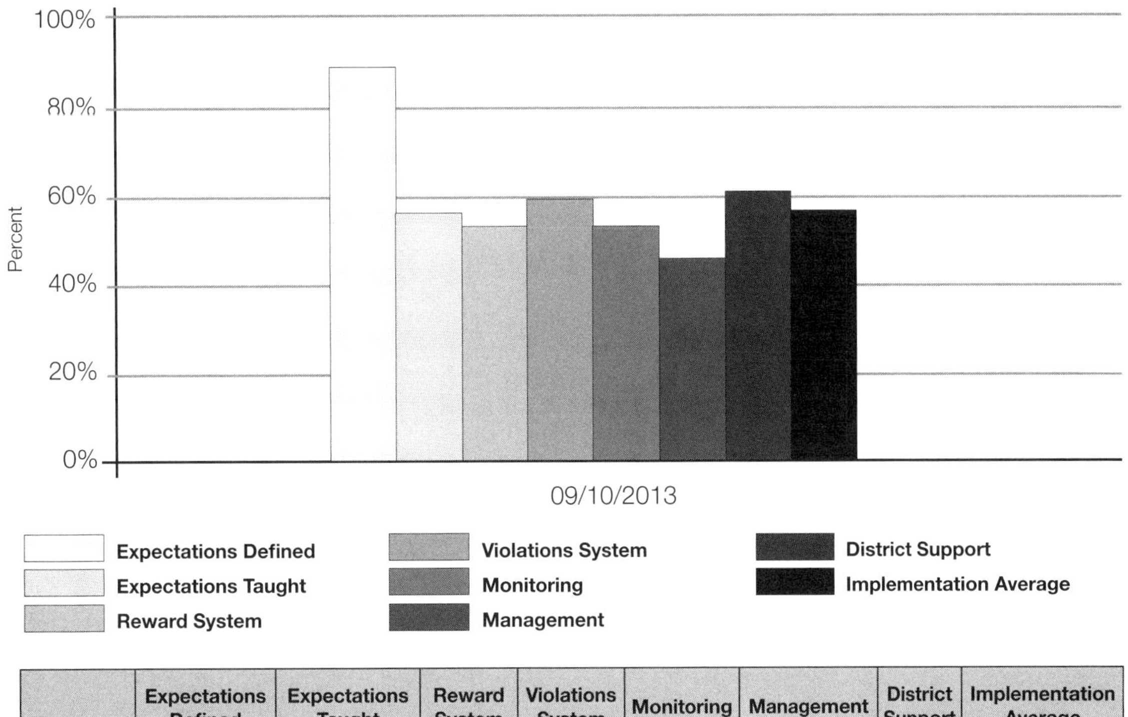

	Expectations Defined	Expectations Taught	Reward System	Violations System	Monitoring	Management	District Support	Implementation Average
9/10/2013	90%	57%	53%	59%	53%	47%	61%	58%

Figure 4.7

Sample SAS Item Report—Example 1

School Year			Number of Responses	Date Collected		
2013–14			102	9/10/2013		
Current Status			Feature	Improvement Priority		
In Place	Partial	Not	System: schoolwide	High	Medium	Low
80%	19%	1%	**1.** A small number (e.g., 3–5) of positively and clearly stated student expectations or rules are defined.	27%	26%	47%
26%	62%	12%	**2.** Expected student behaviors are taught directly.	63%	32%	5%
16%	74%	10%	**3.** Expected student behaviors are rewarded regularly.	42%	47%	11%

continued →

Figure 4.7

Sample SAS Item Report—Example 1, continued

School Year			Number of Responses	Date Collected		
2013–14			102	9/10/2013		
Current Status			Feature	Improvement Priority		
In Place	Partial	Not	System: schoolwide	High	Medium	Low
26%	59%	14%	**4.** Problem behaviors (failure to meet expected student behaviors) are defined clearly.	59%	25%	16%
20%	56%	24%	**5.** Consequences for problem behaviors are defined clearly.	64%	24%	12%
17%	57%	27%	**6.** Distinctions between office v. classroom managed problem behaviors are clear.	44%	44%	13%
28%	63%	9%	**7.** Options exist to allow classroom instruction to continue when problem behavior occurs.	40%	48%	12%
75%	24%	1%	**8.** Procedures are in place to address emergency/dangerous situations.	40%	19%	42%
33%	55%	13%	**9.** A team exists for behavior support planning & problem solving.	51%	38%	11%
46%	43%	11%	**10.** School administrator is an active participant on the behavior support team.	58%	23%	19%
27%	61%	12%	**11.** Data on problem behavior patterns are collected and summarized within an ongoing system.	45%	40%	15%
13%	38%	49%	**12.** Patterns of student problem behavior are reported to teams and faculty for active decision making on a regular basis (e.g., monthly).	59%	35%	5%
43%	51%	6%	**13.** School has formal strategies for informing families about expected student behaviors at school.	53%	27%	19%
10%	45%	45%	**14.** Booster training activities for students are developed, modified, & conducted based on school data.	38%	53%	9%
22%	37%	41%	**15.** Schoolwide behavior support team has a budget for (a) teaching students, (b) ongoing rewards, and (c) annual staff planning.	47%	36%	17%
22%	54%	24%	**16.** All staff are involved directly and/or indirectly in schoolwide interventions.	61%	27%	12%
20%	52%	28%	**17.** The school team has access to ongoing training and support from district personnel.	44%	40%	16%
60%	38%	2%	**18.** The school is required by the district to report on the school climate, discipline level, or student behavior at least annually.	31%	35%	33%

KEY: Items fully in place; Items partially in place; Items not yet in place a baseline means: basic status before implementation. Often our role is to help staff relax, avoid anxiety related to the data, and gain confidence in its use. Reframe your reaction to the report and you can look at it and see all the opportunities that lie ahead: so many choices. Leadership teams and staff can look at the Improvement Priority column to help decide where to put their energies. Some of the tasks tend to occur in a logical order of implementation, but the SAS gives you good information on what your staff thinks and supports, and this also helps guide your order of implementation.

When you get beyond all the dark gray in Figure 4.7, you will notice immediately that item 1 is white. Remember, white corresponds to the items that are completed and in place. In this example, item 1 relates to the subscale for Expectations Defined (see Figure 4.6). This tells you the staff perceive that expectations are defined. The lowest subscale in Figure 4.6 is labeled "Management." If you look at the SAS subscale description in Figure 4.2, page 54, you see that this subscale is made up of items 14–16, which include, according to Figure 4.7, the school providing booster training sessions for students (item 14); having a budget to teach students, continue team planning, and implementing student acknowledgment systems (item 15); and implementing a process to involve all staff in doing the interventions (item 16). These items are things we would not expect a school that is just starting PBIS to have in place. Remember, this school has been implementing PBIS for only a few weeks. And, since they have not even begun the initial teaching of expectations, it is normal that a lot of items are not even started, let alone in place. This is good to know in advance: when you view your school's baseline SAS Item Report, expect to see lots of red items.

Subscale Report for the SAS—Example 2

Now, for comparison, let's look at another school further along in implementation. **Figure 4.8** on page 62 shows an SAS Subscale Report for a school that has completed two years of structured team training. Notice that their Implementation Average is at 86 percent. That is terrific. All but one of the subscales are above 80 percent. Again: terrific. The subscale for the Violation System is at 75 percent. Let's go to the Item Report and see what that tells us.

Item Report for the SAS—Example 2

A quick view of the Item Report reveals *a lot* less dark gray (or red when viewed online). The only dark gray item suggests the staff perceive that consequences are not clearly defined. To deepen this understanding, refer to the chart on pages 62–63, which includes the items that make up the subscales; in this case, the Violation Systems subscale is comprised of items 4–8. Glancing at these items reveals that these are all light gray (yellow) except for item 5, which is dark gray (red). For this item, the ratings for "in place" versus "partially in place" are close—43 percent of respondents rate it "in place," 53 percent rate it "partially in place," and only 3 percent rate it "not started." In general, the items on the Violation Systems subscale have to do with clear delineations of behaviors and practices. Staff perceives that student behavioral problems are not clearly defined and, similarly, the distinctions between office-managed and classroom-managed behavior are not clear.

These data can be a springboard for great discussion at staff meetings. The report findings are not surprising to us; we encourage schools from the beginning to clearly define problem behaviors and distinguish between office-managed versus classroom-managed problems. Defining and implementing consistent practice is an incredible challenge that requires ongoing monitoring and acknowledgment of staff. Monitoring progress and achievement in this area of behavior management may require you to devise some additional informal measures, such as observations and extended conversations at staff meetings. Consistency will pay off; consensus requires patience and commitment from everyone.

Figure 4.8

Sample SAS Subscale Report—Example 2

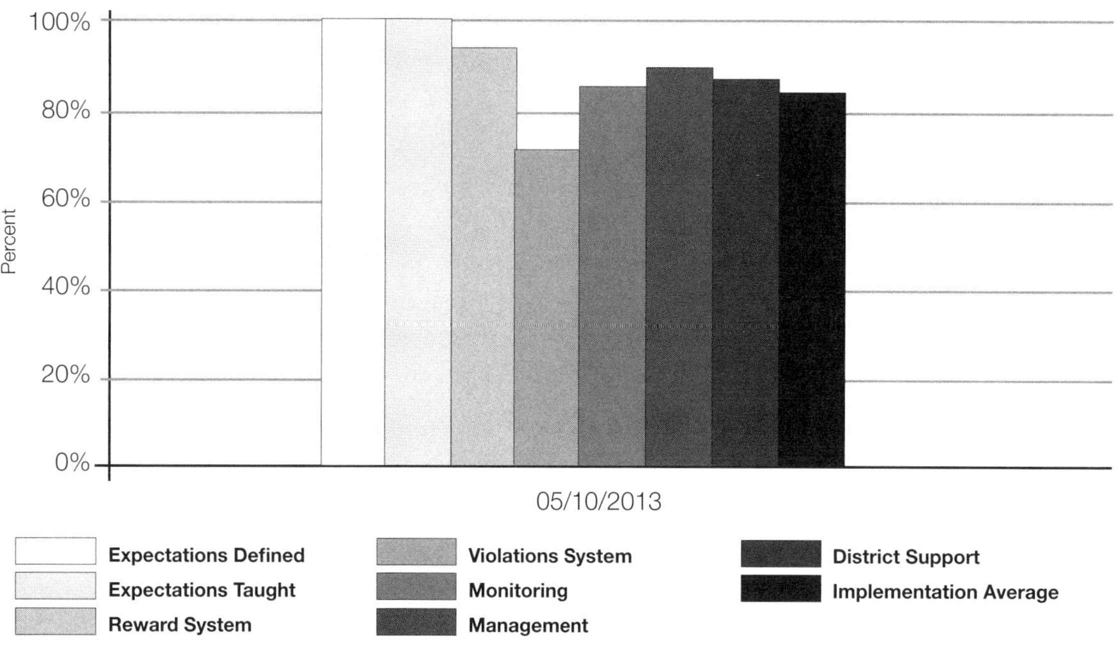

	Expectations Defined	Expectations Taught	Reward System	Violations System	Monitoring	Management	District Support	Implementation Average
5/10/2013	100%	100%	94%	75%	86%	90%	88%	86%

Figure 4.9

Sample SAS Item Report—Example 2

School Year			Number of Responses	Date Collected		
2012–13			34	5/10/2013		
Current Status			Feature	Improvement Priority		
In Place	Partial	Not	System: schoolwide	High	Medium	Low
100%	0%	0%	**1.** A small number (e.g., 3–5) of positively and clearly stated student expectations or rules are defined.	12%	8%	80%
100%	0%	0%	**2.** Expected student behaviors are taught directly.	16%	24%	60%
88%	12%	0%	**3.** Expected student behaviors are rewarded regularly.	4%	20%	76%

continued →

Figure 4.9

Sample SAS Item Report—Example 2, continued

School Year			Number of Responses	Date Collected		
2012–13			34	5/10/2013		
Current Status			Feature	Improvement Priority		
In Place	Partial	Not	System: schoolwide	High	Medium	Low
56%	41%	3%	**4.** Problem behaviors (failure to meet expected student behaviors) are defined clearly.	15%	52%	33%
43%	53%	3%	**5.** Consequences for problem behaviors are defined clearly.	31%	46%	23%
59%	37%	4%	**6.** Distinctions between office v. classroom managed problem behaviors are clear.	26%	35%	39%
57%	37%	7%	**7.** Options exist to allow classroom instruction to continue when problem behavior occurs.	21%	42%	38%
64%	21%	15%	**8.** Procedures are in place to address emergency/dangerous situations.	28%	32%	40%
85%	15%	0%	**9.** A team exists for behavior support planning & problem solving.	16%	24%	60%
79%	21%	0%	**10.** School administrator is an active participant on the behavior support team.	10%	33%	57%
83%	17%	0%	**11.** Data on problem behavior patterns are collected and summarized within an ongoing system.	0%	30%	70%
67%	22%	11%	**12.** Patterns of student problem behavior are reported to teams and faculty for active decision making on a regular basis (e.g., monthly).	11%	42%	47%
84%	16%	0%	**13.** School has formal strategies for informing families about expected student behaviors at school.	0%	48%	52%
85%	11%	4%	**14.** Booster training activities for students are developed, modified, & conducted based on school data.	10%	35%	55%
94%	6%	0%	**15.** Schoolwide behavior support team has a budget for (a) teaching students, (b) ongoing rewards, and (c) annual staff planning.	0%	46%	54%
66%	31%	3%	**16.** All staff are involved directly and/or indirectly in schoolwide interventions.	14%	38%	48%
70%	30%	0%	**17.** The school team has access to ongoing training and support from district personnel.	6%	31%	63%
85%	15%	0%	**18.** The school is required by the district to report on the school climate, discipline level, or student behavior at least annually.	0%	17%	83%

KEY: Items fully in place; Items partially in place; Items not yet in place

Sample Assessment Reports for School-Wide Evaluation Tool (SET)

Subscale Report for SET

Let's look at an example showing a school's SET results. The Subscale Report in **Figure 4.10** shows where the school is at baseline (pre-intervention). This school has some pieces in place at baseline, but they are far below the criterion score of 80 percent. One of the subscales—for Reward System—is at zero, which means none of those tasks have been started. The Item Report will help us see what is going on here.

Item Report for SET

The Item Report displays all the questions that were assessed and the corresponding score: 0, 1, or 2. The scores for this school are ones and zeroes, which is why the graph indicates partial features are in place. Below each question is a key to help you understand the scoring. Remember that the SET is completed by looking at a variety of sources. These include permanent products (posters, lesson plans, teaching matrices, and action plans); staff interviews (questions about topics such as using data and teaching and rewarding expected behavior); student interviews (asking questions such as, can they recite the expectations?); and observations (visual evidence of schoolwide expectations).

Recall from the Subscale Report in Figure 4.10 that the subscale for Expectations Defined was at 50 percent. A review of the Item Report in **Figure 4.11** on pages 66–67 shows two items that make up this subscale and each was scored a 1 out of 2. According to the scoring rubric (0, 1, 2), there were either too many expectations (>5) or they were negatively focused. So the leadership team for this school can review what they have developed for their expectations and then make changes to their plan accordingly.

For planning purposes, compare Subscale and Item scores to the TIC and SAS. Then identify the priorities that are correlated with one another and important to early establishment of the PBIS features. One clear conclusion from the data in Figures 4.10 and 4.11 is that the leadership team and the school need to determine whether they have too many expectations or whether the expectations are stated negatively. The data show that the reward system is not in place, which makes sense since the school also has only partial accomplishment for Expectations Defined and for Expectations Taught. This would also be a good time to complete and refine the schoolwide expectations and look closely at what needs to be in place to effectively begin teaching the expectations.

A Representative Sample?

When you administer the SAS, you want to secure the highest response rate possible. The sample school in Figures 4.8 and 4.9 had thirty-four respondents. This number may or may not be representative of that school. A representative response rate depends on the size of the school and number of staff. Do your best to obtain a high response rate. This takes effort. Do not assume it will occur without a lot of prompting and encouragement.

Sample Assessment Reports for Benchmarks of Quality (BoQ)

Total Score Report for BoQ

This school is in its fourth year of implementation, two years out of formal team training. The criterion total score for the BoQ for fidelity purposes is 70 percent or greater. As shown in **Figure 4.12** on page 68, this school achieved 80 percent. Let's look deeper.

Subscale Report for BoQ

The BoQ has ten subscales made up of fifty-three items. In the sample in **Figure 4.13** on page 69, eight of the ten subscales are above 70 percent; two are not. The two subscales below 70 percent are Faculty Commitment and Lesson Plans. Let's go to the Item Report and learn more.

Figure 4.10

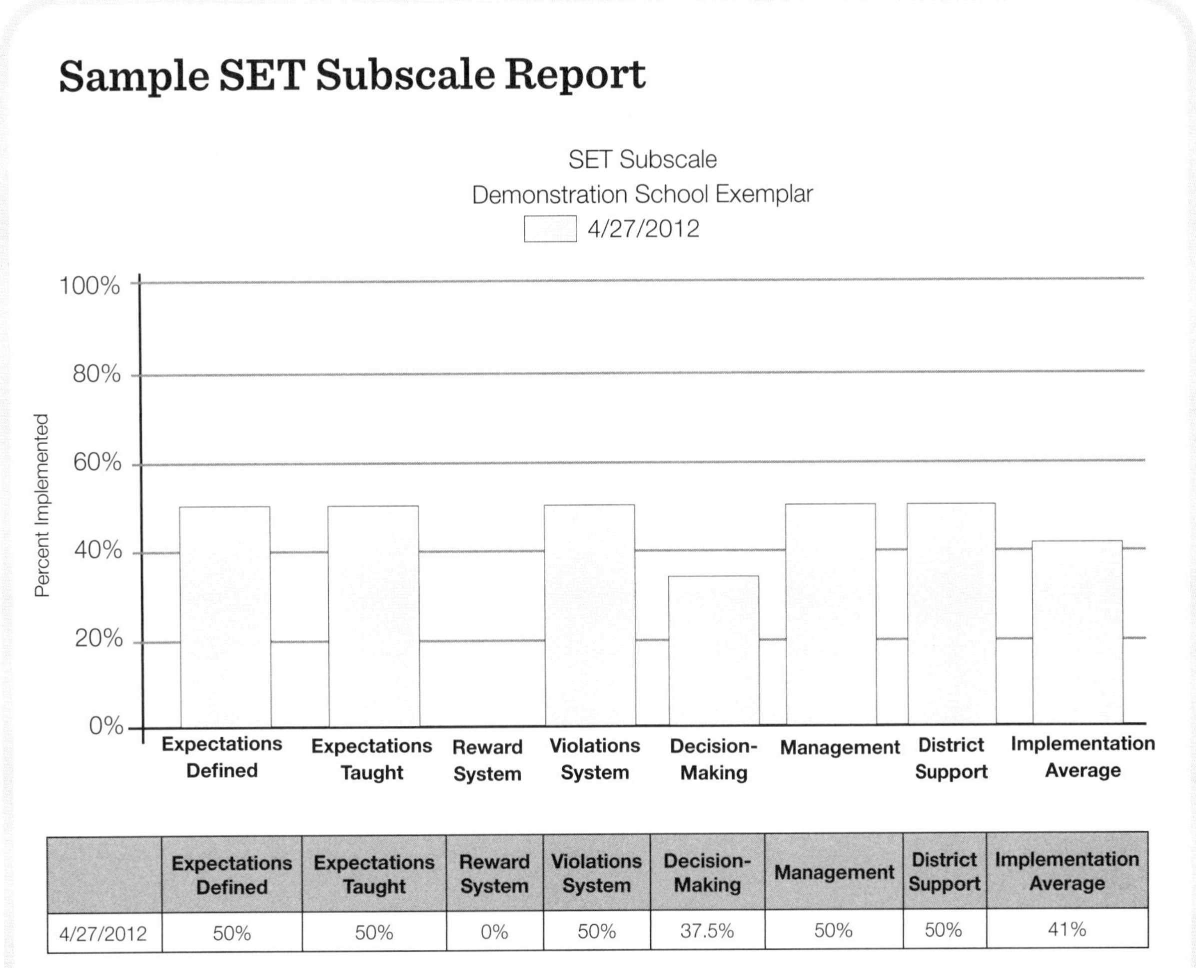

	Expectations Defined	Expectations Taught	Reward System	Violations System	Decision-Making	Management	District Support	Implementation Average
4/27/2012	50%	50%	0%	50%	37.5%	50%	50%	41%

Item Report for BoQ

Under Faculty Commitment in **Figure 4.14** on pages 70–72, a couple of items suggest that the leadership team might not share data regularly with staff and that staff feedback is not sought regularly. Remember, the BoQ is a self-assessment completed by PBIS Leadership Team members, who probably have a pretty accurate reading of their own activities. These two broad tasks to share data and to seek feedback are essential for achieving and maintaining staff buy-in and sustainability. Four years from the beginning, the leadership team should still be reporting data to substantiate successful outcomes and to justify action planning. These tasks should be part of routines established and maintained permanently.

The tasks that stand out related to Lesson Plans in Figure 4.14 suggest that the teaching of expectations has not yet been integrated with core curriculum and that the leadership team feels a need to develop more strategies for teaching these lessons. Another data point suggests the leadership team perceives that they need to improve the strategies for teaching the core features of PBIS to their students' families and community members. Digging deep into these data reports provides leadership teams with more

Figure 4.11

Sample SET Item Report

School Year	Number of Responses	Date Completed
2011–12	1	04/27/2012

Feature	Score (0, 1, 2)
Expectations Defined	
1. Is there documentation that staff has agreed to 5 or fewer positively stated school rules/behavioral expectations? (0=no; 1=too many/negatively focused; 2=yes)	1
2. Are the agreed upon rules & expectations publicly posted in 8 of 10 locations? (See interview & observation form for selection of locations) (0=0–4; 1=5–7; 2=8–10)	1
Expectations Taught	
3. Is there a documented system for teaching behavioral expectations to students on an annual basis? (0=no; 1=states that teaching will occur; 2=yes)	1
4. Do 90% of the staff asked state that teaching of behavioral expectations to students has occurred this year? (0=0–50%); 1=51–89%; 2=90–100%)	1
5. Do 90% of team members asked state that the schoolwide program has been taught/reviewed with staff on an annual basis? (0=0–50%; 1=51–89%; 2=90–100%)	1
6. Can at least 70% of 15 or more students state 67% of the school rules? (0=0–50%; 1=51–69%; 2=70–100%)	1
7. Can 90% or more of the staff asked list 67% of the school rules? (0=0–50%; 1=51–89%; 2=90–100%)	1
Ongoing Systems for Rewarding Behavioral Expectations	
8. Is there a documented system for rewarding student behavior? (0=no; 1=states to acknowledge, but not how; 2=yes)	0
9. Do 50% or more students asked indicate they have received a reward (other than verbal praise) for expected behaviors over the past two months? (0=0–25%; 1=26–49%; 2=50–100%)	0
10. Do 90% of staff asked indicate they have delivered a reward (other than verbal praise) to students for expected behavior over the past two months? (0=0–50%; 1=51–89%; 2=90–100%)	0
System for Responding to Behavioral Violations	
11. Is there a documented system for dealing with and reporting specific behavioral violations? (0=no; 1=states to document, but not how; 2=yes)	1
12. Do 90% of staff asked agree with administration on what problems are office-managed and what problems are classroom-managed? (0=0–50%; 1=51–89%; 2=90–100%)	1
13. Is the documented crisis plan for responding to extreme dangerous situations posted in 6 of 7 locations? (0=0–3; 1=4–5; 2=6–7)	1
14. Do 90% of staff asked agree with administration on procedure for handling extreme emergencies (stranger in building with weapon)? (0=0–50%; 1=51–89%; 2=90–100%)	1

continued →

Figure 4.11

Sample SET Item Report, continued

School Year	Number of Responses	Date Completed
2011–12	1	04/27/2012
Feature		Score (0, 1, 2)
Monitoring & Decision-Making		
15. Does the discipline referral form list (a) student/grade, (b) date, (c) time, (d) referring staff, (e) problem behavior, (f) location, (g) persons involved, (h) probable motivation, & (i) administrative decision? (0=0–3 items; 1=4–6 items; 2=7–9 items)		1
16. Can the administrator clearly define a system for collecting & summarizing discipline referrals (computer software, data entry time)? (0=no; 1=referrals are collected; 2=yes)		1
17. Does the administrator report that the team provides discipline data summary reports to the staff at least three times/year? (0=no; 1=1–2 times/year; 2=3 or more times/year)		1
18. Do 90% of team members asked report that discipline data is used for making decisions in designing, implementing, and revising schoolwide effective behavior support efforts? (0=0–50%; 1=51–89%; 2=90–100%)		0
Management		
19. Does the school improvement plan list improving behavior support systems as one of the top 3 school improvement plan goals? (0=no; 1=4th or lower priority; 2=1st–3rd priority)		1
20. Can 90% of staff asked report that there is a schoolwide team established to address behavior support systems in the school? (0=0–50%; 1=51–89%; 2=90–100%)		1
21. Does the administrator report that team membership includes representation of all staff? (0=no; 2=yes)		1
22. Can 90% of team members asked identify the team leader? (0=0–50%; 1=51–89%; 2=90–100%)		1
23. Is the administrator an active member of the schoolwide behavior support team? (0=no; 1=yes, but not consistently; 2=yes)		1
24. Does the administrator report that team meetings occur at least monthly? (0=no team meeting; 1=less often than monthly; 2=at least monthly)		1
25. Does the administrator report that the team reports progress to the staff at least four times per year? (0=no; 1=less than 4 times per year; 2=yes)		1
26. Does the team have an action plan with specific goals that is less than one year old? (0=no; 2=yes)		1
District-Level Support		
27. Does the school budget contain an allocated amount of money for building and maintaining schoolwide behavioral support? (0=no; 2=yes)		1
28. Can the administrator identify an out-of-school liaison in the district or state? (0=no; 2=yes)		1

information for planning and improving PBIS implementation, and for sustaining support and buy-in. At this stage, four years into implementation, the leadership team at this school should be regularly assessing implementation status, documenting fidelity, and sharing clear evidence of positive changes in student behavior.

Baseline Data

Baseline data is supposed to reflect where a school is prior to implementation, to give schools a starting point. We have noticed, however, that administrators and leadership teams are extremely sensitive about baseline scores. Team trainers are sometimes reluctant to share the data with schools out of fear that it will be too discouraging. This line of thinking among trainers can have the unfortunate consequence of reinforcing the notion that data are bad and that only top scores should be shared or reported. This thinking suggests that trainers are not doing a good job of teaching people a deep understanding of data and data-driven decision making.

Try this informal observation: The next time you are present when someone teaches a module or segment on data, pay attention to their choice of words for introducing the topic. Are they apologetic? Are they enthusiastic? Do they set the tone of being excited? Are they bored? What message sets the stage? If it were possible to change the views about the meaning and use of baseline data before administering assessments, this reframing might prevent a lot of unnecessary stress. Having said that, if your baseline score were the same as your score on a SET after five years, when you had supposedly achieved full implementation, then you would have another whole list of concerns and plans to address.

Figure 4.12

Sample BoQ Total Score Report

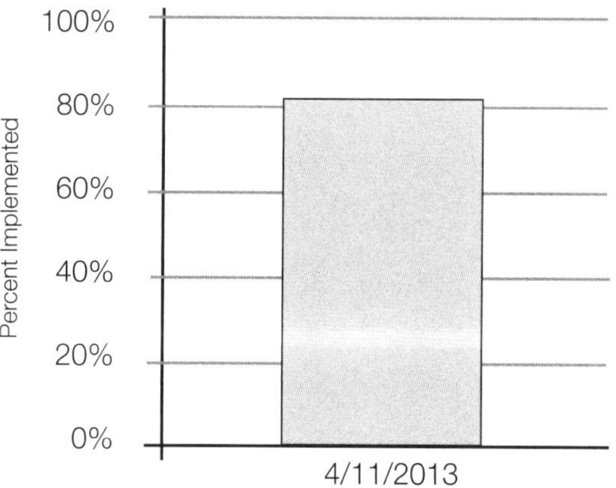

School Year	Date Completed	Total Score
2012–13	4/11/2012	81%

Figure 4.13

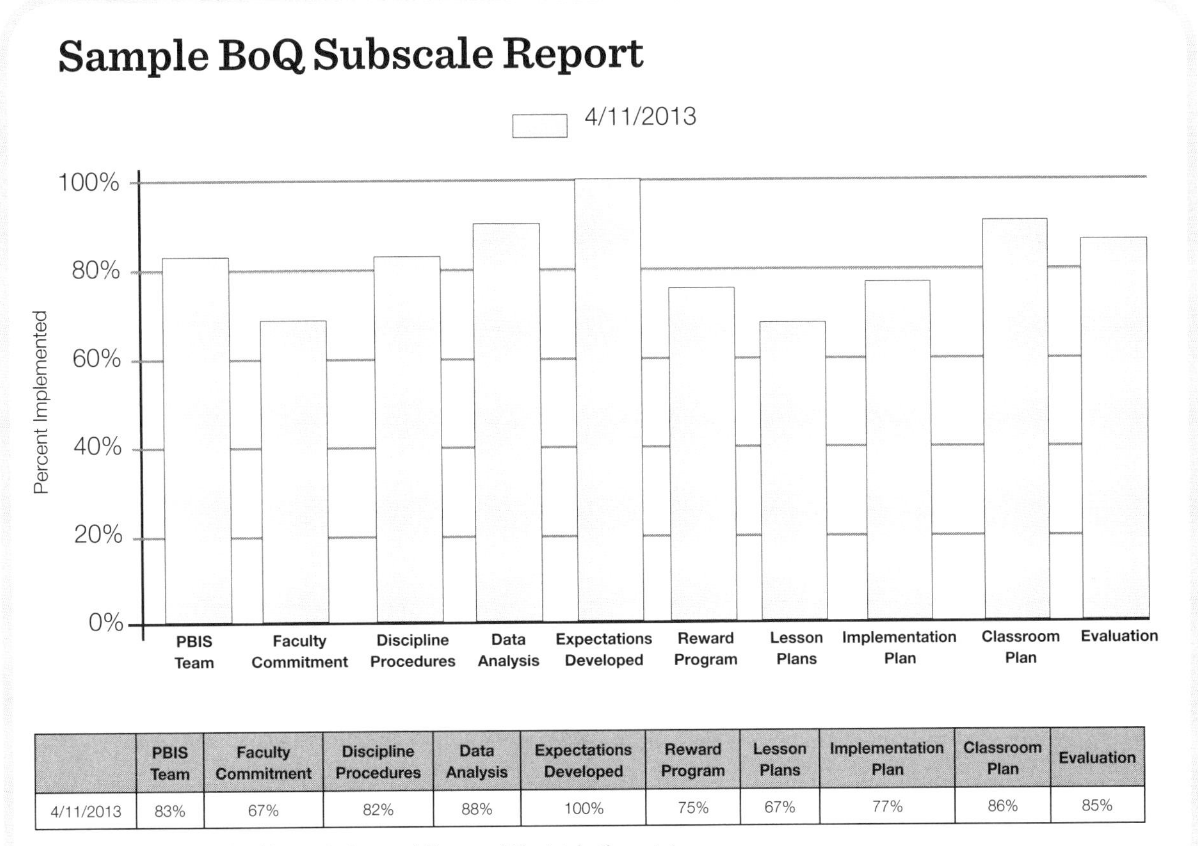

	PBIS Team	Faculty Commitment	Discipline Procedures	Data Analysis	Expectations Developed	Reward Program	Lesson Plans	Implementation Plan	Classroom Plan	Evaluation
4/11/2013	83%	67%	82%	88%	100%	75%	67%	77%	86%	85%

PBIS Implementation Inventory

Before closing this section on assessment tools, we want to introduce you to a new PBIS tool that is emerging from the OSEP Technical Assistance Center. In January 2014, Rob Horner and others shared the beta draft of the Positive Behavioral Interventions and Supports Implementation Inventory (PBIS Inventory).[13]

The PBIS Inventory is a tool that can be used during initial and sustained implementation of schoolwide PBIS. The instrument was developed to measure features assessed by previously existing tools used at all tiers. It is laid out in three sections (Tier 1, Tier 2, Tier 3), which can be completed separately. The intended purpose is for schools to use the inventory to assess progress at initial implementation, as a planning guide for implementation of all three tiers, as a measure of sustained PBIS practice, and finally as a tool to identify and recognize high-achieving and sustaining schools. The scoring criteria are like other PBIS assessment tools (0 = not implemented; 1 = partially in place; 2 = fully implemented). The inventory builds in specific data sources for scoring and brief rubrics associated with each.

The PBIS Inventory is a very promising instrument because it offers a single tool that serves multiple purposes across all tiers of implementation and sustainability, and with standardized scoring throughout. Early indications suggest that this tool will provide both practical information for leadership teams and schools to use, as well as a good source of data for evaluations across schools and for subsequent research related to PBIS practice and outcomes. Upon further testing, the PBIS Inventory may replace other tools or be integrated with existing tools. It is anticipated to be available at no cost at www.pbisasssessment.org or downloadable at www.pbis.org. Stay tuned for more information about this new tool at www.pbis.org and www.pbisapps.org.

[13]Algozzine, et al., 2013.

Figure 4.14

Sample BoQ Item Report

School Year	Number of Responses	Date Completed
2011–12	1	04/11/2013
Feature		**Score (0, 1, 2, 3)**
PBIS Team		
1. Team has administrative support		2 of 3
2. Team has regular meetings (at least monthly)		2 of 2
3. Team has established a clear mission/purpose		1 of 1
Faculty Commitment		
4. Faculty are aware of behavior problems across campus (regular data sharing)		1 of 2
5. Faculty are involved in establishing and reviewing goals		2 of 2
6. Faculty feedback is obtained throughout the year		1 of 2
Effective Procedures for Dealing with Discipline		
7. Discipline process is described in narrative format or depicted in graphic format		2 of 2
8. Process includes documentation procedures		1 of 1
9. Discipline referral form includes information useful in decision making		2 of 2
10. Problem behaviors are defined		2 of 3
11. Major/minor behaviors are clearly differentiated		1 of 2
12. Suggested array of appropriate responses to major (office-managed) problem behaviors		1 of 1
Data Entry & Analysis Plan Established		
13. Data system to collect and analyze ODR data exists		3 of 3
14. Additional data is collected (attendance, grades, faculty attendance, surveys)		1 of 1
15. Data is analyzed by the team at least monthly		2 of 2
16. Data is shared with team and faculty monthly (minimum)		1 of 2
Expectations & Rules Developed		
17. 3–5 positively stated schoolwide expectations are posted around school		3 of 3
18. Expectations apply to both students and staff		3 of 3
19. Rules developed and posted for specific settings (settings where data suggest rules are needed)		2 of 2
20. Rules are linked to expectations		1 of 1
21. Staff are involved in development of expectations and rules		2 of 2

continued →

Figure 4.14

Sample BoQ Item Report, continued

School Year	Number of Responses	Date Completed
2011–12	1	04/11/2013
Feature		Score (0, 1, 2, 3)
Reward Recognition Program Established		
22. A system of rewards has elements that are implemented consistently across campus		3 of 3
23. A variety of methods are used to reward students		1 of 2
24. Rewards are linked to expectations and rules		3 of 3
25. Rewards are varied to maintain student interest		1 of 2
26. Ratios of reinforcement to corrections are high		2 of 3
27. Students are involved in identifying/developing incentives		1 of 1
28. The system includes incentives for staff/faculty		1 of 2
Lesson Plans for Teaching Expectations/Rules		
29. A behavioral curriculum includes teaching expectations and rules		2 of 2
30. Lessons include examples and non-examples		1 of 1
31. Lessons use a variety of teaching strategies		1 of 2
32. Lessons are embedded into subject area curriculum		1 of 2
33. Faculty/staff and students are involved in development & delivery of behavioral curriculum		1 of 1
34. Strategies to share key features of SWPBIS program with families/community are developed and implemented		0 of 1
Implementation Plan		
35. A curriculum to teach the components of the discipline system to all staff is developed and used		1 of 2
36. Plans for training staff how to teach expectations/rules/rewards are developed, scheduled, and delivered		1 of 2
37. Develop, schedule, and deliver plans for teaching students expectations/rules/rewards		3 of 3
38. Booster sessions for students and staff are planned, scheduled, and delivered		2 of 2
39. Schedule for rewards/incentive for the year is planned		1 of 1
40. Plans for orienting incoming staff and students are developed and implemented		1 of 2
41. Plans for involving families/community are developed & implemented		1 of 1

continued →

Figure 4.14

Sample BoQ Item Report, continued

School Year	Number of Responses	Date Completed
2011–12	1	04/11/2013

Feature	Score (0, 1, 2, 3)
Reward Recognition Program Established	
42. Classroom rules are defined for each of the schoolwide expectations and are posted in classrooms	2 of 2
43. Classroom routines and procedures are explicitly identified for activities where problems often occur (e.g., entering class, asking questions, sharpening pencil, using restroom, dismissal)	2 of 2
44. Expected behavior routines in classrooms are taught	2 of 2
45. Classroom teachers use immediate and specific praise	1 of 2
46. Acknowledgment of students demonstrating adherence to classroom rules and routines occurs more frequently than acknowledgment of inappropriate behaviors	2 of 2
47. Procedures exist for tracking classroom behavior problems	1 of 2
48. Classrooms have a range of consequences/interventions for problem behavior that are documented and consistently delivered	2 of 2
Evaluation	
49. Students and staff are surveyed about PBIS	1 of 2
50. Students and staff can identify expectations and rules	2 of 2
51. Staff use discipline system documentation appropriately	3 of 3
52. Staff use reward system appropriately	3 of 3
53. Outcomes (behavior problems, attendance, morale) are documented and used to evaluate PBIS plan	2 of 3

Office Discipline Referral (ODR) Data

The ODR is ubiquitous; or, more precisely stated, sending students out of class for disruptive behavior is ubiquitous. The process for doing so and the monitoring of the practice may be as unique as each student affected by it. Referring students out of class is a practice used from coast to coast, in small one-school districts through large multi-school districts. For that reason, it is a common and somewhat standardized measure of student behavior or general building climate.

As mentioned previously, ODRs are also key measures of both progress and outcome data in the PBIS implementation process. ODR data can be used in different ways at different times. For example, ODR data may be part of the initial discussion of whether a school has a problem, part of problem solving, and part of evaluating outcomes and effectiveness.[14] In this section, we'll look at ways to track and organize ODR data so that your team can make the best use of it. These methods include the Schoolwide Information System (SWIS), other student information systems, and systems you can develop on your own to track data, such as spreadsheets.

[14]McIntosh, Frank, Spaulding, 2010.

ODR Data for Screening and Progress Monitoring

The ODR is not only a strong measure of outcomes, but also it can be used for screening and for monitoring progress of individual students and schoolwide PBIS efforts. How can ODRs be useful for screening? In Chapter 1 we depicted the conceptual basis of PBIS as a triangle. (See Figure 1.1.) Recall that a successful Tier 1 system includes easy and efficient interventions that result in 80 percent or more of students having zero to one ODR per school year. As you move up the triangle, Tier 2 interventions target students with two to five ODRs, essentially screening those students who need this extra assistance. At the top of the triangle is Tier 3, with the most intense interventions, which flags students who have six or more ODRs.

A terrific piece of research illustrates the potential in using ODRs as part of screening and early intervention with individual students. Researchers Kent McIntosh, Jennifer Frank, and Scott Spaulding have found that students who have two referrals in the fall tend to escalate to six or more by the end of the school year. The research demonstrates how monitoring ODRs and intervening early, at no more than two referrals, can stabilize behaviors earlier in the school year.[15] This finding supports the importance of using ODR data early and often and the significant effects of early intervention. This means more instructional time, less time out of the classroom, and more efficient use of resources.

On a schoolwide level, the leadership team can look at ODR patterns to help guide systems interventions, such as where to intervene. Many referrals across many settings may mean that the team needs to look at how solidly the features of PBIS implementation are in place. Conversely, a few students with a high number of referrals suggests looking at the Tier 2 and Tier 3 interventions or the individual student system. Using a solid, data-driven problem-solving approach enables leadership teams to define problems with precision and to establish goals, solutions, and outcomes. ODRs are the primary data source to measure the efficacy of interventions in specific settings over time.

ODRs and Disciplinary Procedures

ODRs can only help you monitor progress and outcomes if they contain accurate data that is collected on a consistent basis. Be sure to define the behaviors you are tracking very clearly, so that staff knows the difference between using inappropriate language (considered a minor behavioral issue) and being verbally abusive (considered a major issue).

If your school does not already have an effective ODR form in place, we recommend designing the form to require very little writing. Checkboxes are ideal—quick and easy. Also include a few lines for teachers and other staff to give a brief summation of what happened. They can describe the behavior trigger (e.g., students were asked to complete a worksheet) as well as the behavior (e.g., student crumpled worksheet, swearing). If administrators need more information, they can ask the staff member who filled out the form.

Some schools design the referral form without much thought. They simply ask who did what to whom and maybe the date and teacher involved. They may also include a section about what consequence the office handed out (e.g., call home, apology, detention, or suspension). The drawback to this approach is that it allows you to track only who is doing the behavior, what it was, and who it affected. It doesn't provide enough information to determine if your schoolwide interventions are really working or identify potential weak spots in your practices.

The ODR form is a key piece of data collection for your school, and staff must be able to complete the form accurately, uniformly, and quickly. The data collected from the form needs to be entered in a timely fashion. We recommend including the following items on your form:

[15] Ibid.

- student name
- date
- time of the incident
- student's classroom or advisory teacher (optional)
- student grade level
- referring staff member
- location of the incident
- problem behavior
- possible motivation
- others involved
- administrative decision and signature

If your school has signed up for SWIS (see below), these items cover information that SWIS asks for. The SWIS data fields lead to graphs and reports that support effective problem solving. Predefined fields ensure standardization of your process schoolwide. Even if you aren't using SWIS, the preceding list provides good information to have if your data entry system can support it. Page 75 is a reproducible **Office Discipline Referral (ODR) Form.**

Figure 4.15 on page 76 shows a sample filled-out ODR form.

Develop a Data System

ODRs should be gathered, summarized, and reported consistently. This information should be regularly available to the PBIS Leadership Team, at least monthly, in a format and depth that enables the team to solve problems. The information should also be shared with the entire staff at least quarterly so they fully understand the school's progress. The data collection system that your school uses should allow this sharing of information to happen easily.

Schoolwide Information System (SWIS)

Although numerous information systems are available to schools, we use the Web-based data collection system called SWIS to illustrate how the ODR is used in measuring progress and outcomes and in daily, active, data-based problem solving. We are not pushing SWIS over other programs, but schools have ready access to it and SWIS generates many reports that enable us to present thorough examples. This section is introductory; more detailed use and illustration with data-driven problem solving is covered in Chapter 5.

Rob Horner, one of the founders of PBIS, recognized the need to create a system that makes ODR data accessible and useful to staff. Based on experience and sound theory, Horner and University of Oregon staff developed SWIS in 1999 as a systems-change strategy to ensure that staff have easy access to the right data at the right time and in the right format to make the best decisions.Today, SWIS is used from coast to coast in thousands of schools. Schools pay an annual subscription licensing fee to use SWIS. In order to get SWIS, schools must work with a SWIS facilitator to meet certain readiness requirements and to participate in formal training.

When Char first started her position as the state PBIS coordinator for Minnesota in 2005, she had the opportunity to become a SWIS facilitator in order to train schools in using the SWIS database. She helped all of the new PBIS schools learn the program. One of her first schools was in a small town in the northern Minnesota, and the experience was unforgettable. This was the first school where she trained the PBIS Leadership Team in using SWIS. The administrator showed her the shoebox in which he securely kept their current ODRs. The principal commented on how much easier it was to go to the school board meetings with their data in that box. The shoebox may surprise you, but since then, Char has trained many schools and worked with many SWIS facilitators, and still she hears things like, "This school doesn't have a referral form; they just send kids to the office. Or we think that's where they go."

Beth consulted with a school that didn't even have a referral system—meaning no documentation of any kind regarding behaviors. Students were sent out of the room, mostly

Office Discipline Referral (ODR) Form

Student ______________________ Grade ________ Date ________ Referred by ______________________

Time ________________ Others involved: ☐ Peer ☐ Staff ☐ Teacher ☐ Guest teacher ☐ None

Location:
☐Playground ☐Cafeteria ☐Hallway ☐Classroom ☐Media center ☐Bathroom ☐Arrival/dismissal
☐Bus ☐Office ☐Nurse's office ☐Assembly ☐Other ______________________

Problem Behavior	Redirections	Possible Motivation	Administrative Decision
Minor: *Kept w/teacher; three minors of the same behavior = Major* **1.** Inappropriate language **2.** Defiance/disruption **3.** Property misuse **4.** Other ***Major:*** *Requires immediate administrative attention* **5.** Abusive language **6.** Fight/physical aggression **7.** Defiance/disrespect/noncompliance **8.** Harassment/bullying **9.** Property damage/vandalism **10.** Other	Take a break Proximity conference Parent phone call Move seat Assignment modification Other	**1.** Obtain peer attention **2.** Obtain adult attention **3.** Obtain item or activity **4.** Avoid peer attention **5.** Avoid adult attention **6.** Avoid task or activity **7.** Other	Loss of privilege Time in office Conference with student Parent phone call Act of apology Behavior room In-school suspension Out-of-school suspension Other Referral to: School psychologist School social worker Nurse Other

Comments: ____

____

____

Student response: ____

____

Administrative signature and date: ____

Figure 4.15

Sample Office Discipline Referral (ODR) Form

Student: Johnny Jones **Grade:** 6 **Date:** 10/12/13 **Referred by:** Ms. Nelson
Time: 9:45 **Others involved:** x Peer ☐Staff ☐Teacher ☐Guest Teacher ☐None

Location:
☐Playground ☐Cafeteria x Hallway ☐Classroom ☐Media center ☐Bathroom
☐Arrival/dismissal ☐Bus ☐Office ☐Nurse's office ☐Assembly ☐Other ____________

Problem Behavior	Redirections	Possible Motivation	Administrative Decision
***Minor:** Kept w/ teacher; three minors of the same behavior = Major* **1.** Inappropriate language **2.** Defiance/ disruption **3.** Property misuse **4.** Other ***Major:** Requires immediate administrative attention* **5.** Abusive language **6.** Fight/physical aggression **7.** **X** Defiance/ disrespect/ noncompliance **8.** Harassment/ bullying **9.** Property damage/ vandalism **10.** Other	**X** Take a break **X** Proximity conference Parent phone call Move seat Assignment modification Other	**1.** **X** Obtain peer attention **2.** Obtain adult attention **3.** Obtain item or activity **4.** Avoid peer attention **5.** Avoid adult attention **6.** Avoid task or activity **7.** Other	Loss of privilege Time in office **X** Conference with student **X** Parent phone call Act of apology Behavior room In-school suspension Out-of-school suspension Other Referral to: School psychologist School social worker Nurse Other

Comments: In the classroom, Johnny said "who cares?" when I asked him to name the capital of Canada. I asked him to take a break in class. These two things got the class laughing.
Student response: "Yes I said it. I was bored in class."
Administrative signature and date: Mrs. Gustavson 10/12/13

One PBIS portal provides all PBIS-related tools, including the SWIS Suite, PBIS Assessment, PBIS Evaluation, and SAMI (SWIS Account Management Interface). Visit www.pbisapps.org and select "Resources;" this will take you to a series of locations for each application. There you can find a list of resources, watch a demo, and get more information about subscription fees and setup.

to an administrator; sometimes to the school social worker. These schools had no data to track what behavior was causing the greatest challenge in the school or how many times students had been referred out and for what behavior. Administrators were basing their needs on assumptions about what was happening in their school. The tradition was just to send students out as the teachers deemed necessary. Beth gave these schools a sample referral form and asked them to start collecting data about behaviors. The staff was enthusiastic to learn more about their school.

Now, when implementing PBIS, we recommend that schools start completely from scratch with their ODR process, rather than competing with a current referral form, or rather 3,000 printed Rediforms. We discourage schools from keeping ODRs in a shoebox and strongly encourage them to use technology as holder of and processing tool for the data, which allows for immediate and active use of ODR data for decision making.

As an information system, SWIS is designed as a user-friendly tool for decision making about student behavior. It is one of the best and most efficient tools we have seen. Char still uses SWIS as a state trainer, and she works with coaches and building administrators who use it daily. She also works with many schools that are using other student information systems; these alternatives do not seem as clearly defined and accessible for the type of decision making done at the school level. A system like SWIS has a very different purpose than larger student information systems that schools use because it is strictly related to student behavior and was created for school-based decisions.

We both like using SWIS because it allows for easy data entry and easy monitoring of behavioral data. If your school is going to use another data system, make sure you can quickly find the big five areas of behavioral data and ensure that you can "drill down" with custom reports to develop precision statements about the behavior in your school. Another key feature of SWIS and embedded within its training is an in-depth, effective

What Are the "Big Five" Core Behavioral Data Reports?

When the University of Oregon initially developed and launched SWIS, they created and installed what was known as the "big five" data reports needed for effective problem solving:

1. Average number of referrals per day
2. Referrals by location
3. Referrals by time of day
4. Referrals by type of problem behavior
5. Referrals by student

These big five reports have been our best friends for a number of years. In August 2010, SWIS 5.0 launched a new version, which soon became SWIS 5.1. This is a huge modification of the application, reflecting a great deal of feedback since SWIS was first launched. It is more user-friendly and effective. The new dashboard (see **Figure 4.16** on page 78) provides the viewer with the big five Core Reports, plus two new additions: referrals by day of the week and referrals by grade level. The dashboard greets the viewer with up-to-date data on all seven areas, plus a chronological listing of referrals. This dashboard provides a picture of what has happened in your building. Based on this picture, you might choose to hold a student assistance meeting, create a drill-down report for a particular student, schedule a meeting with a grade-level professional learning community (PLC), or open your custom template for your fifth-grade classrooms. We will talk more about SWIS in the context of problem solving in Chapter 5.

Figure 4.16

SWIS Dashboard

problem-solving model. The basic components of this model are derived from a multiyear research project conducted by the University of Oregon and produced under the title Team-Initiated Problem Solving, or TIPS. (See Chapter 5 for details on TIPS.)

One of the barriers to some schools readily adopting SWIS is that they have to double enter some of the information: once into SWIS and a second time into their district's student information system. Many schools, however, have contacted us after using their district system asking how to get started with SWIS because it allowed them to get the data they so desperately needed. SWIS developers are well aware of these concerns; in fact, they have begun development on ways for different information systems to integrate with SWIS without loss of integrity.

Using a Spreadsheet to Track ODR Data

If your school does not use a behavior monitoring system (such as SWIS or another formal data-based program), you can use a spreadsheet. Doing so will allow you to arrange and sort the data in many different ways. **Figure 4.17** presents a sample spreadsheet with all the necessary parts of data collection.

When all of the referrals are recorded on the spreadsheet, they can be sorted by date (how many referrals on average per day?), by student (which students have the most referrals?), by behavior (which behaviors should we target?), by time, by location, and by action taken on the referral. You can also calculate the total number of referrals to monitor whether the total number of ODRs is going up or down. Multiply the total number of referrals by twenty minutes (the average length of time spent dealing with each referral) to see just how much academic time is lost to behaviors and how much administrative time is spent dealing with behaviors. Visit the Maryland PBIS website at www.pbismaryland.org and look for the Cost/Benefit Worksheet that will do this for you.

As a framework to change systems, PBIS requires schools to collect baseline data about student behaviors. But remember, it can take two to three years to set up a solid foundation with PBIS Tier 1. *Patience is key.* Begin collecting some data as your school prepares to implement PBIS, and then continue the practice. Over time, as you follow the data trail, you will start to notice trends and patterns in your school.

Figure 4.17

Sample ODR Spreadsheet

Date	Student Name	Behavior	Time	Location	Outcome
9/10/12	Mark	Disrespect—minor	12:30	Art room	Reflection sheet
9/12/12	Kevin	Tech. violation	9:45	Comp lab	No computer for a week
9/13/12	Mia	Dress code	8:30	Front entry	Changed clothes
9/13/12	Juan	Inappropriate language—minor	12:15	Math class	Reflection sheet
9/14/12	Kierra	Inappropriate language—minor	9:50	Office	Reflection sheet
9/14/12	Fred	Fighting	1:30	Gym class	Suspension—two days
9/14/12	John	Fighting	1:30	Gym class	Suspension—two days

Chapter 5

Effective Data-Based Decision Making

In Chapter 4, we talked in detail about the various assessment tools for measuring progress, fidelity, and outcomes in PBIS implementation. In this chapter, we discuss data-based decision making using these tools. This step relies on a solid foundation and fluency with the tools that your team uses. We offer the following advice to new PBIS Leadership Teams:

1. **Learn the data tools right from the beginning.** Learn the name of the tool, the purpose, the source, the content, what the tool measures, and how to interpret it and use it in planning. In Minnesota, teams complete a Team Implementation Checklist (TIC) on the first morning of training. Sometimes, however, the simplest obstacle can block use of this tool and others. For example, the team or data manager may not have the school's identification number to access online surveys. This minor barrier can prevent schools from entering data.
2. **Read through each tool and ask questions about any item or scoring that you do not understand.** For example, leadership teams often struggle with some of the wording on the Team Implementation Checklist (TIC). One item (#5) refers to conducting an audit of school committees. Without some clarification, teams don't know that this refers to the Working Smarter Matrix activity that helps schools identify and integrate or disband current activities and committees that have outlived their usefulness to the school.
3. **Make sure that the PBIS Leadership Team is fluent with the tools.** Everyone on the team needs to spend time to become as fluent as possible. When one person, the principal or the coach, is the holder of the access or the understanding, then the team may not buy in or have the knowledge to effectively use the information when that person is gone.
4. **Have a clear practice for ensuring transmission of information to team members.** You don't want information to get lost with turnover of team members and staff. For example, I have had teams contact me after a year of looking for passwords and consequently missing out on opportunities to gather and use data.
5. **Learn the tools and translate them to outcomes, goals, and action plans.** Each of the tools we discussed in Chapter 4 has multiple reports available that provide details about the scores. Understand these reports so that you can use the information to plan actions and to answer questions from team or staff members. Once, during a district PBIS planning day during which several school PBIS Leadership Teams presented all of their data, one team member asked how two subscales compared on different instruments. No one

knew the answer, or even what content was included on each instrument. If your team doesn't understand how to translate the tools, how will team members be able to present data to the staff and others?

6. **Adopt an action planning routine.** We give examples of such routines in this chapter. Some schools don't use data either because the data are not available or the team doesn't know how to translate it to an action plan. This requires new skills and a broad base of buy-in. Without action planning skills and consensus, it can be easier and more fun to focus on posters, T-shirts, tickets, celebrations, and other visible pieces of PBIS implementation *without* having the data to support these efforts.
7. **Have the ability to "drill down" into data.** In Minnesota, for example, we promote systematic use of office discipline referral (ODR) data right away. When you have established the eight PBIS features and are problem solving with the student data, you will need to be able to refine that data. This is very challenging for many schools, even if they are using SWIS. Some PBIS coaches do not have access to student data, or the data system cannot easily provide the information needed. This is a huge barrier, but it can be overcome with practice, coaching, support, and patience.

With these thoughts in mind, Chapter 5 focuses on some specific routines for engaging your team in data-based decision making or problem solving. We will talk about some simple problem-solving approaches and then briefly review the TIPS model.

What Is Data-Based Decision Making or Problem Solving?

The concept of problem solving is very common in fields such as education, business, and health care. The most basic approach suggests that you identify the problem, develop and implement solutions, and then evaluate the results. It sounds easy and straightforward, and it is—except for the human factor. In a group process, the group can be hijacked and taken off course by group dynamics. Perhaps the facilitator or leader is less experienced in facilitating a group, or conflict develops as strong personalities among group members clash. Carrying out effective problem solving is definitely a skill.

Along with the skills required, it helps to have a model that clearly delineates the problem-solving process. In the course of implementing PBIS as a team-led model, you will be problem solving with data both to do basic planning and implementation, and to develop detailed solutions for schoolwide interventions. This problem solving relies heavily on all the data sources and methods discussed in Chapter 4.

If you look across states at different PBIS websites, you will find numerous examples of problem solving. **Figure 5.1** on page 82 shows the decision-making model that the state of Missouri uses. Note their six-step decision-making process:

1. Identify the outcomes
2. Identify the current status
3. Analyze the current status
4. Develop a plan
5. Implement the plan
6. Evaluate the plan

The Missouri model includes the PBIS data tools that are related to each step. This decision-making approach aligns with the eight key features of PBIS (see page 9 in Chapter 1) and illustrates a planning model for PBIS implementation. The Missouri graphic provides a great starting point for decision making. In addition, teams need a process and routines to guide team behavior in order to accomplish the planning.

Minnesota also uses a graphic to depict a data-based planning and problem-solving model, as shown in **Figure 5.2** on page 83.

Figure 5.1

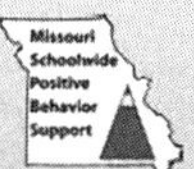

Missouri Schoolwide PBS State Initiative. Reprinted with permission from pbismissouri.org.

Minnesota uses seven planning steps that are similar to Missouri's. Notice both models include the names of data tools to use at each step. In addition, Minnesota builds some questions into each step. Both models provide a graphic prompt that might help PBIS coaches and teams adopt a logical sequence and routine for using various tools at different steps in problem solving.

These simple, data-based decision models for action planning are really effective throughout PBIS implementation. In the initial stages, the leadership team focuses the action planning on establishing the eight key features of the PBIS framework. The assessment tools we discussed in Chapter 4—TIC, SAS, SET, and BoQ—are the data measures you will use to evaluate your implementation progress, fidelity, and outcomes. In addition, ODR data will also help you assess progress and make decisions about next steps.

Identifying Outcomes

Evaluators say to start with the end in mind and to determine where you want to end up as a result of performing x, y, and z. When PBIS cofounder George Sugai and others do training, they charge teams to always start with the outcome. That outcome is the beginning of the roadmap. Schools generally decide to pursue PBIS implementation for particular reasons related to the social climate. This is the basis for your desired PBIS outcome, mission, vision, and so on. Most leadership teams that participate in formal training develop a very clear statement of purpose. Here's an example:

> The purpose of Elm Creek Elementary's Schoolwide Positive Behavioral Interventions and Supports Program is to establish and maintain safe and effective

Figure 5.2

Minnesota Problem Solving and Data-Based Action Planning Model

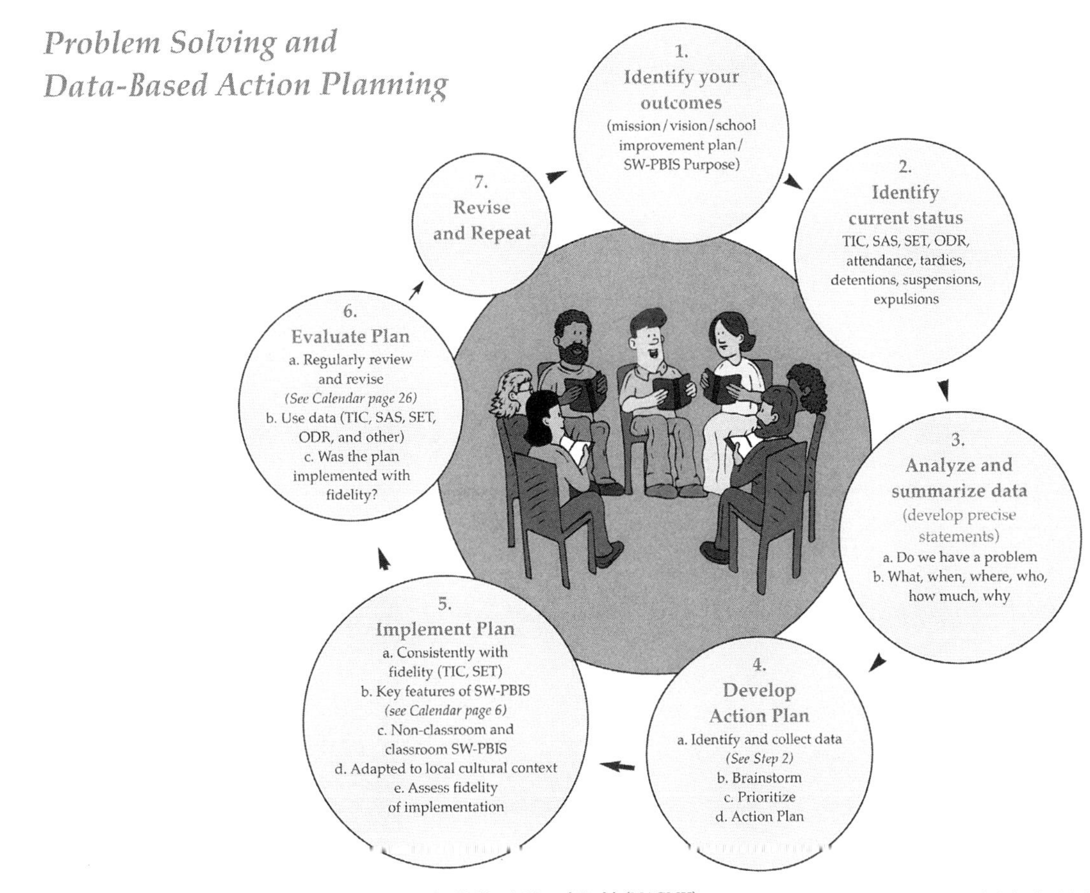

Reprinted with permission from the Minnesota Association for Children's Mental Health (MACMH). MACMH Coach Calendar 2013-2014

school environments that maximize academic achievement and the social competence of all students.

Current Status

Once you have determined a clear outcome, assess where you stand in relation to that outcome. This is essentially a gap analysis. Use some of the data you gathered when your school first considered adopting PBIS. For example, did your school see a larger than desired number of student absences, tardies, detentions, suspensions, expulsions, or ODRs? Something created the momentum for change, the impetus to seek an even better learning environment. Schools frequently say they were doing pretty well but wanted to be even better. A school does not have to be in dire straits to seek change.

In the early stages of implementation, leadership teams use three of the four tools we discuss during year one. The state your school is in will determine which tools are used as part of a standardized statewide approach. Initially, schools find the Team Implementation Checklist (TIC) to be a very useful tool to assess the presence of Tier 1 features. You can complete the TIC during the course of a team discussion. Also in the early stages, you may elect to conduct a

Self-Assessment Survey (SAS) to see how school staff members perceive your school in relation to the eight key features of PBIS. The schoolwide portion of the SAS is especially helpful for comparing and assessing progress. It helps you recognize what PBIS features may already be partially in place, helps you gather staff input, and provides an opportunity to involve staff and build buy-in. Depending on your statewide approach, your team will likely use the SET or the BoQ to measure progress and fidelity.

Analyzing and Summarizing Your Data

Once you have gathered your data, you need to develop and answer questions. The data should help you do this. First, do you think, from looking at the data, that you have a problem? This can be, for example, the gap between your desired outcome and your current status. In the early stages of PBIS implementation, your questions will focus on the eight key features of PBIS and the extent to which your school has some of these features in place. Again, the TIC is a very useful tool here. Comparing your TIC and SAS data will enable you to identify specific areas where you need to focus implementation efforts.

> A school does not have to be in dire straits to seek change.

For example, your TIC data may indicate that your school has defined a small number of behavioral expectations, but the SAS responses may indicate that these expectations are not in place. This reveals a discrepancy between what your leadership team and your staff perceive to be in place. Discrepancies are common whenever you compare data. At this point, you will need to do some exploration to explain the difference in perception: review the data with your staff. Gathering this additional input not only helps tremendously to fill in your understanding but also builds further buy-in from staff. The combined scores from the TIC and the SAS, along with the data-driven conversation you have with staff, will help you begin action planning. (See Figure 4.1 on page 50 for a summary of the different PBIS assessment tools—who uses them, the method of gathering information, and the purpose of each.)

Developing an Action Plan

During the early stage of PBIS implementation, action planning focuses on getting PBIS in place with fidelity. As you progress toward fidelity, action planning focuses more specifically on student behavior. Be sure to build fidelity checks into your action plans. If you don't stop to assess how you're doing and report results, you won't know if you've achieved the outcomes targeted by the action plan. Decide who is going to follow up on the actions and what constitutes a completed task. Determining all of this in advance will go a long way to reinforcing your efforts.

A critical component in action planning is documenting the decisions you make at leadership team meetings. This documentation helps keep team members accountable and focused on tasks, which is what enables them to make progress. The Team Implementation Checklist (TIC) includes an action plan that matches the various sections of the TIC and the eight key features of PBIS. You can download this document at www.pbisapps.org, or create your own planning format.

A word of caution: One common omission in action planning is forgetting to record decisions and accountability. Adopt an action planning format that ensures that you document each leadership team meeting, the issues discussed, the participants, the action steps and tasks, and the task specifics—including the who, what, where, and by when to be accomplished. See pages 168 and 176 in the Appendix for examples.

Let's look at how you can form an action plan using the TIC. In the example that follows, we have TIC reports from a school in its first year of implementation. The school completed two TICs, one at the beginning of implementation and a second one after three months. **Figure 5.3** shows the TIC Subscale Report that tracks the eight

PBIS features over both checklist dates. Beneath the graph is the table showing the percentage of items in place. Using these data allows the leadership team to see areas of improvement, progress in establishing PBIS features, and areas of need. This school started with a strong commitment and an established team. It made excellent progress in increasing its use of assessment tools and in further defining its expectations. One area that still needs attention is developing an action plan based on the TIC—a very important step, as noted previously in the discussion about using TIC data for early implementation (see page 84).

This school also has needs in the area of teaching expectations. The scores in a subsection of the school's TIC Item Report, shown in **Figure 5.4** on page 86, demonstrate the teaching tasks that need strengthening. The four items are all rated as a 1, which means they are only partially in place. The PBIS Leadership Team can use this data to begin an action plan for teaching. **Figure 5.5** on page 86 illustrates a plausible plan based on two items related to teaching: (1) developing teaching plans and (2) developing a teaching matrix for the non-classroom areas identified.

Implementing the Action Plan

The ultimate goal of your school is to implement PBIS with fidelity. As we discussed earlier, this occurs in stages over several years. With each step you accomplish, consider how you will check the fidelity of that component (using TIC, SET,

Figure 5.3

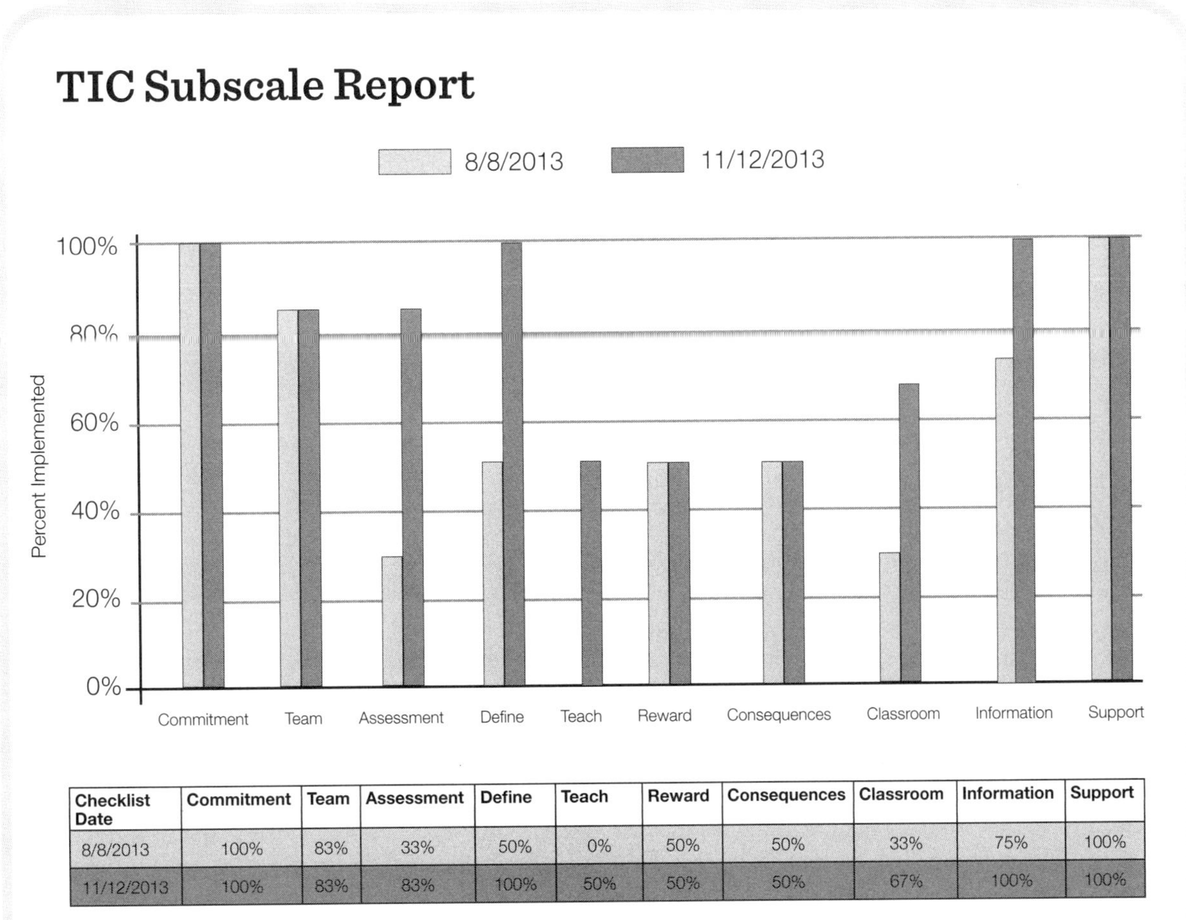

Checklist Date	Commitment	Team	Assessment	Define	Teach	Reward	Consequences	Classroom	Information	Support
8/8/2013	100%	83%	33%	50%	0%	50%	50%	33%	75%	100%
11/12/2013	100%	83%	83%	100%	50%	50%	50%	67%	100%	100%

Figure 5.4

Item Report November 2013

Establish Schoolwide Expectations	
1. Teaching plans for schoolwide expectations are developed.	1
2. Schoolwide behavioral expectations are taught directly and formally.	1
3. System in place to acknowledge/reward schoolwide expectations.	1
4. Clearly defined and consistent consequences and procedures for undesirable behaviors are developed.	1

Figure 5.5

TIC Action Plan

TIC Action Plan			
Date: November 15, 2013 Participants: Carol, Jared, Indira, Susan, Jackie, Nassar, Barbara, William			
Activity/Task	**Activity/Task Analysis**	**Who**	**By When**
1. Develop teaching plans for schoolwide expectations	Will prepare 5 specific lesson plans, one for each expectation, that are relevant to grades 4–6 for hallways and lunchroom to be measured by document review and TIC follow-up.	Jared, Susan, Indira	2/15/14
Fidelity check for Task 1	The coach will check in with the subgroup to identify progress on task, resources needed, and adherence to timelines. The subgroup will rate its progress on a scale of 1–5, with 5 being on time.	Jared	1/15/14
2. Develop a schoolwide teaching matrix	Carol and Jackie will work with team 1 to develop a teaching matrix.	Carol and Jackie	3/15/14
Fidelity check for Task 2	The coach will check in with the subgroup to identify progress on task, resources needed, and adherence to timelines. The subgroup will rate its progress on a scale of 1–5, with 5 being on time.	Jared	2/1/14

or observations, for example) and also how you will sustain it (for example, ongoing teaching for staff and students and planning for team member turnover). You'll ask questions such as these:

- When the team and the school staff adopt the expectations and begin to teach these, do we see follow-through?
- Are all staff and all students involved?
- How and where do the lesson plans and supports come for teaching staff?
- Who works with the non-licensed staff?

You'll also look at how to achieve consistency and then maintain it. This may involve asking questions such as these:

- Are we involving staff in all decisions?
- Are we providing refresher training to new and existing staff?
- Are we observing staff to ensure that they are teaching expectations?

Evaluating the Action Plan

Once you have given your school time to implement the plan, you need to decide how you will evaluate it. The overall framework and standard for comparison are the eight key features of PBIS. The PBIS data assessment tools allow you to evaluate implementation and fidelity fairly easily and efficiently. You have to establish the routine for doing so; for example, determine the schedule, person responsible, and tools to be used. Implementation flows throughout your building: schoolwide, non-classroom areas, classrooms, and individual students. Evaluate the key features in all areas of your building.

Revising the Action Plan

Once you have achieved the stated outcomes and followed your evaluation plan to check on implementation and fidelity, it is time to use the data collected to make revisions in your action plan. Update your data from progress and fidelity or ODR. Check your fidelity of implementation for all aspects of your plan. Adapt to changing contextual needs.

Once you have given your school time to implement the plan, you need to decide how you will evaluate it.

Problem-Solving Approaches within the SWIS System

The SWIS system was launched in 1999 with the intention of making ODR data systematic and easily available to school staff in order to improve the efficiency of problem solving. Each school that adopts this data system receives specific training in using SWIS and in data-based problem solving. The SWIS approach to problem solving can work with almost any ODR system, as long as the leadership team can gather the level of data needed. The content and process of SWIS problem solving require your leadership team to follow seven steps:

1. Establish an effective team.
2. Define the problem with precision.
3. Define the goal before the solution.
4. Build functional solutions.
5. Transform solutions into action plans.
6. Measure the fidelity and impact of action plans.
7. Adapt solutions to new data.

In the SWIS training, the trainers do an excellent job of defining and describing what each of these steps means and looks like. Using real examples, the trainers demonstrate each step based on school data. Before concluding, the trainers provide case studies and simulations so that participants can build fluency through practice with active coaching. The materials are excellent and the delivery of the training provides effective teaching and learning outcomes. The seven steps are defined below.

Step 1: Establish an effective team.

An effective team is priceless. Creating one requires very thoughtful planning and recruiting so that the team is representative of the stakeholders it serves. You must spell out roles and recruit staff with the skills, interests, and motivation needed to fulfill their assigned role. (See Chapter 2 for more on this topic.)

Step 2: Define the problem with precision.

A requirement for good problem solving is clearly defining the problem so that everyone is working to solve the same problem. The SWIS model uses the term "precision statement" to articulate a problem in a very specific and concrete way so that the team can focus its efforts on a solvable problem. Many groups start working with a problem description that is too primary (or generalized) and consequently difficult to develop an appropriate solution. Precision statements are built on the who, what, where, when, how, and why questions. You'll develop your precision statements using the big five behavioral data reports (referrals by average number per day, by type of behavior, by time of day, by location, and by student), referred to as the Core Reports in SWIS 5.1, which adds two additional reports on referrals by grade level and by day of the week.

Following is a chunk of data from which a problem can be defined:

> The total number of ODRs from last year was 243. The most frequent referral was "disruption to class" (65 percent, or 159), which breaks down like this: 15 percent during advisory from 8:15–8:45 a.m., and 35 percent were from ninth graders, 30 percent from tenth graders, 20 percent from eleventh graders, and 15 percent from twelfth graders. Regarding the remaining referrals, 40 percent occurred after advisory and before lunch, 10 percent were during lunch, and 35 were percent were after lunch.

The chart in **Figure 5.6** shows how this data can be framed in generalized primary statements or phrased in precise, evidence-based language to make precision statements that clearly define a problem.

Drilling even deeper could tell you who the students are and in which classrooms the disruptive behavior occurs during the rest of the day. The PBIS Leadership Team for this school has

Figure 5.6

Primary versus Precision Statements

Primary Statements	Precision Statements
Too many referrals. September has more suspensions than last year. The advisory period isn't working. There are too many referrals for disruptions.	The most frequent referral from last year was disruption to class (65 percent or 159) [answers what]. 15 percent [answers how many] of referrals for disruption occurred during advisory [answers where] from 8:15–8:45 [answers when], 35 percent were from 9th graders [answers who] to gain peer attention [answers why].

chosen to focus on the advisory period for teaching the new skills, with a focus on ninth-grade students. The team will look for an overall reduction in disruptive behavior as students transfer new skills to other classes.

Precision statements are based on refined data, which reduces the guesswork involved with a problem and focuses instead on finding a solution. This puts resources where they are most needed. The PBIS Leadership Team writes precision statements for each problem. (For further guidance on writing precision statements, see reproducible worksheet titled **Data Drill-Down for Creating Precision Statements** on page 171 of the Appendix.)

Step 3: Define the goal before the solution.

Once you have precisely defined the problem, you then define a schoolwide outcome, or smart goal. "Smart" serves as a mnemonic device to remember the factors to incorporate into a goal:

Specific
Measurable
Attainable
Relevant
Timely

Keeping in mind the data sample for disruptive behavior presented in Step 2, the leadership team for this school identified the following SMART goal:

> Ninth graders will represent no more than 1 percent of referrals from morning advisories for disruptive behavior each month for the remainder of the school year.

The team further defined this goal by clarifying how each of the factors in SMART related to the goal:

Specific: The PBIS team wanted to decrease the total number of ODRs from morning advisories by ninth graders to no more than 1 percent.

Measurable: The team will track and count referrals toward this goal level.

Attainable: The PBIS team is looking to decrease the number of referrals to no more than 1 percent by the end of the year.

Relevant: The goal is important because reducing ODRs is in the school improvement plan as one of the top three schoolwide goals.

Timely: This is current data that shows the need throughout the ninth-grade class.

Step 4: Build functional solutions.

Once a SMART goal has been defined, the PBIS Leadership Team can then develop a solution to the problem. Solutions offer steps for action. Precision statements guide this process by enabling the team to focus on very specific areas where the problem occurs, rather than make broad, unnecessary interventions. For the precision statements shown in Figure 5.6, the leadership team might recommend that administration assign more staff to monitor the hallways to encourage students to get to advisory on time; or the leadership team might recommend that students serve on the advisory planning committee to make the activities more relevant to the students.

Without precision statements, leadership team members might make general statements about what they are seeing; for example, "So many of our students are disruptive!" or, "Advisory is a waste of time. No one wants to be there." These statements do not lead to functional solutions. With the limited resources available to schools, PBIS Leadership Teams can't afford to try and guess where the hot spot areas are in their school. Teams need to get it right the first time whenever possible. Using precision statements not only help them get it right but also enable them to build functional solutions.

In addition to precision statements, six components build a foundation for functional solutions. These components are prevention, teaching, recognition, extinction, corrective consequences, and data collection. The solutions worksheet presented in **Figure 5.7** on page 90 shows how these six components can help determine a solution for the example of behavior disruptions.

Figure 5.7

Solutions Worksheet

Solution Component	Action Steps
Prevention	*How can we avoid the problem context?* • Encourage students to be on time to advisory and cause fewer disruptions by arriving late. • Reteach expectations. • Teachers will use the hand signal to get students' attention. Teachers will remodel this with students throughout the day.
Teaching	*How can we define, teach, and monitor what we want?* • Teach 9th graders to associate teacher hand signal with prompt for expectations. • Advisory class will be used to focus on teaching/learning about schoolwide expectations for 9th grade. William is creating this with the advisory sub-group. (The group is also creating advisory lesson plans for grades 10–12 with a focus on college and career.)
Recognition	*How can we build in systematic rewards for positive behavior?* • Increase the ratio to 8:1 for reward tickets given for following schoolwide expectations. • Quarterly the school will have assemblies to recognize students who are demonstrating a positive effect on our school.
Extinction	*How can we prevent problem behavior from being rewarded?* • Reinforce regularly the routine and structure for advisory; write it on board and announce verbally. If advisory class completes routines without delays due to disruptions, class will gain 10 minutes for social interaction at the end. • Teachers can refer chronic disrupters to the student assistance team for help with an extinction plan based on the individual student's motivation for the behavior.
Corrective Consequences	*What are efficient, consistent consequences for problem behavior?* • When students are referred out of class for being disruptive they will go to the behavior room and complete a short packet on meeting schoolwide expectations. • When they return to class they will have a short conference with the teacher or staff member who referred them to the behavior room.
Data Collection	*How will we collect and use data to monitor our efforts and evaluate 1) fidelity and 2) impact on student outcomes?* • Teacher and para will review routines and completion daily. • When staff members fill out a referral form they will complete all boxes, including interventions attempted in the classroom. • The PBIS data team will review data weekly to watch for progress toward decreasing referrals for disruptions.

Step 5: Transform solutions into action plans.

Once you have identified the solution components and the accompanying action steps, you are ready to develop a comprehensive action plan that includes the six solution components as well as action items, persons responsible, timelines, and how you will measure the outcome. **Figure 5.8** on page 92 shows a sample action plan to address disruptive behavior.

Step 6: Measure the fidelity and impact of action plans.

A major part of any successful action plan is evaluation. This process is straightforward. It requires you to monitor outcomes. Ask questions in two areas. First: Did we do what we said we would do? Did we implement the plan? Yes? No? Partially? These are questions about fidelity. They don't have to be complicated but a simple follow-up with those assigned different action steps. You can ask, you can observe, and you can look at data. Whatever way you choose, just make sure you check that you have actually carried out the plan as you designed it.

You may want to take advantage of SWIS and TIPS. The best way to find SWIS materials and information is to go to www.pbisapps.org and, from the Applications tab, select SWIS Suite. The section on the SWIS facilitator includes a link to find a facilitator in your state. You may also contact your local or state SWPBIS entity. If you don't know who that is, you can go onto www.pbis.org and look for the PBIS partners and this will give you contact information for your state.

If you are interested in obtaining training in TIPS, know that this is available to schools and districts through the service of certified TIPS Trainers. The installation process includes training and onsite coaching over a period of months with regular fidelity checks. Again contact your state PBIS entity or you can contact to see where TIPS trainers are located in or near your state.

The second question topic: Did our efforts have an impact? This is the reason you put time, effort, and resources into an action plan. You designed your measures right at the onset so that you could determine whether you achieved the defined outcome. All the data you collect on fidelity of implementation and impact will help you if you need to make adaptations.

Step 7: Adapt solutions to new data.

This is an important step in any continuous improvement. Again, this step is based on the data you have gathered in defining the problem as well as in designing the solution and action plan. Your decisions rest on good data as well as professional knowledge and skills. Whatever the outcome, data informs all of your future actions and adaptations.

Team-Initiated Problem Solving (TIPS)

Over the years as more schools adopted SWIS, it became clear that PBIS Leadership Teams needed further assistance in how to effectively use data for problem solving. Leadership teams were gathering data but not using it in effective ways to create meaningful solutions. This led to research, begun in 2008. The researchers studied leadership teams and determined that the process of a team moving from a problem to a solution required more careful and specific problem solving and solution development, as well as subsequent action planning. Specifically, the researchers determined that schools needed "a clear model with steps for problem solving, access to the right information at the right time in the right format, and a formal process that a group could use to build and implement solutions."[16] To address this need, the researchers developed a specific, comprehensive model for problem solving at the team level. Named Team-Initiated Problem Solving, or TIPS, it includes two major components:

[16] Todd, A. W., et al., 2013.

Figure 5.8

Sample Action Planning Document

Solution Component	Action Steps	Who is responsible?	By when?	How will fidelity be measured?
Prevention	1. Professional development for staff on handling disruptive behavior	William	October 2014	Check schedule and staff feedback
	2. Reteach expectations to students	Advisory teachers	October 2014	Email staff and ask
	3. Student council assist in making posters for hallways/classrooms to promote Expectation for October: Respect	Susan and Marty (student council supervisor)	October 2014	Observe posters
Teaching	1. Teach students to respond to teacher hand signal as cue for expectations	Advisory teachers	November 2014	Review lesson plans and teacher feedback
	2. 9th grade team incorporates lessons on respect in their curriculum	Indira and 9th grade team	November 2014	Review and observe lessons
Recognition	1. Increase Caught in the Act reward tickets during advisories	Fred	November and ongoing	Record number of tickets turned in
	2. School will have quarterly assemblies to recognize students who are demonstrating school expectations	Susan		Document assembly
Extinction	1. Create a structure and routine for advisories with student input to increase engagement 2. Upon early completion of routine students gain 10 minutes of social time	Advisory teachers	October	Review and gather ODR data from revised Advisory structure
Corrective Consequence	1. Review with staff how to have a short student conference for disruptive behavior	PBIS Leadership Team at faculty meetings	October February April	Observe and gather staff feedback at meetings
Data Collection	1. Staff accurately complete ODR forms 2. PBIS team reviews data weekly	PBIS Leadership Team	Weekly	Summarize and report data at PBIS team meeting and faculty meetings Compare trends and levels to 9th grade baseline

1. A model for establishing effective teams
2. A model of effective problem solving with data

TIPS is a formal, evidence-based model that is available to schools, regions, and states through formal training and coaching. As an in-depth model that requires specialized support, TIPS cannot be adequately represented in this short description. Our purpose here is to introduce you to the value and potential of TIPS and to point you to further resources and training for your school, district, or state. As you read the description of TIPS you will notice that it overlaps with the seven problem-solving steps in SWIS. That is because TIPS incorporates the successful component of SWIS while also adding new emphasis on what research shows is needed to make problem solving effective in real school settings.

Effective Teams

The first components of TIPS involve creating an effective leadership team and using a meeting process that is rooted in the foundations of problem solving. These foundations enable teams to establish effective team functioning in which the roles, responsibilities, tasks, data, plans, and follow-up are understood and implemented by all team members. The goal of this process is to ensure that meetings have predictability, participation, accountability, and communication. Although a lot of it would seem like common sense, as Mark Twain once said, "Common sense ain't all that common." And common sense doesn't necessarily translate to common practice. To facilitate creating an effective team, TIPS defines the essential roles and tasks for meetings, shown in **Figure 5.9** on page 94.

Teams use an established agenda, review data at the onset, review progress from previous meetings, document decisions and changes, and start and end on time. Participation requires 75 percent of the team members present. Team members develop and adhere to agreed-upon norms, and meeting minutes are available to all team members within twenty-four hours, including the time and location of the next meeting.

Effective Problem Solving with Data

Figure 5.10 on page 95 illustrates the TIPS foundations for PBIS Leadership Teams to have effective meetings in which problems are solved. With this foundation, the TIPS model provides teams with a structure for using data in problem solving. The structure enables teams to develop the knowledge and skills needed to define problems in a manner that leads to solutions. This includes learning how to define problems with precision, using precision statements, as we discussed in the second SWIS problem-solving step (see page 88). It also includes the creation of SMART goals: goals that are specific, measurable, attainable, relevant, and timely (discussed in the third SWIS problem-solving step, page 89). From the SMART goal, teams adopt a focus on solutions that includes six parts, as presented in Figure 5.7.

The goal of this process is to ensure that meetings have predictability, participation, accountability, and communication.

In summary, one of the major benefits that TIPS offers is its model for meeting foundations, which facilitates team development toward an effective, high functioning group. The content of this model is not typically available but so essential to teach success. A second major benefit of TIPS is that teams receive detailed training and ongoing support in problem solving. This includes the seven steps of problem solving: how to identify behavioral problems with precision, define a goal for change, build a solution with action steps to achieve the goal, implement a comprehensive action plan, monitor outcomes, and evaluate and adapt the solution. TIPS offers this professional development to PBIS Leadership Teams to help them fulfill tasks with fidelity. Training takes place onsite at your school, with continuous coaching over several months to ensure that you acquire TIPS skills

Figure 5.9

Roles and Tasks for Meetings

Roles	Tasks
1. Meeting facilitator	Asks questions Implements norms Keeps to agenda Progresses through agenda Starts and ends on time
2. Data analyst	Likes data Is fluent in navigating dataset to generate reports Discriminates features/labels for creating custom reports Creates a story from data summary (for both old and new problems) Generates data summaries and summary statements 15–20 minutes before meeting
3. Minute-taker	Uses computer during meeting to take notes Listens to discussion and paraphrases critical information in written form Is fluent with meeting summary forms Keeps chronological records of meetings and accomplishments
4. Timekeeper	Keeps track of time on agenda items Communicates time used as meeting progresses
5. Participants	Attend at least 75 percent of meetings Listen to and consider all perspectives Maintain a sense of humor Show mutual respect Cooperate and support the group

and maintain them with fluency. We strongly encourage teams to consider obtaining TIPS training. Contact your local PBIS entity to find access to TIPS training in your state.

This chapter has presented examples of problem-solving frameworks using data within a PBIS system. You can use these approaches with implementation data from the SET, TICS, SAS, BoQ, and in the future the PBIS Implementation Inventory, as well as ODR data. Although using SWIS is not essential to monitor ODR data, whatever system you do use should allow you to easily access very specific data in order to develop precise problem statements. We have included a "Data Drill Down for Creating Precision Statements" in the Appendix (see page 171). This sheet is designed so that PBIS teams can use it to determine if they can

Figure 5.10

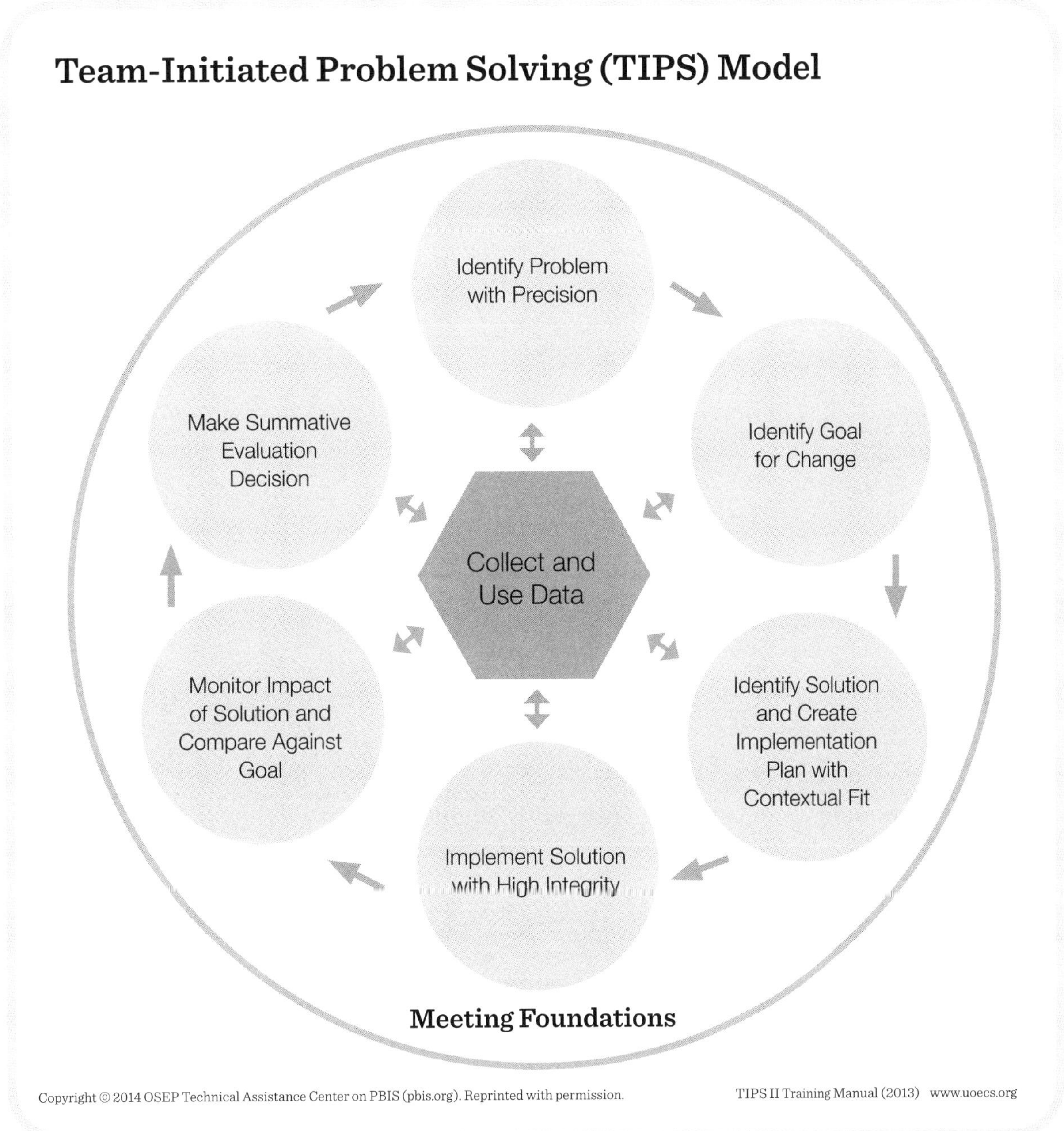

access the specific data needed to create precision statements with their own ODR system. Some of these examples are simple and logical approaches. We have added a specific model, TIPS, that contains a general problem-solving approach; in addition, we described the advantage of focusing on "meeting foundations." Schools that successfully sustain PBIS must have effective PBIS Leadership Teams. It is essential for coaches and teams to review and select the problem-solving framework that will ensure their school can achieve its important outcomes. At the end of the day, schools want to be able to say, "We did what we said we would do and we achieved the important outcomes. We made a difference for kids and our school."

Part Two
Implementing PBIS Tier 1

The chapters in Part Two of this book detail all the actions and desired outcomes of each stage of PBIS Tier 1 implementation. Be sure to complete all of the checklist items and assessments noted in each section. It may seem like too much information at first, but eventually you will see how everything flows together.

The word "implementation" means to put something into action. In PBIS, implementation refers to putting in place a framework schoolwide that is defined by the eight key features outlined in Chapter 1 (see page 9). Studies on implementation across various fields help us understand that putting new behaviors into practice is a process that occurs over time rather than a singular event that happens all at once.[17]

The more you understand the big picture and the process, the more likely you are to achieve full implementation and long-term sustainability.

In 2005, the National Implementation Research Network (NIRN) published a cross-disciplinary review of research on implementation that also identified a progression of stages in the process of implementation. PBIS has adapted and incorporated this stage-based concept to guide efforts toward facilitating and sustaining full implementation.[18] **Figure 6.1** offers a conceptual view of these stages in PBIS.

As you can probably surmise from looking at Figure 6.1, the stages of PBIS implementation require a full-scale effort. In Part 2 of this book, we devote a whole chapter to each stage. Before we delve into these chapters, however, let's consider three overarching messages that are implied in Figure 6.1's outline of stages.

First, the time estimated from initial adoption to achieving PBIS as "business as usual" with a continuous improvement process fully in place is between three and five years. Everyone involved needs to remember this timeframe. It means that you are committing to a long-term relationship with the process and outcomes, and that PBIS is not something that will be accomplished within a single or even two academic years. Support and resources need to be available for a long time. Temporary funding with grants may be helpful initially but need to be replaced with stable funding that matches the real timeframe. Roles and functions need to be incorporated within existing positions to ensure stability and continuity of support.

Second, as you get started with implementation, you need to pace yourself, your leadership team, your staff, the district, and the community. Embrace realistic expectations for progress and outcomes. This outlook will affect your communications, assessments, and reporting to everyone concerned. Understanding how much time and effort is involved helps you better understand and respect the process that leads to important outcomes. We frequently see the great enthusiasm that new PBIS schools embrace and the ensuing disappointment when they cannot demonstrate outcomes after a short period of implementation.

Finally, your understanding of the process will empower you to plan for the frequent changes and challenges that are inevitable in any kind of human system. Expect staffing and funding changes and build in the capacity to accommodate these so that you support continuity from day one. Stage-based approaches suggest a linear progression that is generally accurate. Yet in PBIS, you may at times feel like you are stepping backward even as you try to move forward. Rather than interpreting this as negative, view your implementation performance level as an indicator that informs your actions. Progress in any stage necessarily includes infrastructure maintenance as well as staff buy-in. The more you understand the big picture and the process, the more likely you are to achieve full implementation and long-term sustainability.

[17] Sugai, 2013.
[18] Goodman, 2013; Fixsen, et al., 2005; Horner and Sugai, 2006.

Figure 6.1

Stages of PBIS Implementation

Stage	Description	Implications
Stage 1: Exploration and Adoption	Deciding to commit to adoption and implementation of PBIS	• Determine if your school has any need for behavioral intervention. • Become informed about what PBIS is. • Discuss how PBIS might meet the need in your context. • Discuss whether or not to adopt it. • Secure support and sufficient staff buy-in.
Stage 2: Installation—Getting Ready	Establishing necessary infrastructure to support the implementation	• Get system support. • Demonstrate priority. • Build leadership team. • Review existing resources. • Develop action plan.
Stage 3: Initial Implementation—Getting Going	Putting key features of PBIS actively in place	• Carry out action plan. • Evaluate and compare plan to PBIS eight key features. • Problem solve. • Move toward achieving all eight features with fidelity.
Stage 4: Full Implementation—Up and Running	Expanding the framework across people and settings	Expand from a few to many: • across staff, families, and community • across schools in district
Stage 5: Sustaining and Continuous Improvement	Maintaining and improving	• Evaluate implementation fidelity and outcomes. • Revise based on implementation data. • Improve efficiency. • Adapt to change. • Embed within school or district routines.

Adapted from the work of Fixsen & Blase (NIRN) and Sugai & Horner (OSEP Technical Assistance Center on PBIS).

Chapter 6
PBIS Stage 1: Exploration and Adoption

Prior to adopting and implementing PBIS, most schools spend a period of time exploring the practice and considering the process for developing school readiness. The decision to implement PBIS in your school should not be taken lightly. It requires dedication and risk taking. PBIS asks educators to let go of old ideas (for example, that suspension will change a student's behavior) and grab on to new ideas (for example, that we need to help students learn the expected school behaviors they don't already have in their toolbox of social skills and then reinforce and maintain those skills). Resources to gain PBIS awareness and readiness vary across districts and states; nevertheless, an intentional approach to this beginning stage is beneficial for coaches and school staff.

Tasks

Core objectives of stage 1:

1. Determine if your school has a need to address issues regarding student behavior and school climate; look at your data and staff concerns.
2. Gather information about options; research PBIS and decide whether this is a good fit for your school.
3. Review information with staff and get a sense of buy-in and commitment to move ahead.
4. Decide whether or not to proceed.

Determining Need

Consider Learning Outcomes and School Climate

How do you know whether PBIS is needed in your school? The school leadership and staff need to determine whether or not they have a problem or concern with the social behavior or safety in the school.

Begin by honestly answering these two questions:

1. Are at least 80 percent of your students fully engaged in the learning process?

To answer this question, do a little data research: How many students have office discipline referrals (ODRs), and what percentage is that of your total student population?

2. Are at least 80 percent of your students progressing on the learning continuum?

To find this answer, dig a little deeper into your data: How many students are on target with their reading and math skills to meet school, district, and state academic goals?

If you answered "No," or "I'm not sure," or possibly "I don't think so" to either of these questions, then your school would definitely benefit from PBIS. This data-driven approach will help you answer these questions with ease. Schools that use PBIS benefit by becoming more aware

Coaching During Stage 1

Ideally, your school's PBIS coach is selected even before the school has formally decided to adopt PBIS. This allows for continuity in leadership throughout the entire process of system change. (For more details on selecting a PBIS coach, see Chapter 3.)

In this first stage, coaches can:

1. Gather data about your school's needs. For example, look at attendance, behavior, exclusionary practices, staff and student perceptions of safety, achievement, and so on.
2. Gather data on current perceptions of satisfaction among parents, staff, community, and students.
3. Gather and present information about PBIS—what it is, what implementation looks like (for example, from model schools), what outcomes have been demonstrated, and how PBIS would meet your school's identified need. Research shows that when staff have a good understanding of PBIS, they are more likely to buy in to the program.[19]
4. Gather information on necessary supports for PBIS implementation; for example, administrators, staff, funding, district-level commitment, and time commitment for building readiness and infrastructure.
5. Assist administrators and others to achieve buy-in from school staff. For example, gather and present practical, local examples, visit other schools using PBIS; or talk to other school or district PBIS coordinators).
6. Assist your school in adopting a process for decision making—that is, determine how your school will decide whether or not to adopt PBIS.

of where their students stand academically; most also report significant drops in the number of ODRs, suspensions, and expulsions. With all of those students being back in the classroom, you can bet that academics are improving, teachers are teaching more, and administrators have time to do other administrative duties besides disciplining students.

What's more, the overall health of the school environment, or culture, improves once the entire school encourages the same set of positive student behaviors. Educational researcher Kathleen Cotton, in her journal article "Schoolwide and Classroom Discipline," shared her findings from reviewing numerous articles and criteria on what it means to be a safe school. She found the following characteristics showed up consistently in safe schools:[20]

- The **staff** is committed to creating and maintaining an environment that is, above all, conducive to learning and that does not tolerate inappropriate student behavior.
- High **behavioral expectations** are communicated to all students and staff.
- **Rules and procedures** for dealing with discipline problems are clearly conveyed and known to everyone in the school, students and staff.
- A warm **school climate** makes students feel welcome and cared for as individuals.
- The **principal** is visible to students and staff daily and is generally supportive; the principal is not just a disciplinarian.
- **Teachers** are trained and authorized to handle minor behavioral problems in the classroom, with referrals being made to the principal or other administrator for serious behavioral infractions.
- Close ties with the **community** keep parents involved with the school and the wider community updated on school goals and activities.

The PBIS framework incorporates all these characteristics. They develop through the implementation process—your school doesn't need to have these pieces in place when you start to implement PBIS. Prior to participating in state cohort training, however, some states require an agreement from 80 percent of staff that they are willing to commit to creating a safe school that engages students in learning and that encourages staff to raise their standards of effective teaching.

[19] Filter and Sytsma, 2013.
[20] Cotton, 1990.

Collect and Review Baseline Data

Another step in the decision-making process involves collecting some baseline data. The easiest way to do this is to look at your office discipline referrals (ODRs). Count the total number of referrals for a set period and then start breaking them down. For example, look at how many referrals have been written for certain behaviors, how many referrals per month, by grade, by boys versus girls, by race and ethnicity, and so on. Doing this will help you move from seeing the data as just a number—perhaps one that is big and scary even—to seeing the students who are behind those numbers and beginning to examine the underlying issues and circumstances that may be involved with the problem behavior.

Are there too many referrals? Do students feel unsafe? Do staff need more classroom management skills?

Once you have taken a look at your discipline data, consider your school's practices regarding behavioral problems and how those practices affect the problem and the students involved. Then, answer the questions on the worksheet titled **Current Practices for Behavioral Problems** on pages 103–104 to think about whether your school is working up to its potential.

The bottom line of whether your school will ultimately decide to adopt PBIS likely comes down to a perception of need: Are there too many referrals? Do students feel unsafe? Do staff need more classroom management skills? Another way to look at this is to consider whether the top three priorities in your school improvement plan address student behavior, school culture, or other related issues. If none of these are a priority in your improvement plan, then staff may not perceive PBIS as a priority for your school to adopt.

Learning About PBIS

As a framework for improving school climate and reducing behavioral problems, PBIS offers both structure and flexibility. Part of deciding whether to organize your school efforts toward creating a safer environment that promotes learning involves examining the possibilities of using this approach. At this point, it is often helpful to review the ways that other schools have implemented PBIS. For example, if your district has implemented PBIS in other schools, it should be easy to visit them. If your state or nearby PBIS agency has a website, you may find examples of other schools at the same grade level who have implemented PBIS. Inviting PBIS Leadership Teams and administrators to come talk to staff is a great idea. When Char was a state coordinator, she invited key exploration committee members to PBIS information meetings to "tell the real truth" to administrators and staff so they hear what it's really like and not just hear her passion for PBIS.

Coach's Tip from Beth

I scoured the Internet looking for examples of PBIS implementation before my school adopted it. The PBIS website offers slide presentations, research articles written by academics in the field, and videos created by schools and school districts that explain how and why they decided to use PBIS and what outcomes they experienced.

Early Commitment and Buy-In

When schools decide to adopt PBIS, they need to understand the long-term commitment required to implement the framework. PBIS coaches, exploration committees, and leadership teams—once they are developed—are agents of change. You will face the challenge of staff buy-in not only before your school decides to adopt PBIS but also as a constant factor throughout implementation.

Current Practices for Behavioral Problems: Staff Systems, Student Practices, and Data Practices

Staff Systems

1. What insights about our students do we gain from looking at behavioral data?

2. How are teachers handling disruptive behaviors in the classroom? Do we have a consistent procedure for this? For example, does one teacher allow gum chewing and another refer the student out for having gum?

3. Where do the students go once they get referred out of the classroom? What does the referral process look like in our school?

4. Who tends to the students in the office or the behavior room, and what happens once they arrive?

5. What happens when a student returns to the classroom?

6. Where does the paper referral go once the student returns to class?

7. What type of training does our school provide to teachers in positive classroom management procedures?

continued →

Current Practices for Behavioral Problems: Staff Systems, Student Practices, and Data Practices, continued

Student Practices

1. How are students learning the skills they need to stay in class? Are students being taught pro-social behavior?

2. How is our school promoting positive behaviors between students and staff?

3. How are positive behaviors being reinforced and acknowledged in our school?

4. What kind of interventions are in place for students who have three or more referrals?

Data Practices

1. How is our school tracking behavior problems?

2. Who is looking at the data?

3. Who is actively monitoring the school improvement plan?

4. How does our referral data correlate to the racial makeup of our school?

Don't assume that initial buy-in to an initiative means that level of commitment will remain constant. Anticipate this issue and pre-correct before buy-in flags. This topic is addressed in all the chapters in Part 2, to consider what type of buy-in is required at each stage of the implementation process.

Understanding Reluctance

System change is difficult. Unfortunately many teachers and other school staff have had the experience of starting many new initiatives and then watching them disappear slowly or quickly after changes in leadership or other new circumstances at the school. This creates a sense of revolving-door initiatives, which can leave many feeling cynical. For example, have you ever attended a training, taken notes all day and maybe done some role-playing, all the while knowing in your heart it wouldn't last beyond next Monday morning? Such experiences naturally leave staff questioning whether to invest at all, or at least wondering when they should get on board the next time something new comes along.

It's very helpful for PBIS coaches, exploration committees, and leadership teams to be familiar with the history of a school, especially how many initiatives have started and failed in years past. Knowing at the outset what you're up against in your efforts to gain buy-in will help you develop strategies and realistic expectations for convincing staff that this time will be different. When Beth worked on staff and new models were introduced, the prevailing message from old-timers was that if you didn't like what they were doing, just hold on—because it would be something else in about three years. And they were right!

Char has encountered teachers who don't want to invest themselves in the model for numerous reasons. Frequently, both coaches and staff talk about colleagues who just don't buy in. This happens in nearly all schools, regardless of the situation. There are always team or community members who hesitate. Some teachers even refuse to participate in PBIS, arguing, "Kids should already know what to do in school—sit down, be quiet, and do their work." PBIS acknowledges that some students simply don't know what they are supposed to do, for various reasons, or they need help managing their feelings.

If, after explaining the fundamentals of the framework as well as the plans for implementation, you encounter anyone unwilling to budge from their viewpoint, it's often best to simply extend the invitation for them to join the effort if they change their mind. We typically encourage exploration committees and leadership teams to focus on those staff members who have already bought in and are working with the process. Still, it's helpful to gain a general understanding of the psychological aspects of learning and change and how this affects buy-in.[21]

- **Change means uncertainty.** That uncertainty may be about the specifics—or the lack of specifics—of what and how things are changing and who is directing or facilitating the change. Uncertainty may also be a reflection of whether the direction of change is viewed as positive, or some people may not believe they can successfully implement the change.
- **Uncertainty is a powerful trigger for anxiety.** This reaction is natural and people vary in their response to uncertainty. Some may thrive and others may experience a lot of fear.
- **Anxiety may lead to avoidance.** Some people will go to great lengths to avoid feeling anxious. Anxiety is an unpleasant emotion. Sometimes we label this avoidance behavior as willful resistance and respond negatively to those who exhibit it. However, it might be more useful to recognize that adults, like kids, might be trying to protect themselves by responding this way. This recognition allows you to work toward easing the natural discomfort rather than blaming the person.
- **Lack of information and understanding can lead to a negative outlook.** This is really important, because you want to start off building positive expectations among staff and families. The good news is that this is

[21]Bandura, 1977.

something you can work to change—namely, by providing good information early and often.

- **Resistance is a natural human response to uncertainty.** Framing resistance in this way allows you to be proactive and positive in your interactions with others rather than to blame or focus negative attention on people who are slow to buy in.

How to Achieve Buy-In

One of the questions that repeatedly surfaces across the stages of implementation is how to get and maintain buy-in. We approach buy-in with prevention logic and good teaching and planning. Attention to buy-in should occur early and often and include specific tasks.

During the five stages of the implementation, there are seven possible audiences from whom we need buy-in:

1. Administrators
2. PBIS Leadership Team
3. School staff
4. District staff
5. Students
6. Families
7. Community

First, let's talk about what we mean by staff buy-in, which is necessary even before the decision to officially commit to PBIS has been made. Staff buy-in, sometimes called staff investment, means that teachers and other school employees engage in decision making and planning, behave consistently with decisions, and continue to follow through and support all aspects of the initiative. They understand what PBIS is, how it will fit the school context, and what it will mean in terms of their time and effort.

Often when a school is considering adopting PBIS, there is usually a presentation to all school staff about the initiative and then some type of vote. A supportive vote more than likely represents staffs' understanding and sense of need at that point in time. In other words, it's a snapshot. What unfolds during implementation is the realization that the adults in the environment have to change the way they do business. And change translates to time and effort.

Indeed, the implementation period of change begins to take more time, effort, and commitment from staff. That's where coaches and leadership teams begin to see more issues with buy-in. For example, staff members who initially voted for PBIS may now be slow to make changes in the way that they handle classroom behavioral problems.

Leading people through change requires a roadmap and coaching. PBIS implementation means changing the system and relies heavily on changing adult behavior. Coaches and leadership teams take on the role of guiding their colleagues through the process, so that they are part of and understand the direction, the outcomes, and the specific steps they'll need to take along the way.

It's important to demonstrate confidence in people's ability to change. This means conveying belief and support for the staff's ability to adopt the actions necessary to reach full implementation.[22] Coaches, exploration committees, and leadership teams have the job of helping staff see this possibility. This is done by modeling, sharing examples, and visiting and networking with other schools further along in the process.

Positive acknowledgment of each step is also helpful. New behavior needs a lot of reinforcement. When we teach kids, we increase the ratio of reinforcement. Typically educators hear that classrooms should have a 4:1 ratio of positive comments to negative comments. When teaching new skills to students, however, educators are encouraged to reinforce a lot more—7:1 or even 8:1 in the beginning, because kids need to be praised when they are learning something new, and they tend to increase use of the new behavior to get the positive attention from adults. The same applies when teaching adults—we have to increase the ratio of reinforcement and acknowledgment.

[22]Bandura, 1977.

Steps toward Gaining Staff Buy-In

The following steps can help you gain staff buy-in while you are exploring PBIS.

Involve staff from the beginning. Invite several staff members to be on the PBIS exploration committee, and, later, the leadership team. Communicate decisions. Make the process of implementing the features of PBIS transparent and shared. Consciously and frequently solicit staff input. This can be done in formal ways, such as staff surveys, as well as through informal conversations that occur naturally in the school setting.

Create and maintain ongoing communication. Build a communication plan and share the story of PBIS implementation. Use multiple methods for sharing news about PBIS with all key stakeholders, including face-to-face communication, presentations to small and large groups, blog posts, websites, and newsletters. Work to create a sense of community around this initiative. Share action plans and decision making with staff and show them the data that demonstrate progress and outcomes.

Build trust. Listen to staff and work to build rapport with everyone, regardless of their position. Keep planning and teamwork transparent. Avoid any in-group/out-group dynamics. Demonstrate to staff how their input is used.

Regularly acknowledge all staff. Plan and show appreciation for staff efforts with notes, awards, drawings, preferred parking, errands, breakfasts, and so on. Develop a plan to acknowledge staff members who are working to implement PBIS; you can do this daily, weekly, or on an ad-hoc schedule. Communicate confidence in all staff and in their ability to contribute toward the desired outcomes. Provide supports to staff quickly when needed.

Remember, buy-in doesn't come automatically and doesn't continue without conscious effort.

Provide visible leadership support. Ensure that your administrator publically supports the PBIS initiative with verbal, written, and visual statements. It is helpful when administrators are present and participating at trainings and meetings and are open to visiting classrooms. The administrator plays a key role in communicating success to the district as well as the community. We have heard principals presenting their outcome data at PBIS conferences and thought: If that principal is willing to stand in front of a crowd talking about PBIS at his school, then that's a school where we would want to work!

Celebrate successes regularly. If you are a member of the PBIS Leadership Team, be sure to acknowledge and celebrate success in achieving and advancing implementation. Though success is gratifying, it is still a lot of work. Share successes with the whole school, staff, and students at planned celebrations. For example, when the number of discipline referrals drops, congratulate students on their success in following school expectations and celebrate with a fun school activity. We've heard of such crazy activities as inviting kids to the auditorium to throw a pie in the principal's face because the number of referrals dropped by 10 percent!

Remember, buy-in doesn't come automatically and doesn't continue without conscious effort. If you had some staff buy-in during the fall, that doesn't mean it will still be there in the spring. Buy-in is not a single event but an ongoing process. It may feel a bit like herding cats; support ebbs and flows, and not everyone is going to champion this effort. Even so, most staff members will support practices that make their job more effective and efficient. As a PBIS coach or leadership team member, you have the job of enabling your colleagues to experience such outcomes.

Buy-In During Stage 1

While buy-in continues throughout PBIS, during the exploration process it may include these specific steps:

1. The administrator commits to adopting and implementing PBIS with all the implications for staff time, resources, and so on.
2. Staff members demonstrate initial buy-in, or commitment, to implement PBIS. This buy-in may be established through a vote following a presentation about PBIS, a school visit, and so on. Most often an informal vote will be taken, but some schools use staff surveys, ballots, or lists of staff supporting it. With good explanations from administrators up front, staff see the need for initial buy-in; they have lived through the negative consequences of starting an important initiative without full buy-in.
3. District support is established. When a school is the first, or the only, school in a large district to adopt PBIS, gaining strong support from the district is key. Often, when other schools see support from the district, they come on board, too. The district structure helps ensure continuity and sustainability, so staff won't view PBIS as an initiative that will last a year or so until the next newest, latest, greatest one comes along.

Figure 6.2 charts a way to break down these tasks into specific measures and delegate responsibility for them.

Deciding to Adopt PBIS

There are many ways a school or district can come to the decision to use the PBIS framework. A principal might read some research about it and decide it's just the thing she's looking for to improve the school. A teacher in graduate school may decide to research PBIS and passionately discuss it with anyone in the district who will listen. District administration could be looking for ways to improve the safety of the school to make it more enticing to prospective students and their families. Some teachers have brought PBIS to their schools after seeing it in action in their own child's school in a different district.

Part of making the decision to formally adopt PBIS includes being sure that your school is prepared to take on the implementation process. There are resources available to help you determine your school's readiness. Check to see if your state department of education has a readiness checklist on its website. If not, take a look at the Florida PBIS website (flpbs.fmhi.usf.edu); click on the Procedures and Tools tab to find a readiness checklist that schools can use as they prepare for PBIS. Some items on the list are:

- district leadership and support
- a school improvement plan that includes schoolwide discipline
- commitment from principal to provide support and make discipline decisions
- a commitment from at least 80 percent of staff and administration to implement PBIS knowing that it may take three to five years to fully implement PBIS
- a PBIS Leadership Team that agrees to meet at least two times per month and includes members who have a background in behavior (such as a school psychologist, school social worker, counselor, or special education teacher)
- faculty has received an overview presentation of PBIS
- the district agrees to provide funding to support PBIS initiatives
- an internal school coach has been identified by the principal or district administration

Figure 6.2

Exploration and Adoption—Buy-In Roles and Measures During Stage 1

Person/Group Responsible	Buy-in Tasks	Measures
Building administrator	Identifies school leaders and committee members to explore PBIS Supports exploration and adoption efforts	• Allocates funding—paying for subs so committee members can attend trainings; money for posters; hiring reinforcements • Grants time—for exploration committee to meet and attend trainings • Provides resources—posters, lesson plans, community-building curriculum, large poster paper, various other supplies
Exploration committee	Shares knowledge of PBIS with school and district staff	• Researches PBIS • Presents and promotes knowledge with school and district staff
School staff	Decides if PBIS is right for their school	• 80 percent staff agreement needed to implement PBIS
District administration	Identifies school leaders and committee members to explore PBIS	• Agrees to support implementation of PBIS—funding, time, resources
Families and community	Decides if PBIS is right for the school	• Agrees to support PBIS in the school as part of the school community

Telling Your School's Story

A helpful activity as you adopt and prepare to implement PBIS is to articulate what we call your school's story. This activity means thinking about how you will communicate the changes your school is making to your staff, your families, your district administration, your community, and any other stakeholders.

We recommend that you develop a narrative based on your data (which you update regularly as you progress), a narrative that you can share during each stage of implementation. In this and the following chapters on the stages of implementation we provide a worksheet that includes an example to help you tell your story. Use your own creativity to add details that make it your school's story. Reviewing your school story periodically can also help you learn more about what's working and what may need to be fine-tuned. For example, when Beth was a school PBIS coach, she kept a three-ring binder that stored everything created around PBIS—the purpose statement and expectations; TIC, SAS, and SET scores; an informal survey done with students; photos of student-of-the-month celebrations; photos of students collecting trinkets at the school prize box; emails the principal sent to staff regarding the implementation of PBIS; and team meeting minutes. This binder contained all the elements of her school's journey with PBIS. When Beth looked back at this binder as the implementation continued, she could see things she might have done differently, like *not* trying to start everything at once!

One way to tell your story is with data on a spreadsheet or a graph. This might become a poster hung in the teacher's lounge, a report to your school board, a presentation to your community members at open house night. Some schools hang graphs in the hallway so the kids can keep an eye on referral numbers. Others make funny videos with staff and students to share with the school, the school board, the community, and maybe even the national PBIS conference.

Whatever method of storytelling you decide to use, be honest about your starting point. Sometimes when you see how many ODRs your school has written in a year, you may want to shave a few points off so you don't look so bad. Resist this urge—it's unethical and a bad idea! Start exactly where you are starting. Keep a running record of the data to demonstrate ups and downs that occur. Don't be surprised if the number of ODRs actually goes up during the second year—this seems to be a common occurrence. That may simply indicate that you are counting behaviors better, that teachers are following the behavior flowchart better, or that more students are being referred. That could be a part of your school's story, in a section called "The Year Our Referrals Doubled." Embrace and accept what is happening in your data and your school.

However you choose to do it, it's important that you tell your story. You have regular, valid measures of progress, implementation, and fidelity with PBIS. Let your audiences and stakeholders know that implementation occurs across stages and years. To tell your story at this stage in the process, work through questions similar to those in the sidebar Our School's Story—PBIS Stage 1 (see page 111).

Resources

If your school is considering using PBIS, or if you are planning to propose it to your school or district, there are many tools and resources available to help you get started. First, look at and make use of the PDF presentation included in the digital download of this book. (See page x for details.) Also, check with your state for an organized system of training and support for schools and districts using PBIS. Many states have related information on their department of education website. If your state does not have an organized system for training schools, visit www.pbis.org for resources. Another option is the Association for Positive Behavior Supports, www.apbs.org. They have listings for state networks and can help you get PBIS established in your school or district.

Our School's Story—PBIS Stage 1

In this stage of our story, we focus on why our school began exploring PBIS.

Why did our school get involved in PBIS?

Note: Include the reasons that your school decided to move ahead, e.g., *School climate was perceived by staff and students as unsafe* . . . (elaborate); *ODRs were rising significantly over the previous two years* . . . ; *Student achievement was below district/state/national norms* . . . (elaborate with number from state's department of education website)

Example: "During the school year, our school saw an increase in disruptive student behavior with a significant rise in ODRs for serious student behavior problems, which we think led to declines in perceptions of safety and academic achievement by our students. Therefore our school adopted a school improvement goal of reducing major behavior referrals. We chose to accomplish this by implementing a daily advisory period for all students and by starting a peer mentoring group."

Chapter 7

PBIS Stage 2: Getting Ready—Installing the Infrastructure

Once you have formally decided to implement PBIS, the next step is to get ready by installing the groundwork for implementation. This includes some of the eight key features of PBIS that were noted in Chapter 1. During stage 2 you will identify initial tasks and take some first steps. These tasks involve creating the basic infrastructure that will build capacity to support further actions. This intentional planning and prioritizing of tasks to fit the particular needs of your school—rather than jumping into all of the elements at once—will go far in setting the tone and pace of implementation. What's more, it will help you achieve early successes and thus build momentum and gain additional buy-in for PBIS.

Tasks

Core objectives of stage 2:

1. Establish a leadership team that will guide implementation.
2. Develop a process to communicate at all levels.
3. Establish a system of technical assistance that will support the leadership team, staff, and community in accomplishing the tasks related to the practice of PBIS.

Key Features at Stage 2

As you prepare to begin PBIS during the installation stage, you'll start to assemble and develop items from the eight key PBIS features. The three boldfaced items in the following list highlight those features that are part of the process at the installation stage.

1. **Establish the PBIS Leadership Team.**
2. **Develop a statement of purpose.**
3. **Identify three to five schoolwide positive behavioral expectations.**
4. Develop teaching procedures.
5. Develop lesson plans.
6. Develop procedures for acknowledging positive student behavior.
7. Develop procedures for discouraging rule violations.
8. Develop data systems for monitoring implementation, fidelity, and outcomes.

Establishing a PBIS Leadership Team

An important first step during the installation stage is for the coach and administrator to work together to identify potential members for the PBIS Leadership Team. This diverse group of people from your school will be instrumental in every facet of implementation. They will gain support and buy-in from other school staff, help with PBIS training, and collect and use data to ensure that PBIS is being implemented with fidelity. Ultimately, leadership team members help ensure that PBIS reaches its potential to promote a safe school and a positive learning environment while decreasing behavioral problems. (See Chapter 2 for step-by-step information on forming a leadership team.)

Once all members of the leadership team have been chosen, consider attending PBIS trainings as a team. This not only helps you guide your school through the PBIS implementation process but also allows the team members to become cohesive, learning about each other as they become a unit.

Once the leadership team is established and initial roles have been assigned, the team can begin developing plans and procedures that will become the backbone of PBIS in your school. But first, it's important to get a feel for how teachers and other staff see the current state of behavior at your school.

Coach's Tip from Beth

Be sure to involve all members of your PBIS Leadership Team right away. Ask team members if they have particular areas of interest and assign them related tasks when possible. Team members want to feel that they are contributing, so make use of their skills and talents. To do this, you can:

- rotate note-taking (use a consistent form and process)
- invite team members to submit agenda items for meetings (always follow up on previous agenda and action items before tackling new topics)
- rotate data presenters at faculty meetings
- create subgroups that might include staff not on the PBIS Leadership Team (for example, form a reinforcement committee to plan an award system, gather prizes or rewards, and set up how they will be distributed)

Coaching During Stage 2

Coaches can:

1. Talk with the principal about establishing a working and representative team.
2. Identify and clarify your role as a coach so that you and your principal can communicate this to staff and the wider school community.
3. Assist the administrator and the leadership team in the assignment of team roles (team leader/facilitator, note-taker, data manager, timekeeper, and archivist).
4. Identify the PBIS assessment tools and data monitoring system the school will use. Connect your school or district with your local PBIS coordinator for help in getting started with the PBIS assessment tools. (See Chapter 4 for more on assessment tools.)
5. Assist the administrator in providing clear, tangible directions to guide the PBIS Leadership Team in making action plans that include data collection and progress monitoring.
6. Become fluent in using, analyzing, and reporting data that tracks implementation progress, fidelity, and outcomes.
7. Become fluent in understanding and using the school's (or district's) office discipline referral (ODR) system.
8. Acquire technical assistance to build personal fluency in using data tools. (See Chapter 4.)
9. Build personal fluency in the team problem-solving process. (See Chapter 5.)
10. Establish a regular meeting time and place for the leadership team.
11. Ask for a regular time slot on the faculty meeting agenda across the year.
12. Determine your process for communicating and sharing your school's story about PBIS. Every decision, accomplishment, and change should be shared with staff to encourage their engagement and buy-in.

Remember, your job is to oversee these areas, not to do it all! Work with your principal to select a strong leadership team and then divide the jobs. Know your strength and pull others onto the team who can dedicate their skills and expertise in implementing PBIS.

PBIS Team Training Tip from Char

My experience at the regional and state levels has been in a state that provides an opportunity to engage in so-called training cohorts. The schools selected for this program received two years of very structured support with training and infrastructure building around data, systems, and practices. Formal training and coaching support a scope and sequence of training and practice. The training model will look different in each state, but the training content tends to be consistent and faithful to the PBIS model suggested by the national Office of Special Education Programs (OSEP) Technical Assistance Center. In my personal experience, the most effective and efficient training approach is through an organized and systematic structure.

Districts and schools can certainly choose to move ahead with adoption and implementation without participating in any external formal training system. My caution with this approach is that the district team must become extremely fluent in their understanding of the entire system of PBIS and its components. When districts or schools hire an outside trainer who comes just once or twice, the staff hears about the eight primary features of PBIS much like they would in other conferences. Often, however, they don't receive the assistance needed to build a system that ensures the availability and accuracy of coaching, evaluation, training, and behavioral support. As a result, some people adopt some features but often there is no data system used to assist in measuring implementation and fidelity. In other words, although it can be less expensive to hire a single trainer and limit the amount of time teachers and others are out of the classroom or building, doing so may fail to build the architectural system that holds the whole framework in place.

It's very difficult to change a complete system without a good roadmap and feedback systems to keep you on track. Even when schools and districts go through prolonged and systemic training and coaching, there are enough naturally occurring challenges that sustainability often fails. From what I have seen, districts or schools that work in isolation are less successful in meeting these challenges.

Collecting and Examining Baseline Data

One of the first tasks of the PBIS Leadership Team is to review the behavioral practices currently being used in the school. They ask all staff members—including office support, paraprofessionals, custodians, and cafeteria workers—to complete the Self-Assessment Survey (see Chapter 4). This survey includes a section called the "classroom system," which will help you assess current behavioral practices.

During this installation stage, the team can also look at behavioral data currently being collected to get an objective view of how the school handles disruptive behaviors. It's important to have this type of baseline data in hand and use it as a starting point before fully implementing PBIS. This information is frequently found on ODR reports (see Chapter 4). Use the data to guide your team to determine areas of strength and concern.

As your team sifts through the staff survey results and behavioral data, keep the following questions in mind:

- Who are your students?
- What is working well for students and staff?
- Where are the trouble spots in the building?
- What do your students need to achieve greater academic success?
- What do staff members need to achieve more successful teaching experiences?
- How does what you are doing now align with your school improvement plan?

Developing an Action Plan

All of the data collected can be used to develop an action plan, which is a more detailed, ongoing list of what the PBIS Leadership Team is working on. Teams can update the action plan as they go, checking off items as they are completed and then adding new tasks. **Figure 7.1** presents a sample action plan.

Figure 7.1

Sample PBIS Action Plan

Key PBIS Feature	Action/Activity	Person Responsible	Start Date	End Date	When/How It Will Be Evaluated
#1	Establish the PBIS Leadership Team	Administrator and Coach	5/8/14	5/8/14	Team will represent each grade level and include 2 paraprofessionals, 2 specialists, and 2 from other areas
#2	Develop the purpose statement	PBIS team	5/22/14	5/24/14	PBIS team will draft a purpose statement for review at final staff meeting
#3	Develop expectations	PBIS team	5/22/14	5/24/14	PBIS team will draft expectations for review at final staff meeting

Coach's Tip from Beth:

When I started coaching, my action plan was long and complicated. I tried to implement everything that was missing all at once. This is a huge mistake, not to mention an exhausting and impossible endeavor! It's better to focus on implementing a few things really well. As things get done, add something else to your action plan. Remember, it usually takes three to five years to fully implement Tier 1.

Also, from the beginning, be sure to delegate various jobs and tasks on the action plan to all PBIS Leadership Team members. This keeps your to-do list from overflowing and builds the capacity of the whole team. It is really important to reinforce that PBIS is a team-guided process at all levels and not person dependent.

Establishing Schoolwide Behavioral Expectations

Using the data collected thus far, and focusing especially on the areas of need identified by staff, your next step is to define three to five schoolwide behavioral expectations. These will be the expectations that all students are held to and will be followed in both classroom and non-classroom settings. Often a first step in this task is to write a purpose statement.

Write a Purpose Statement

The purpose statement lays your school's foundation for the PBIS framework; the statement should support the academic and behavioral goals of your school. The purpose statement guides all the work of the team; it says why you do what you do. The purpose statement should be:

- positively stated
- two to three sentences in length

- supportive of academic achievement
- contextually and culturally appropriate (for age, language, community)
- agreed upon by at least 80 percent of school staff
- communicated to families, community members, and district administrators

Include the purpose statement on newsletters, websites, posters, referral forms, and anything else your school prints or publishes. It keeps the purpose statement clearly in focus and puts it out into the community.

Sample Purpose Statement

The following purpose statement is from a hypothetical school named Evergreen School:

The Evergreen School is a community of learners. With school staff supporting us, we come to school to become our best selves by studying hard and becoming good citizens in a safe and friendly school environment.

Write the Schoolwide Expectations

Now, use your purpose statement as a guide to write schoolwide expectations. The expectations should reflect the values of your school community. *Note:* We recommend using the word "expectations" instead of "rules" because rules seem stiff and threatening. Rules seem to say, "You will do . . . " and "You will not do . . . " Using the word expectations puts the onus back on the students. It says, "This is what we expect from you and we know you can live up to these expectations." Some schools like to have students assist in the process of writing the expectations. One way to do this is to invite each homeroom to write three things that are important to school and that support the purpose statement. Each homeroom can send a representative to a meeting, much like the founding fathers writing the Constitution, to share, vote, and agree on the expectations for the school. The representatives then bring the final expectations back to homeroom and explain how the group came up with the expectations. The adult facilitating the large group of representatives can guide the conversation and may set meeting ground rules, such as use positive statements, use expected school language, and every idea is considered.

Sample Schoolwide Expectations

Using the Evergreen School as an example again, here is how their schoolwide expectations might look:

At Evergreen School:

We come to school to learn.
We respect ourselves and others.
We are responsible for our actions.

Writing open-ended expectations allows them to be used in numerous settings (hallway, gym, lunchroom, and so on) and tailored to the different grades. These expectations should be displayed all over the school—in classrooms, hallways, entrances, cafeteria, and so on. This allows a staff member who encounters a student running in the hallways to simply point to the expectations and ask the student, "Where in our expectations do you think running in the hallways is okay?" These expectations will have been taught and retaught and reinforced to students, so the student knows that running in the hallways doesn't fit into your expectations. She can quickly make amends and, as long as no one was harmed and she was running to avoid being late to class, can go off to class walking. It's likely that the student will receive a tardy note and thus still be held responsible for her actions. For more examples and blank forms your team can fill out, see the Appendix and the digital download for this book.

Cultural Diversity and Behavioral Expectations

In establishing expectations, think not just about your students but also about your staff and the backgrounds they bring to the classroom. Perhaps teachers also need some training about expected behaviors. Here's a story about a time when Beth had to reevaluate her own expectations of desirable behaviors:

> I was raised in a white, Catholic, German-Norwegian family. Every Sunday morning, we went to Mass, which started at 10:30 and ended at 11:30. We were taught to be very punctual. This is how I experienced school as a student and, later, as a schoolteacher—be on time and in place, quietly waiting for the next direction. These were the expectations I had for myself and my students.
>
> Then one Sunday a dear friend invited me to attend her predominately African American church. The service started at 10:30, so I thought we should get in and sit down so we would be prepared for the service to begin. My friend laughed when I said this and mentioned that the service had already started. "Can't you hear the music?" she asked. Finally, we went in to take our seats—five minutes late according to my watch. I noticed that some people drifted in during the service, while others seemed to be leaving. Throughout the service, some people walked across the aisle to socialize with friends and family. There were times when we were all standing and singing and clapping, and other times when we were seated and listening, punctuated by shouts of "Amen" and "That's right!" All in all, the service lasted about three hours.
>
> Afterward, my friend, who works with a school district, asked me what I thought. "I could have written 100 behavioral referrals!" I responded in shock. Yet this church service was loud and joyous and full of love and energy. Although many people went out of their way to welcome me, it felt like a community that I didn't quite belong to. I didn't know the rules or the system; I felt out of place. My friend then pointed out that this is the environment many African American students come from—call and response with the pastor, arriving to church when you get there, and leaving your seat to socialize with friends a few rows over: the very things that drive many teachers crazy.

Many students walk into classrooms not knowing the school's system or expectations. Using PBIS creates what some educators refer to as "institutionalized rules," the behaviors students need to be successful in the world.

> When implementing schoolwide expectations, keep in mind the culture of your students and the communities they come from, the traditions and rituals.

I recently spoke with an African American teacher about PBIS. She admitted that she didn't like it in the beginning but said it grew on her as she realized that students needed to know the basic rules to get along in society. For example, many schools expect students to walk on the right side of the hallway. She thought that when students learned this expectation, they could apply it to driving, as well, because we drive on the right side of the road. When asked about blurting out answers and comments as an offshoot of the call and response learned in many African American churches, she commented that there is a time and place for blurting as well as a time to refrain from doing so. (She also had been in the military, an organization that isn't appreciative of blurting.)

This teacher also spoke about the importance of students learning to be bicultural, living between two worlds. When we go home we talk one way; and when we go to school or college, apply for jobs, or enter the military, we talk another way. I, too, think it is important for students to know when to communicate spontaneously, or "call and respond," and when to be quiet and listen. Implementing PBIS can help teach all students the difference between the two.

When implementing schoolwide expectations, keep in mind the culture of your students and the communities they come from, the traditions and rituals. One school in Minneapolis has a predominately American Indian student population and writes their schoolwide expectations in Dakota as well as English. Another school has a predominately Hmong student population. Their posters of schoolwide expectations incorporate a design common in Hmong embroidery. In the traditional Somali culture, boys and girls cannot touch hands. We began to rethink some of the activities that involved shaking hands as a greeting (bumping elbows, for example). We also know schools whose students made their schoolwide expectations into a rap and filmed a video to go along with it. What's important is that you involve your students, parents, and community members in creating the expectations for your school, or at least give them a hand in helping teach the expectations. This creates ownership and buy-in for the students, making your PBIS program relevant to them, and it increases involvement from families and the greater community.

Implementing the PBIS framework with fidelity, then, can also help schools decrease racial disparity in behavioral referrals and suspensions by opening conversations about how teachers handle behaviors in their classrooms and coming up with solutions to prevent the behavior from happening again. You can also use data to compare the referrals among racial and ethnic groups in your school. For example, how many African American and Latino students are being referred out of class compared to white students? What behaviors are those referrals for? How did the teacher respond to the behaviors prior to referring them out of the classroom?

In conversation with a white teacher, Beth mentioned her frustration with the disproportionate number of African American students who had ODRs. He responded, "I don't refer students out because they are black; I refer them out because they are disruptive." This opened a discussion about race in the classroom but offered no solutions.

Of course many teachers build wonderful relationships with students and their families. These are the teachers (many of whom are white) who allow call and response, are glad to see students come to their class (even if they are a few minutes late), and celebrate successes with their students. Many of these teachers have high expectations for their students and cheer them on to greatness. They get to know the families. Students do well in these classes because the teacher accepts them, listens to them, corrects them, and honors them. And these are the teachers who typically refer very few students out of their classrooms.

Staff should have conversations about the data and discuss why racial disparity is happening in their schools. These conversations can lead to soul searching for some teachers, while others may dig their heels in deeper, resisting the idea that they should have to teach students how to behave in their classrooms. Perhaps some professional development around cultural diversity that includes coaching in the classroom would benefit schools struggling with racial disparity in their referral process.

Develop and Publically Post a Schoolwide Behavioral Matrix

A behavioral matrix is based on your schoolwide expectations and is distributed to all staff. **Figure 7.2** shows a sample matrix that continues the example of the Evergreen School. Notice how this matrix uses Evergreen's purpose statement and expectations to guide the work. This matrix provides the basis for increasing consistency throughout school settings and classrooms because it is taught to all students, and all staff are responsible for implementing the matrix. On page 120 is a reproducible **Behavioral Matrix Template** that your team can use to create your own matrix.

Figure 7.2

Sample Behavioral Matrix—Evergreen School

Expectation	Classroom	Hallways	Cafeteria	Office	Bathrooms
We come to school to learn.	Be on time. Have materials. Pay attention to the teacher.	Quiet in the hallways—voice level 1. Wait patiently for your teacher to open the door.	Go to class when dismissed. Bring class materials with you to lunch so you will be on time to class.	Get a pass from your teacher if you need to go to the office.	Do your business and get back to class.
We respect ourselves and others.	Ask for help if you don't understand something. Pay attention to the assignment.	Use respectful words with custodians. Greet others in a friendly way. Use walking feet for safety.	Use respectful words with cafeteria workers. Eat your fruits and vegetables.	Respect others' privacy. Be polite to office staff.	Respect others' privacy.
We are responsible for our actions.	Complete and turn in assignments.	Throw trash in trashcans. Walk on the right side.	Take only what you will eat. Throw away trash.	Quietly wait your turn in line.	Flush and throw away paper towels.

Developing a Process to Communicate at All Levels

As you get everything ready for PBIS implementation, think about how you will communicate the implementation plans with staff at your school and at the district level as well as with school families and the larger community. For example, how will you share with staff the purpose statement and the expectations? How about the new referral system? The PBIS implementation plans would be a good topic for a professional development day led by your principal or possibly your district. The schedule could look like this:

1. PBIS overview for staff: 1 hour
2. Behavior basics (what are behaviors?): 30 minutes

Behavioral Matrix Template

Expectation	Classroom	Hallways	Cafeteria	Office	Bathrooms	____ (other area)	____ (other area)

Figure 7.3

Getting Ready—Buy-In Roles and Measures During Stage 2

Person/Group Responsible	Buy-In Tasks	Measures
Administrator	Invites staff to be on PBIS Leadership Team	Allows staff development time for the PBIS team
Leadership team	Sets the team meeting schedule for the year Defines team roles	Team members agree to participate for at least three years
School staff	Schoolwide behavioral matrix is shared with staff and they vote for approval	Final products are produced
District	Agrees to provide funding for PBIS Leadership Team	District leadership team is identified

3. Present the purpose statement, behavioral expectations, and lesson plans: 1.5 hours
4. The referral process, including the flowchart for handling behaviors and the behavioral matrix, minor and major behaviors: 1.5–2 hours
5. Reward system, natural and logical consequences: 1 hour

How will you let parents and families know that the school is making a major systems shift from a punitive approach to a pro-social, learning skills approach? Many schools host an open house near the beginning of the school year. Perhaps you can set up a table with various resources for families and distribute a pamphlet about PBIS that introduces your purpose statement, behavioral expectations, and how you plan to implement the framework. If possible, have someone from your PBIS team at the table who can share information with families and answer questions about it. The principal could also give a short talk to families about the changes for the coming school year.

Buy-In and Support

At each stage of implementation, keep revisiting the ongoing concern of how to keep support for PBIS strong and what steps need to be taken to continually sustain buy-in. Until recently, the topic of buy-in has not been studied systematically. In 2013, a report of innovative research on this topic reveals two factors that appear to predict greater staff buy-in: (1) an opportunity to have input into PBIS-related activities and (2) an understanding of what PBIS is.[23] Keeping these preliminary findings in mind, we suggest that at team meetings you discuss which team members need to take which actions and add those to your action plan. Consider every meeting and interaction as an opportunity to explain, demonstrate, answer questions, and ask for input. Also consider how school staff and the district can contribute to PBIS as a way to increase their buy-in. **Figure 7.3** outlines buy-in tasks for the installation stage by person or group responsible.

[23] Filter and Sytsma, 2013.

Telling Your School's Story

In Chapter 6, we introduced the idea of beginning to tell your school's PBIS story, once you have decided to adopt PBIS. Now you have taken the steps to install PBIS infrastructure in your school, having put in place the first three of the eight key PBIS features: you've formed a leadership team and developed both a purpose statement and behavioral expectations. In addition, you've started an action plan and established a process for communication. Your story has expanded.

Take some time now to share this part of your story, or experience, with your staff, your families, your district administration, and your community. Once again, you can develop a narrative based on your current data as you prepare to implement PBIS in your school. This update to your story can be shared in a poster, a report, a newsletter or newspaper article, a presentation, or some other method of communication. Remember to use your own creativity. Following are some questions to consider as you work to develop your continuing story.

Our School's Story—PBIS Stage 2

In this stage of our story, we focus on sharing how our school is doing with the installation of PBIS.

Where did we start?

Here's an example:
In August, we met during team training and completed the Team Implementation Checklist (TIC). Our first TIC looked like this: Of the ten subscales, our two highest were "commitment" and "support." We achieved 75 percent on the Commitment subscale, which measures administrative and staff support.

A narrative for this school might be:
Our principal is fully supportive of this PBIS effort in our school. She attended meetings describing PBIS, met with principals in other schools using PBIS, and invited a PBIS Leadership Team from another school to our faculty meeting to describe their experiences and results. She has stated her commitment to this effort for the next five years. Our staff voted and 90 percent of staff is in favor of this initiative. Our other high score was on the Support subscale, which measures the behavioral support we have in our school. We have several staff members, including a leadership team member, with special training and skills in conducting functional behavioral assessments and developing behavioral support plans. This will be a great asset as we move further along on the implementation of PBIS.

Chapter 8

PBIS Stage 3: Getting Going—Initial Implementation

The initial implementation stage involves putting the remaining features of the PBIS framework in place and then measuring their implementation progress. As your school gets going on PBIS, the leadership team needs to ensure that all eight PBIS features are described clearly to the entire school staff. Then, as implementation continues, your school should exhibit tangible evidence of the presence and practice of the eight features. Using PBIS assessment tools, the leadership team confirms that each feature is in place with fidelity.

Tasks

Core objectives of stage 3:

1. Help the school staff understand the eight key features of PBIS.
2. Understand the leadership team process as the core of PBIS implementation.
3. Understand and conduct action planning based on progress, fidelity, and outcome data.

Key Features at Stage 3

During stage 2 you installed the first three features of PBIS. Now, as you get going on the initial implementation in stage 3, you'll put in place the remaining five features of the framework. The boldfaced items in the following features list highlight the five that are part of the initial implementation process.

1. Establish the PBIS Leadership Team.
2. Develop a statement of purpose.
3. Identify three to five schoolwide positive behavioral expectations.
4. **Develop teaching procedures.**
5. **Develop lesson plans.**
6. **Develop procedures for acknowledging positive student behavior.**
7. **Develop procedures for discouraging rule violations.**
8. **Develop data systems for monitoring implementation.**

Coaching During Stage 3

Coaches can:

1. Review the eight key features of PBIS with the PBIS Leadership Team, with other teams in the school, and with staff. Ensure that all staff members understand what the features are and what they look like in your setting.
2. Identify and use a tool for assessing progress. (See Chapter 4 and www.pbisapps.org.)
3. Select a process for making team decisions—including who, what, when, and how. For example, will your leadership team make decisions through consensus, majority vote, fist-to-five consensus, or something else? The decision-making process should always start by reviewing the current data.
4. Assist the PBIS Leadership Team in adopting and using a process for action planning and implementing the plan. For example, how will you assign specific tasks and how will you document the who, what, when, and how?
5. Teach the leadership team about assessment tools that measure progress, fidelity, and outcomes. Build a team routine for assessing and for reviewing results and using them to update the action plan.
6. Develop a series of questions that your team can use to actively and effectively engage in problem solving.

Training School Staff in the Features of PBIS

Training staff members on the PBIS framework includes helping them understand the eight key features of implementation. This is a process that is not accomplished all at once. It typically begins with a presentation of PBIS basics that occurs before the staff vote on whether or not to adopt the behavioral framework in the school. Then it continues in formal and informal ways throughout the school year; indeed, it continues on as part of the long-term operating system of the school.

It's also important that all staff members are trained to teach the schoolwide behavioral expectations identified in the matrix in Chapter 7 (see page 120 and Figure 7.2). PBIS does not produce a manual for this training because the framework allows leadership teams and school staff to determine the content details and order of implementation to best fit the situation. Consequently, the behavioral expectations that your school uses are developed and taught by school staff, and sometimes also the students, to reflect your school's culture and values.

Many schools using the PBIS framework create their own lessons to teach the expected school behaviors. Consider creating a subgroup of your PBIS Leadership Team to develop formal lesson plans to be distributed to staff. We have found that consistency of teaching the expectations increases when a small subcommittee designs formal lesson plans for the whole staff. Lessons can address sections of the behavioral matrix (how to walk in the hallways, for example). These lessons can be incorporated into a morning meeting or advisory, where students greet one another and share or participate in a short activity. **Figure 8.1** presents a sample lesson plan for teaching cafeteria behaviors. A reproducible **Lesson Plan Template** is on page 126.

Some schools or districts prefer using a published, research-based curriculum on social skills to assist in teaching general social skills to students. Examples include Second Step, Responsive Classrooms (for elementary), and Developmental Designs (for middle schools). If you use a published curriculum, consider tailoring parts of the curriculum to support your behavioral matrix. For example, if the week's lesson is on making and being a friend, bring that back to the cafeteria column on the matrix by encouraging students to invite other students to sit with them at lunch.

Whatever methods your school chooses to use to teach behavioral expectations to students, there must be opportunities for staff to demonstrate the information and for students to learn, practice, and receive feedback. Some schools teach the expectations during morning meetings for younger students or advisory time for older students. Mondays could become "Remodel

Figure 8.1

Sample Lesson Plan

Lesson Plan for: *Evergreen School*

Schoolwide Behavioral Expectations:
We come to school to learn.
We respect ourselves and others.
We are responsible for our actions.

Area: *Cafeteria* **Date:** *October 1, 2014*

Behavioral Expectation	*We come to school to learn.*	*We respect ourselves and others.*	*We are responsible for our actions.*
What It Means	*Go to class when dismissed.*	*Invite others to sit with you.* *Eat your fruits and vegetables.*	*Keep the cafeteria clean.* *Throw away trash.*

Purpose of the Lesson:
To remodel, practice, and remind how we are expected to behave in the cafeteria

Supplies and Resources:
Whiteboard
Markers
Y chart (looks like/sounds like/feels like) on large paper
Old magazines, scissors, and glue sticks

Student Activities:
Discuss with the students expectations for the cafeteria.
Discuss the need for the expectations (safety, enjoyable lunch time, orderly—so everyone can eat, and so on).
Ask students to share their ideas about why we have the expectations; fill in the Y chart.
Have the students cut out pictures of a healthy lunch and glue them around the border of the Y chart.
Display the chart in the classroom as a reminder of expected cafeteria behavior.

Reinforcement Activities:
Give the lunchroom monitors reward tickets to hand out to students who are following the expectations.

Lesson Plan Template

Lesson Plan for:

Schoolwide Behavioral Expectations:

Area: **Date:**

Behavioral Expectation			
What It Means			

Purpose of the Lesson:

Supplies and Resources:

Student Activities:

Reinforcement Activities:

Mondays" where staff and students can practice skills on the behavioral matrix. The PBIS Leadership Team could set up a year-long schedule for teaching and reviewing behavioral skills. Routine practices like these increase consistency among staff and provide opportunities for them to reinforce the expected school behaviors. Remind staff to model and demonstrate the positive behavioral skills, and to acknowledge students using desired skills.

Typically, the school PBIS Leadership Team creates a general plan for school staff to introduce the expectations to students, which includes answers to who, what, when, and where. Expectations are taught to students at the beginning of the year, with multiple booster sessions throughout the year, before and after breaks, in large and small groups, as well as with individual students.

Coach's Tip from Beth:

If your school is using a published curriculum, be sure to check out the publisher's website. It may offer tips, ideas, and lesson plans related to PBIS. For example, Responsive Classroom and Developmental Design use CARES (cooperation, assertion, responsibility, empathy, and self-control) as the foundation of their social skills program. This approach supports the framework of PBIS very well. You can incorporate the CARES into your schoolwide expectations and behavioral matrix. Indeed, CARES promotes consistency and eliminates the need for your PBIS Leadership Team to spend a lot of time creating something that already exists.

Develop a System to Acknowledge and Reward Students for Meeting Expectations

When you teach students new academic skills, the pattern usually goes like this:

1. Teacher models or demonstrates.
2. Student practices.
3. Teacher provides feedback.
4. Student tries again or corrects mistake.
5. Teacher praises student for learning a new academic skill with a star and sticker, a high five, or a grade.

These same steps should be followed to teach a new behavioral skill. When students have demonstrated a new skill, acknowledge it. In the classroom you can use high fives, verbal praise, or a thumbs-up. Monitor positive verbal comments versus negative comments made to students. In general, try to keep the ratio four positive comments to one negative comment. When teaching brand-new behavioral skills, increase reinforcement initially to as much as eight to one.

Many schools design a ticket program where teachers hand out tickets when students demonstrate use of a new skill. Sometimes these can be traded in for something the students find valuable—a free homework pass, trinkets, or maybe even a pair of tickets to a dance or sports game. Some schools select a student of the month and tie the selection criteria to the behavioral matrix; students who exhibit outstanding behavior or new behavior identified on the matrix are recognized at a school assembly. This is a topic for which your PBIS Leadership Team may want to solicit ideas from the staff. The idea of rewarding good behavior can be a major turnoff to some people and they may require some gentle persuading. To others, they see rewards as a natural part of learning and will happily jump on board. Personally, we like non-tangible rewards. Not only are they free, but they can also provide some students with much desired social time with friends or favorite staff members. See pages 182–183 in the Appendix for reward ideas.

Develop Procedures that Discourage Rule Violations

PBIS implementation starts with Tier 1 interventions that will affect, encourage, and support all students. Being proactive rather than reactive in handling disruptive behaviors takes some preparation. The following ideas may help you discourage rule violations:

- Be diligent and consistent in enforcing schoolwide expectations with all students.
- "Pre-correct" students, which means reminding them about school routines. For example, you might say to a class: "Who can tell me where we put completed homework?" or "What do we need to remember about using the computer lab?"
- Be prepared each day with an academic lesson plan and keep it moving. The more time students are on task, the less time they have to goof around.
- Give very clear instructions—say what you want the students to do, not what you *don't* want them to do. For example, say: "Remember to walk on the right side of the hallway."
- Redirect students for misbehavior. Use simple reminders rather than a lecture, such as: "Remember when we talked about expected school language yesterday? Can you say that in another way?"
- Use minor behavior infractions as teachable moments, such as a quick lesson on how to walk in the hallway or when to sharpen a pencil. Allow for re-dos; then praise the positive behavior.

Respond to behaviors in predictable ways; this reinforces the schoolwide expectations for students and may reduce the amount of time teachers spend responding to disruptive behaviors. The PBIS Leadership Team may decide when an infraction warrants an ODR. For example, if a student exhibits three minor behaviors with no behavioral change, this might be cause for a referral. If the student's behavior moves from a minor to a major behavior, it is probably time to write a referral. The flowchart in **Figure 8.2** includes a list of minor behaviors that are managed in the classroom and major behaviors, which incur a visit to the office.

Clear definitions of acceptable and non-acceptable behaviors are critical for schoolwide expectations. For example, when Beth was a teacher of students with serious behavioral issues, what she considered inappropriate language may have been viewed as abusive language by other teachers. While developing these behavioral tools and definitions, keep in mind different teachers' classroom management styles and tolerance levels for classroom disruptions. The goal is to increase consistency in how adults deal with student behavior throughout the school.

Using the definitions from the PBIS website may reduce discussions or arguments among staff over what is a major and minor offense. You can find a complete list of behaviors and definitions in the SWIS materials and resources at www.pbisapps.org. Or you might ask your staff to determine the list of major and minor behaviors. We did this with a school and it went pretty smoothly. We broke staff into groups and made a list of major and minor behaviors. Each group shared their list and together we created a master list of major and minor behaviors for the school. This can be a lot of work, however, and can cause some people grief; but it can also increase the buy-in from staff to follow the lists because they helped create them. *Note:* For students who are receiving special education services, be aware of what their Individual Education Plan (IEP) and intervention plan say; these documents may supersede your school behavioral plan.

Develop Data Systems That Monitor Progress

During stage 2, the installation of PBIS infrastructure, you developed an action plan, and you have been updating this plan continuously since then. Monitoring the completion of action plan steps is essential to fully implementing PBIS. You also want to ensure you are implementing these steps with fidelity—in short, that everyone is handling situations in the same way. For example, think back to stage 2, when you developed schoolwide behavioral expectations: How will your PBIS Leadership Team be sure that every teacher has a poster of the expectations displayed in their classroom? The coach or a PBIS team member could go around and count, or staff could photograph the posters in the classrooms and other areas

Figure 8.2

Sample Behavioral Discipline Flowchart*

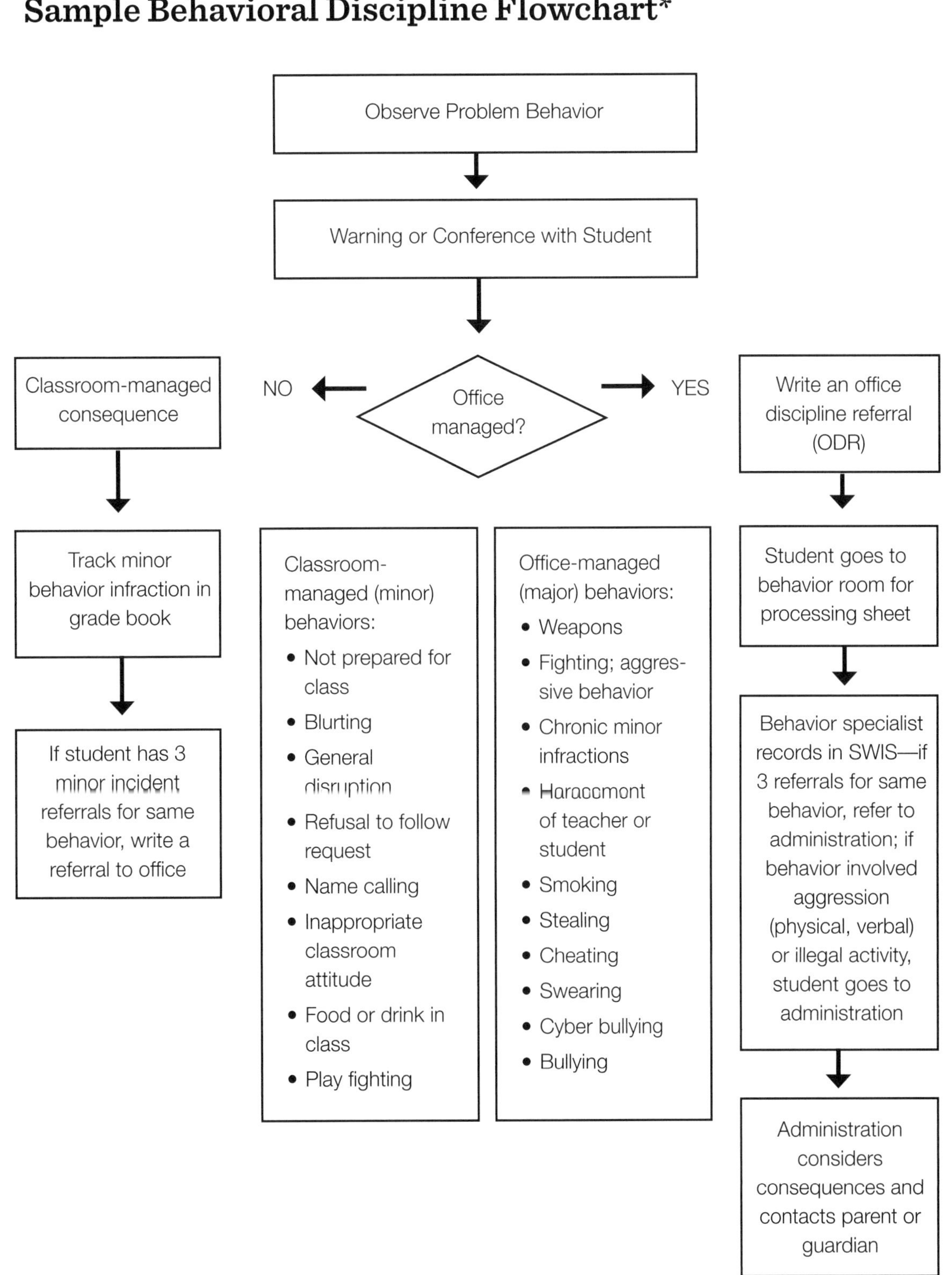

*Teachers/staff should try at least 3 interventions to change minor behaviors before sending students to the office. Administration is expected to relay consequences back to the referring teacher.

(save the photos for your archive book). Using the SET or the BoQ can help your leadership team assess the progress of implementation.

Other parts of your action plan may take longer to implement and the progress may not be immediately evident. Be patient. Set deadlines that are doable. If your initial deadlines appear to be unrealistic, move them out a bit and note the changes on your action plan. Keep track of your action plan items at each PBIS Leadership Team meeting.

We know from research that it is imperative that the schoolwide expectations be replicated in individual classrooms.

Problem Solving

As the PBIS Leadership Team develops an action plan and works to accomplish each item, problems will undoubtedly arise. Some of these may concern the timeline you have established, and you'll need to decide whether or not it can be adjusted. Other problems that occur may involve the actions of other people and, thus, may be more difficult to resolve. For example, in a perfect world, every teacher will willingly take a copy of the behavioral expectations poster and hang it in a prominent location in their classroom. Yet experience tells us that some people refuse or simply don't follow through with this. What to do? This is an issue for the coach to handle. Gracefully and tactfully, the coach can remind the teacher of his or her commitment to the initiative and ask that the teacher hang up the poster. Staff refusal to buy in to PBIS initiatives could be a topic for a PBIS Leadership Team meeting. This topic might spur your team to use the TIPS problem-solving model (see Chapter 5). Ultimately, as a very last resort, this particular issue could be one for the principal to resolve.

Refining Your Action Plan

As Chapter 7 explained, the PBIS Leadership Team formulates an action plan both to guide and to track PBIS implementation. Assessment results from the Team Implementation Checklist (TIC), the Self-Assessment Survey (SAS), and the Benchmarks of Quality (BoQ) provide concrete items for action planning. The leadership team prioritizes action items and considers how to accomplish them, who will take charge of each item, and by when it will be completed.

As you move forward in the implementation process, be sure to update and refine the action plan continually. Also, consider sharing the action plan with all school staff at a faculty meeting and explain how staff will be involved in completing action items. For example, if your team has determined that the three to five behavioral expectations need to be posted in every classroom, hallway, cafeteria, gymnasium, and office, what will the plan be to accomplish this? We know from research that it is imperative that the schoolwide expectations be replicated in individual classrooms.[24] Classroom teachers may adapt the behavioral matrix to the classroom setting, but the matrix still needs to mirror the schoolwide expectations. Some leadership teams decide to print the posters and hand them to teachers to hang in their classrooms; team members also ask school volunteers to display the posters in other areas of the school.

Buy-In and Support

Stage 3 is about putting the pieces in place. Teams often find, at this stage, that they need to take a step back and move at a slower pace. Remember: PBIS is a long-term commitment. The goal is to establish a solid Tier 1 with fidelity. Doing this can only occur with ongoing staff buy-in and schoolwide commitment. To sustain buy-in, it's best not to compare your process or progress with other schools. Implementing PBIS means adapting it to your individual school culture. Take time

[24]Mathews, et al., 2013.

to do it well. Consider how you'll keep support for PBIS strong during this stage. What steps need to be taken to sustain buy-in? How will you determine which team members need to take action to support buy-in? **Figure 8.3** outlines the buy-in tasks for stage 3.

Telling Your School's Story

During the initial stage of implementation, your school's story will expand from sharing baseline data and information about PBIS infrastructure to reporting on how the implementation process is moving along. While you may still include baseline data in your narrative, you may also choose to

Figure 8.3

Getting Going—Buy-In Roles and Measures

Person/Group Responsible	Buy-In Tasks	Measures
Administrator	• Rallies staff • Arranges for staff development time for training	SET, TIC
Coach	• Prompts team to complete data tasks • Engages staff in discussions • Prompts team to update and stay focused on the action plan	TIC
Leadership team	• Train and coach the staff in teaching behavioral expectations to students • Review with staff the schoolwide system for handling problem behaviors	SET, SAS, TIC
School staff	• Agree to behavioral matrix and schoolwide expectations • Agree to schoolwide system for handling behavioral problems	SET, SAS
Students	• Participate in learning behavioral expectations and reinforcement systems • Describe behavioral system for expected schoolwide behaviors	SET
District	• Monitors implementation of PBIS	Invites PBIS Leadership Team to present to school board
Community	• Behavioral systems and practices are explained to the families and community to assist with their buy-in	Newsletters, school and district websites

add some of the reports and graphs that illustrate your progress in teaching the expectations and rewarding students. Following are some questions to consider as you develop your continuing story.

Our School's Story—PBIS Stage 3

In this stage of our story, we'll focus on sharing how our school is doing with the initial implementation of PBIS.

What is our midyear progress?

Here's an example:
We are two thirds of the way through year one of initial implementation. We have measured our progress using the TIC twice and we have surveyed staff with the SAS.

This might be demonstrated to others by sharing a report, shown in **Figure 8.4.**
Our second TIC shows that we have made progress in establishing the key features of PBIS. Under Define Expectations, we increased from 33 percent to 67 percent, and for Teach Expectations, we went from 0 percent to 50 percent.

Figure 8.4

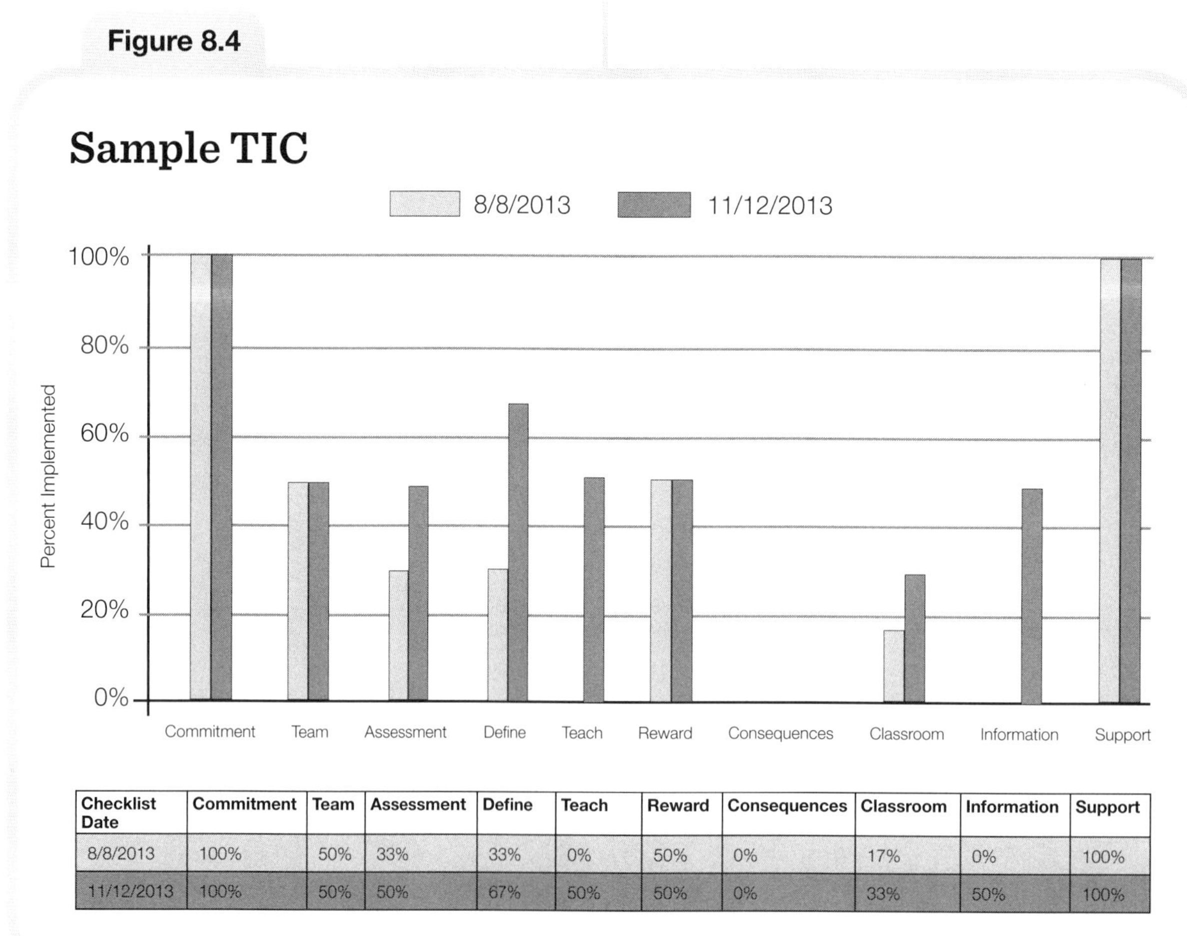

Checklist Date	Commitment	Team	Assessment	Define	Teach	Reward	Consequences	Classroom	Information	Support
8/8/2013	100%	50%	33%	33%	0%	50%	0%	17%	0%	100%
11/12/2013	100%	50%	50%	67%	50%	50%	0%	33%	50%	100%

Chapter 9

PBIS Stage 4: Up and Running—Full Implementation

By the time you reach implementation stage 4, all eight PBIS features are fully in place and fully operational—meaning they are visible and used by all staff with all students, all of the time, across all settings within the school.* The eight features are visible in school reports, newsletters, videos, press releases, policy, and procedures, and this communication extends to the district as well. So while initial implementation means that schools and teams are selecting and adapting PBIS to their particular setting, full implementation means that your school's specific version of the PBIS features are used by all and that speed bumps, migrations, and adaptations during the initial implementation have improved the fit and fidelity of these practices. By stage 4, PBIS has become an established routine in your school.

Schools typically make great strides toward initial implementation during the first year with PBIS, but full implementation takes longer. It may be three to four years after the exploration and adoption stage before the school has fully implemented the PBIS framework. This is long enough for the honeymoon to pass and for several rounds of staff turnover and other political shifts to occur. During the course of stage 4, schools should be seeing evidence of changes in student behavior and school culture. Staff confidence and enthusiasm for the PBIS initiative should also be evident. The PBIS Leadership Team continues to assess implementation fidelity and student outcomes reflecting the school and district routine. In general, PBIS features should be solidly in place and demonstrate measures of fidelity at designated criteria levels. If you are one of the first schools in your district to implement PBIS, you may have the added pressure of being the demonstration site that others will visit to decide if they will also implement PBIS. Telling your story and showing your data are priceless.

Tasks

Core objectives of stage 4:

1. Achieve and document implementation fidelity.
2. Continue to measure support and buy-in from administration and staff.
3. Measure and communicate fidelity and outcomes.

*All staff is the ideal. However, best practice is to have at least 80 percent of staff committing prior to implementing PBIS; in most cases, some staff choose not to participate. The administrator and PBIS coach may work with these staff members and eventually get them on board with PBIS.

Coaching During Stage 4

Coaches can:

1. Work with the PBIS data manager or subgroup to use the instruments that measure implementation fidelity (such as TIC, SET, SAS, and BoQ; see Chapter 4).
2. Remain connected with district, regional, state, and national resources that offer support and guidance.
3. Facilitate continued regular communication with staff, administration, and community about implementation, fidelity, and outcomes.
4. Ensure that the PBIS Leadership Team continues to meet on a regular basis to monitor implementation, system changes, and so on.
5. Be prepared to quickly redirect any missteps that occur. Use your data.

Full Implementation in Action

Let's follow one student, Johnny, on a typical morning to see how PBIS might look when it is fully implemented in his school:

Johnny is in fifth grade in Evergreen School. When he arrives at school on the bus, the bus driver (who has been trained in PBIS) reminds Johnny to wait his turn to get off the bus and then thanks him for doing so. Johnny turns to the bus driver and says, "Thank you!" The bus driver smiles and says, "Have a good day, Johnny. I'll see you after school. I want to hear a good report!"

Johnny races his friend into the building, where the principal, Mrs. Garcia, asks the two students to slow down, reminding them of the school expectation to walk in the hallway. She also says, "Have a good breakfast! Johnny, come and see me after lunch and tell me how your day is going!" He agrees to stop and see Mrs. Garcia later in the day and then goes to the cafeteria with his friend.

The cafeteria worker greets the students. She gives Johnny an extra big smile as he takes the egg roll-up and a carton of milk. When she is finished serving breakfast, she finds Johnny and compliments him on walking in the cafeteria and throwing his trash away. She also gives him a "Caught Ya" ticket that can be turned in for a prize at the end of the week. After a healthy breakfast, the students go to their classrooms.

Each classroom starts the day with twenty minutes of community-building strategies. Mr. Moe, Johnny's teacher, has the students gather in a circle on the floor. This month's theme is friendship and the lesson includes an activity to help the students get to know each other better. Mr. Moe encourages the students to invite other students to join them at lunch today; he also refers to this item on the behavioral matrix. The lesson ends with a game of Silent Ball. Johnny wins and is feeling pretty proud. Mr. Moe congratulates him with a high five and words of praise. "Wow, Johnny, that was a great game of Silent Ball. You were awesome. Next time we play, you can start."

The students are dismissed from homeroom and Johnny heads with his class to the science lab. Posters in the hallways remind the students of the school's behavioral expectations: *We come to school to learn. We respect ourselves and others. We are responsible for our actions.* Teachers and other staff members monitor the hallways between classes and remind students to walk and bring down their voice levels. One staff member pats Johnny on the back for following the expectations and gives him another "Caught Ya" ticket (to reinforce his new and improved habit of walking in the hallway). The science teacher, Mr. Smith, is standing in the doorway greeting the students. When Johnny shows off the pencil he has remembered to bring to class (a rarity for Johnny), Mr. Smith gives Johnny a high five.

Mr. Smith has a solid lesson plan, with learning targets posted on the board. He also has the schoolwide behavioral expectations posted in the front of the room to be visible at all times. Mr. Smith has built a routine: students come in, get their science notebook, and try to figure out the brainteaser on the board. Johnny goes to the bin where the science notebooks are and grabs his as well as two other students' notebooks. Play fighting over the notebooks starts, and Mr. Smith directs Johnny to hand over the notebooks. Mr. Smith quietly reminds Johnny of the routine and asks him to take his seat. Johnny sits at a table with three other students. Johnny moves his chair right next to Omar, who pushes Johnny away while trying to solve the day's puzzle. Johnny laughs until Mr. Smith comes over and reminds Johnny of the "We respect ourselves and others" expectation. He also quickly quizzes Johnny about what that looks like in the science lab and then requests that Johnny apologize to Omar, which Johnny does and Omar accepts. Mr. Smith thanks Johnny for showing his respect by apologizing to Omar.

Mr. Smith reads the learning targets for the day. Meanwhile, Johnny flips his pencil and hits Omar in the head. Johnny laughs out loud while Omar rubs his head. Mr. Smith asks Johnny to move to a seat near the front of the classroom and continues with the lesson. Johnny turns around in his seat trying to get Kia's attention. She ignores Johnny. Mr. Smith tells Johnny to face the front and be respectful to the other students by following the lesson. Johnny soon turns around again and makes faces at Kia. Realizing that he has redirected Johnny four times, Mr. Smith writes a referral for Johnny to go to the behavior room, per the discipline flowchart the faculty created. The ODR has blanks and checkboxes for the date, student, grade level, time of day, where the behavior occurred, who was involved, and what the behavior was. Mr. Smith signs it and sends Johnny out the door.

Johnny walks down the hallway to the behavior room. When he arrives, Mrs. Dillard greets Johnny warmly and firmly, and she takes the referral. She immediately enters the data into a SWIS spreadsheet for data collection. Then she talks to Johnny about the behaviors and he completes a processing sheet that asks what expectation he wasn't following, what he was supposed to be doing, and what will happen when he gets back to class. She has him practice what he will say to Mr. Smith. She jots some notes on the referral form for him to bring back to Mr. Smith. Mrs. Dillard encourages Johnny to do well and reminds him that he likes science class. On the data spreadsheet, Mrs. Dillard marks that she processed the situation with Johnny and he returned to class. Upon returning to the classroom, Johnny sees Mr. Smith at the door. Mr. Smith glances at Mrs. Dillard's notes, and he and Johnny discuss Johnny's plan to take his seat as directed and to complete his work. Mr. Smith keeps a close eye on Johnny while the class completes the lab project. He makes eye contact with Johnny a couple of times—once to remind him to work and once to let him know he was doing a good job.

Someone well versed in PBIS will likely be able to pick out the components of PBIS after spending a day in your school.

After school, the PBIS Leadership Team gathers in the media center to review the monthly data. The team also discusses the auditorium program they will have next month to honor the successes of individual students (for which teachers from each grade submit the names of one boy and one girl to honor). They check the teachers' nominations against the ODR data and agree to give the names to the honoring committee so they can print up certificates for the students. It's the fourth grade's turn to perform a skit about the expectations. Mr. Snyder said they are already working on making a short video, which everyone is very excited about.

This is just one example of what PBIS might look like in an individual school. It might look quite different in your school, depending on factors such as the age range of students, the expectations your team has developed, and the cultures and values of your school. Because PBIS is a framework, the scenario above could vary from building to building; even so, someone well versed in PBIS will likely be able to pick out the components of PBIS after spending a day in your school.

Achieving and Documenting the Fidelity of Implementation

Even when PBIS is fully implemented in your building, fidelity continues to be a priority. Failure to watch fidelity and outcomes increases the risk that your school will drift, or lose the accuracy of implementation. Drift can lead to a watered-down version of PBIS. Fidelity assessment is best achieved by using the School-Wide Evaluation Tool (SET) scores. The gold standard for this assessment is 80 percent. In addition, the Benchmarks of Quality (BoQ) is becoming more common; it has the advantage of providing more detail and being completed by the team at the school. The fidelity cutoff score for the BoQ is 70 percent.

Even when PBIS is fully implemented in your building, fidelity continues to be a priority.

Late spring is usually the best time for completing these evaluation tools. At this point in time, staff can complete the SAS survey taking into account how well the school year went and what could be changed for the fall. The PBIS Leadership Team may be able to meet during the summer to do some action planning using this data. (For more information, see the Evaluation Blueprint for SWPBIS at www.pbis.org.)

The PBIS Leadership Team may also review school data (such as ODRs, attendance, grades, and state test scores) along with the SAS and the SET scores to get a well-rounded picture of implementation fidelity. Or, the team could choose to review the data for areas in the school that are doing well (low ODR rates) and other areas that are struggling (high ODR rates). One of the areas that SET evaluators focus on concerns the visibility of schoolwide expectations around the school. If the evaluator notes a lack of posters in the hallways and the data subgroup notices a lot of referrals coming from the hallways, then the hallways would be an area that the PBIS Leadership Team would want to improve. They might, for example, decide to hang up more expectations posters in the hallways and create lesson plans that address how students should behavior in the hallways.

Buy-In and Support

Even during full implementation, it's important to consider how to keep support for PBIS strong. What steps need to be taken to sustain and even improve buy-in? Which leadership team members need to take action in this effort? **Figure 9.1** outlines the buy-in tasks and responsible party during stage 4.

Communicating with the Local Community

Some people may find it odd to see community participation listed in a school behavioral plan. However, if your school is near a local business (convenience stores, drugstores, restaurants), your principal may tire of phone calls detailing the students' antics in their businesses: "*Your* students are stealing candy!" "*Your* students are play-fighting and making the other customers uncomfortable! Keep them out of my store!"

Yet we know that these aren't "your" students; they are "our" students. Students have a place in communities just like adults do. Many students have parents who work in, or even own, these establishments next door to your school. Students may eventually work in these very stores and restaurants themselves. So, wouldn't it be great if we could help students learn to transfer the behavioral skills they are learning in school to their actions in the larger community as well? Many businesses like to support their local schools. For example, Beth's mechanic liked the local school so much that he would donate bikes for a drawing for students who had perfect attendance. To involve your larger community in PBIS, you may choose

Figure 9.1

Full Implementation—Buy-In Roles and Measures During Stage 4

Person/Group Responsible	Buy-In Tasks	Measures
Administrator	• Regularly attends PBIS Leadership Team meetings • Supports ideas agreed upon by the PBIS team	SET, SAS, BoQ
Leadership team	• Regularly attends PBIS meetings • Reports data to staff	TIC, SET, SAS, BoQ
School staff	• Teach and monitor schoolwide behavioral expectations • Acknowledge and reward use of appropriate behaviors	SET, TIC, SAS, BoQ
Students	• Learn and demonstrate behavioral expectations	ODRs, SET, SAS
District	• Invites PBIS Leadership Team to share data results at school board meetings • Sends district representative to school PBIS meetings • Adopts PBIS districtwide • Expands internal capacity for training	Rates for attendance, graduation, enrollment, suspension, and expulsion Districtwide ODR data
Community	• Secure the support of nearby businesses by expanding the behavioral expectations into the community. • Invite families to be a part of the PBIS Leadership Team. • Invite families share in celebrating school successes.	Participating in the reinforcement system, e.g., handing out the school's "Caught Ya" tickets when students follow the expectations in neighboring businesses Attendance at PBIS meetings, parent attendance rates at open house

to ask nearby businesses to hang the school's expectations near the cash register, since "Be respectful," "Be safe," and "Be ready" also apply to the desired behavior of customers. Store owners can be given a pile of "Caught Ya" tickets and be asked to hand them out to students behaving appropriately while in the stores.

Involving the families of your students in your PBIS efforts also includes communicating with them. Families play a huge role in the social and academic development of children. Invite families to attend open house nights to celebrate progress on a schoolwide behavioral goal. Include the behavioral matrix lesson plan themes in monthly newsletters so that parents can encourage the behaviors at home and in the community.

Another way to expand community involvement might be to include a parent on your PBIS Leadership Team or to have the team give updates to the PTA organization in your school. (Due to the confidential nature of some data, you'll need to refrain from sharing student and staff names when discussing the data.) This helps inform parents of the behavioral goals in your building and enables parents to share the progress with other parents and community members.

Schools can use the school website to inform the public about improved academics and behaviors (lower ODR and suspension numbers, improved attendance, and so on) as a result of the PBIS initiative. This would be wonderful for prospective families to see when they are looking at schools for their children. With parent permission, any behavioral videos created by the students about following expectations or what they like about their school could also be posted on the website to show the world your sense of humor and your commitment to creating a safe and calm school environment. Some schools create blogs. As technology advances, so do creative opportunities.

Telling Your School's Story

Once PBIS is fully implemented in your building, you may think that your school's story of the PBIS implementation process is no longer unfolding. However, the work of creating and maintaining a safe school environment that supports learning is not over; it has simply become the norm. To keep the momentum going, it is vital to remind staff and others about the progress that has been achieved and the continual efforts required to keep the school on the right track with student behavior.

As in earlier stages, we recommend that you develop a narrative based on your data and present your story in a variety of creative ways. Following are some questions to consider as you work to develop your continuing story.

Our School's Story—PBIS Stage 4

In this stage, we'll focus on sharing how we are doing now that PBIS is fully implemented in our school.

1. What is our end-of-year progress?

Here's an example:
We completed our first two years of implementation. We have measured our progress using the TIC twice. We have also surveyed staff with the SAS, and we have completed a SET.

We used the TIC and the SET for this purpose. Our results demonstrate our success in words and pictures, as illustrated in **Figures 9.2** and **9.3** on page 140.

Review the TIC scores over the two years. They fluctuate. This is not unusual but is a good reminder of how the TIC can be useful as a checkpoint to see if some of the features are sliding. At the end of the two years of formal training, this school looks pretty good. It will be really helpful for the PBIS Leadership Team to review the TIC and SET data in detail and be prepared to explain what some of the shifts mean. They will celebrate progress and continue to action plan.

Here is this school's SET score at the end of two years of formal training. It is hard to argue with 100 percent across the board. Some team members may find it interesting to compare scores across measures. What we often hear is that the PBIS Leadership Team is more critical or strict than an outside evaluator when scoring their efforts. They know things at a level that might not be obvious to an outside evaluator.

2. What is our year-end summary and action plan? Our narrative might be:

At the end of the second year of implementation, our school made great strides in implementing PBIS. In reviewing our TIC, we achieved 100 percent for implementing the following: well-defined expectations, teaching the expectations, a reward system, and consequences for behavior problems. Two subscales are below 80 percent: the team and the use of information. These issues require further examination and action planning. We will look at the Item Report. At the next PBIS Leadership Team meeting, we will discuss the details presented in the Item Report, which indicates that the PBIS Leadership Team is questioning how representative it is—for example, who is not there who should be. The other items have to do with summarizing and using ODR data. The PBIS Leadership Team rated this partially in place. This is an important item to address soon.

Our action plan for beginning next year is to implement two planned buy-in activities with staff that address teaching the schoolwide expectations as well as implementing our student recognitions system. In addition, we have improved our ODR form and have planned an additional staff training in September to assist in consistency. We will revise our process for handling ODR data at the PBIS Leadership Team meetings so that we are effectively using data-based decision making. Our team has met consistently and will meet twice a month beginning next September. We are seeking parent involvement on the team for next school year. We have planned lessons for the beginning of the school year for all staff and students. We will also develop a presentation that we will give to the school board in October demonstrating the goal, the progress, and student outcomes to date.

See the digital download for a sample PDF storytelling presentation that uses a combination of data and narrative to share a school's PBIS progress. Details for how to access are on page x.

Figure 9.2

Sample TIC Scores

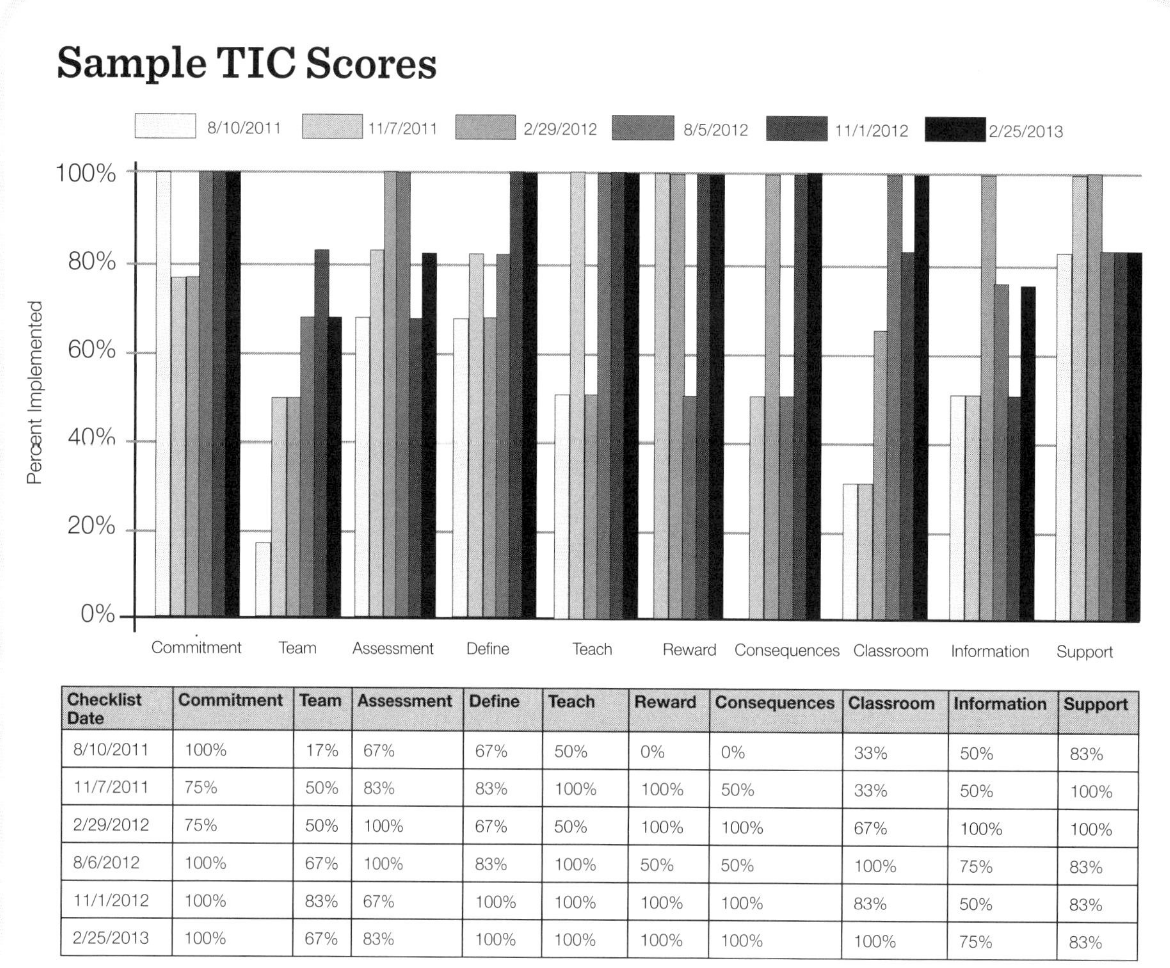

Checklist Date	Commitment	Team	Assessment	Define	Teach	Reward	Consequences	Classroom	Information	Support
8/10/2011	100%	17%	67%	67%	50%	0%	0%	33%	50%	83%
11/7/2011	75%	50%	83%	83%	100%	100%	50%	33%	50%	100%
2/29/2012	75%	50%	100%	67%	50%	100%	100%	67%	100%	100%
8/6/2012	100%	67%	100%	83%	100%	50%	50%	100%	75%	83%
11/1/2012	100%	83%	67%	100%	100%	100%	100%	83%	50%	83%
2/25/2013	100%	67%	83%	100%	100%	100%	100%	100%	75%	83%

Figure 9.3

Sample SET Scores

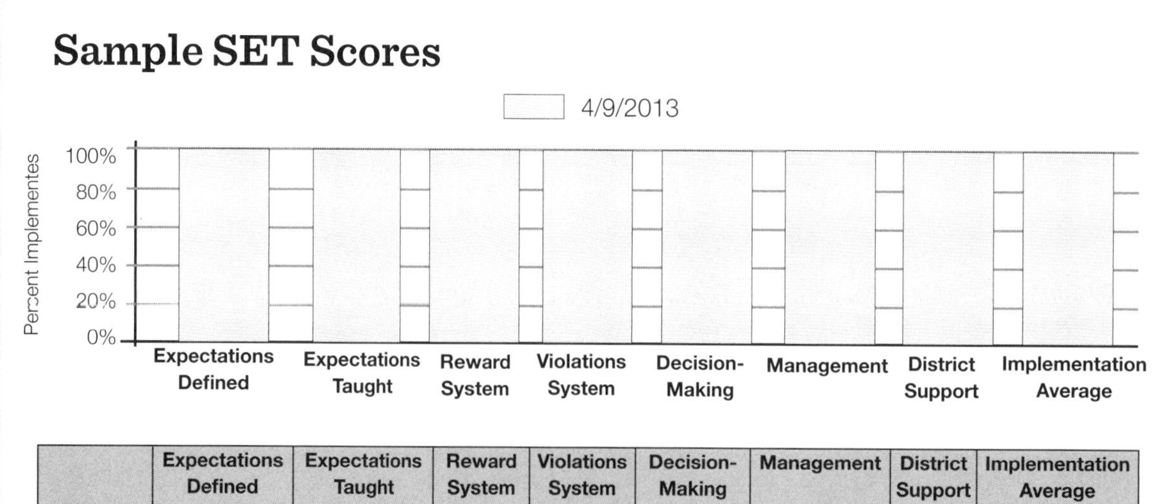

	Expectations Defined	Expectations Taught	Reward System	Violations System	Decision-Making	Management	District Support	Implementation Average
4/9/2013	100%	100%	100%	100%	100%	100%	100%	100%

Chapter 10
PBIS Stage 5: Sustaining and Continuous Improvement

Along the continuum of implementation, schools arrive at a point where PBIS practices are fully in place and stable, for all students, for all staff, in all settings. Staff has gained experience with all aspects of implementation and tackled predictable challenges. It is tempting at this point to rest and declare that the initiative is fully implemented and that the school can now simply coast and continue to reap the benefits of the previous work. But there is still another stage of implementation: sustaining and continuous improvement. Again guided by the PBIS Leadership Team, stage 5 offers opportunities to make further adaptations to fit your specific school and to address any changes that have occurred since the inception of PBIS. These adaptations may include new and more efficient ways to achieve goals and to maintain consistency and fidelity.

One of the key issues during stage 5 is to ensure that there is no drift, or movement away from the eight core features of PBIS. Simple examples of drift include letting go of the acknowledgment and reward system for students who meet expectations, discontinuing the regular teaching of expectations, becoming inconsistent in discipline practices, or other such loosening of key items. While posters, T-shirts, and mottoes may provide visible reminders of expected behaviors, they do not necessarily reflect a deeper, more consistent practice. Studies show that schools that sustain PBIS demonstrate high criteria scores for fidelity on the continued teaching of expectations (80 percent on SET), and they maintain high levels of implementation (80 percent on the composite SET score). Another measure that is commonly used to assess fidelity is the BoQ, which has a criterion of 70 percent.

So, the task for PBIS coaches and teams at stage 5 is to continue to regularly assess the school's outcome data and its faithfulness to core PBIS features. Ensure that PBIS expectations are continuing to be consistently taught throughout the entire school, including within each classroom. This process should be business as usual for every school at stage 5. In addition, coaches and teams must now focus on sustaining practices through buy-in from all stakeholders. Using data, reporting data, and continual communication at all levels are key, as is continuing to acknowledge and celebrate accomplishments.

Tasks

Core objectives of stage 5:

1. Adapt to changing contextual factors, such as staff turnover, team member attrition, enrollment changes, demographic changes, or financial issues.
2. Create more efficient and effective ways to implement core PBIS features.
3. Ensure that new or existing practices continue to match all core features with fidelity.
4. Maintain support, buy-in, and acknowledgment of practices and regular assessment.

Coaching During Stage 5

Coaches can:

1. Continue using data actively in decision making. For example, review your data at the beginning of each meeting to identify questions; gather more data as needed; write precision statements to describe problems; and create goals, solutions, and evaluation measures that ensure appropriate implementation of solutions.
2. Make sure that the PBIS Leadership Team administers and uses regular data checkpoints throughout the year. Use a tool like the BoQ or SAS in Tier 1. Also be aware of upcoming tools, such as the PBIS Implementation Inventory described in Chapter 4. Conduct regular self-assessment of implementation (use the SAS with staff and the TIC with the PBIS Leadership Team).
3. Continue to assess implementation fidelity (SET, BoQ, etc.).
4. Evaluate, report, and problem solve with student data from ODRs.
5. Continue to communicate within the school and throughout the district, region, state, and local community on implementation progress, changes, and outcomes. See the Appendix for some tips and examples to communicate results at various stages.
6. Celebrate and promote successful practices at all levels.

Sustainability

Most of us have probably had the experience of working on a project for a period of months or years and watching it disappear either suddenly when new conditions arise or gradually as staff and constituents change. Sadly, some initiatives are abandoned just when they are on the cusp of making a lasting impact and effecting real change. That is why PBIS is considered a long-term undertaking and why schools are advised about the level of commitment required and the timeline for full implementation before they decide to adopt the framework. Making a substantial commitment like this helps schools achieve buy-in of staff and key stakeholders and assures those involved that their time and efforts are being well spent.

Our purpose in this chapter is to explain what sustainability means within PBIS, talk about why it is important, discuss what researchers tell us about sustainability good practices, and, most important, identify steps that coaches and teams can take to achieve sustainability and protect their important accomplishments.

What Is Sustainability?

Generally, when people find something that works they want to keep it going. They want effective strategies to last over time. They don't want to start over. This thinking is logical but not necessarily easy to carry out. The idea of maintaining practices over time is called "sustainability." Within PBIS this notion of sustainability is really important. PBIS leaders and researchers are spending a lot of time studying what sustainability is and how to do it in real-world situations involving individual schools and school districts. This research will help those who are using the practices of PBIS with success and want to keep them alive and schools continually thriving.

Why Is Sustainability Important?

So what is the big deal about sustainability? The idea of keeping effective practices alive is logical but often very difficult to achieve. Sustaining practices requires a commitment of time, money, support, and emotional investment over the long haul. We believe this can only happen with a good understanding of the PBIS implementation process combined with continuous intentional planning for the future. Sustainability also requires that we accomplish and maintain full implementation of the practices with high fidelity.

So this is the point where the concept and practice of sustainability can get a little complicated. A quick refresher of basic concepts will help: PBIS is a set of clearly defined practices that are embedded within eight key features that have been discussed throughout this book. You can say what these practices are and what they are not. For all of the practices, the two crucial issues are implementation and fidelity. Implementation means that the practices are being done with integrity as they are defined, and you can easily observe adults performing these practices. For example, you can enter a school and observe visual representations of the three to five positive behavioral expectations for students. You can also observe staff actively teaching students what these expectations look like in hallways and other settings. In short, implementation means that the essential, clearly defined practices are regularly used. Fidelity means the practices are true to their original design. Implementation without fidelity is unlikely to produce desired outcomes and reward effort.

Implementation with Fidelity

Once the practices of PBIS are observable, the question is whether they are performed consistently with the manner in which they demonstrated success. You need to ensure that new or existing practices continue to match all core features with fidelity. Let's take an example. "Develop teaching procedures" is one of the eight key features of the PBIS framework. Once a school has identified its expectations, the leadership team or staff develops a behavioral matrix and lesson plans for teaching these expectations in various settings (classroom, hallways, cafeteria, library, and so on). Then all staff proceeds to teach these expectations to all students. Typically, the PBIS Leadership Team develops a plan for doing this as well, which includes the who, what, when, and where involved. Expectations are taught at the beginning of the year with multiple booster sessions throughout the year, before and after breaks, in large and small groups as well as with individual students. The practice of teaching the school expectations is ongoing for all students and all staff.

What can happen with this practice (or any practice in any field) is that drift occurs—the practice is done less frequently and with less consistency to the original standard. So, while the original standard requires teaching the behavioral expectations regularly and consistently, in time, a school may teach the expectations at the beginning of the school year, gradually loosen up their practice of teaching them before or after school breaks, and stop doing boosters or teaching new staff or new students. Such drift leads to a watered-down version of the practice—it is no longer being implemented with fidelity.

When fidelity declines, the associated benefits of PBIS may also decline.

When fidelity declines, the associated benefits of PBIS may also decline. The most efficient way to avoid this gradual drift is to establish a routine pattern for assessing progress, for monitoring sustained practice with fidelity, and for responding to any shifts. Many PBIS experts describe the benefits of a strong coaching system. This directly relates to both fidelity and sustainability. Coaching includes the capacity to quickly redirect PBIS Leadership Teams when fidelity is declining; coaches can also increase their support when the need arises to boost sustainability.[25]

[25]Horner, 2011; Barrett and Duda, 2011; Sugai, 2013.

Barriers to Sustainability

What interferes with sustainability? Numerous challenges may arise. Sometimes the practices were never implemented to full fidelity standards in the first place, so it is impossible to sustain them with fidelity. Perhaps the implementation process stalled in the early stages and the deeper level of practice and change was never achieved. In this case, it is best to regroup and work on an action plan to get the implementation process going again.

Proactive planning for expected events can help prevent loss of progress, time, and efficacy.

Sometimes your own behavior can drift away from the initial high-level practice. For example, the staff and team at one school worked very hard to get the key features of PBIS in place during the first year. Then, when they began their second year, they thought they no longer needed to acknowledge students for following the behavioral expectations because they had done so much of that the first year. As a result, the key feature of regular acknowledgment decreased in frequency and was missing for new students and staff. Implementing with fidelity means that we put the practice fully in place and continue to perform it at the same level.

Think of an analogy with physical fitness. You may be excited when you work out to achieve a new level of competence, like being able to run a 10K, but are dismayed to discover that this optimal level of fitness quickly dissipates when you stop working out regularly. When your behavior drifts away from the level of effective practice, you simply cannot maintain the same fitness level. So it is with PBIS: when you stop putting in the time and effort, the benefits decline.

Other challenges to sustainability include the lack of resources to support the practice. Schools commonly use grant money or special funds to get started with PBIS. Yet, without specific planning for transition, the loss of those funds can undermine ongoing implementation. The PBIS Leadership Team and administrators need to determine which funding needs will be ongoing from the start and include these items in the yearly budget.

Another common challenge is the turnover of staff and administrators. Schools that are able to build and sustain capacity across various teams, the school, and the district have planned for such turnover by sharing tasks within the PBIS Leadership Team, by keeping accurate records of action plans and other related documents, and by establishing a staff training cycle that ensures new staff are initiated into the practices of PBIS and existing staff are reminded of proper protocol.

Sometimes school teams become over-reliant on a single individual "champion" to carry the enthusiasm and effort of the initiative. This can be the principal, the coach, or someone else who is strongly committed. When that person moves on, it leaves a huge void that disrupts the continuity of leadership team and school functioning. This underscores the need to develop fluency among all team members and to share responsibilities for implementation tasks.

In other situations, the PBIS Leadership Team and action plan may lack structures, processes, or system pieces necessary to ensure implementation and fidelity. The failure to self-monitor can cause teams to miss important milestones and opportunities to self-correct. Some very general considerations to address these barriers include awareness and knowledge of sustainability and of the factors that impede implementation and fidelity. Proactive planning for expected events can help prevent loss of progress, time, and efficacy.

Theoretical Model of Sustainability in PBIS

A model of sustainability is emerging based on research specifically related to schoolwide PBIS and its features. This theoretical model, its validation, and the science of implementation offer great promise for the field of sustainability. Kent McIntosh, Rob Horner, George Sugai, and others propose that PBIS sustainability is based on the presence of four factors:

1. PBIS is a priority in the school and district.
2. PBIS is effective; it achieves important outcomes.
3. PBIS is efficient; its efforts target results.
4. PBIS implementers continuously use data to evaluate and adapt to the local context, which enables continuous regeneration.

In their efforts to validate this model, these researchers and others have studied schools implementing PBIS across the country. Two important and practical findings are coming from this work. First, evidence suggests that certain specific actions predict long-term implementation of PBIS with fidelity. Second, they've developed a tool called the SUBSIST Checklist that practitioners can use to self-assess their school's degree of sustainability; the checklist includes an accompanying action plan for responding to identified needs.[26]

SUBSIST Checklist Tool

Kent McIntosh and others have been actively studying how schools can sustain PBIS once it has been fully implemented. They have developed and are testing a research tool called the SUBSIST. A variation of the research tool is the SUBSIST Checklist, a self-assessment for coaches, administrators, and leadership teams to use. This tool allows teams to rank sustainability features as fully, partially, or not yet in place in their schools. Teams can use the results of this assessment to identify strengths, needs, and priorities for action planning. A reproducible version of the checklist appears on pages 178–181 in the Appendix.

Adapting to Changing Circumstances

Change is hard for many people. Often, just when a new project gets rolling along, someone in leadership leaves. For PBIS Leadership Teams, a change in school staffing can affect the makeup of the leadership team. To adapt, teams need to recruit new members. (Perhaps you can entice them with snacks at the meeting, the best parking spaces, or reduced morning supervision duty.) If your PBIS coach leaves, you'll need to adapt by having someone else step into this role. If your school and team planned ahead for this possibility, then you likely already have someone on your PBIS Leadership Team who can easily take over the coaching responsibilities. Even if this change catches your team off guard, your documentation of archived notes and your three-ring notebook of materials will help the next person take on this task. This documentation should include the titles of team roles as well as a description and time commitment for each. Part of planning may include a predictable succession plan, possibly term limits.

Students, too, can change as PBIS initiatives continue. For example, they can tire of the expectations and start to blindly repeat them without knowing what they really are. When staff and team members notice this, it may be time to freshen up the expectations.

Perhaps one of the biggest challenges to sustaining PBIS is when the principal who supports PBIS leaves and is replaced with a principal who does not believe in PBIS and would rather go back to the way things were.[27] To prevent such an awful scenario from occurring, the PBIS coach could proactively approach the new principal to schedule an appointment to discuss the benefits of the initiative; then bring along the three-ring binder of archives, and go over the baseline data (before PBIS) and the current data (reflecting the continued emphasis on the key features of PBIS). Show photos of happy students being honored for being awesome and photos of staff enjoying

[26] McIntosh, et al., 2013.
[27] Strickland-Cohen, McIntosh, and Horner, 2014.

Figure 10.1

Sustaining and Improvement—Buy-In Roles and Measures During Stage 5

Person/Group Responsible	Buy-in Tasks	Measures
Administrator	• Continue to support openly at the school and district level • Secure needed funds to support activities	TIC, SET, BoQ
Leadership team	• Meet regularly • Use data to monitor fidelity • Adapt to changing contexts	TIC, SET, BoQ
School staff	• Assist new staff with continued practice • Acknowledge, support, listen, clarify • Implement schoolwide expectations in classrooms	SAS, SET, BoQ
Students	• Continue to learn and demonstrate behavioral expectations, which are acknowledged appropriately by adults	ODRs, SET or BoQ scores, SAS scores
District	• Provide district leadership with data and information about status and progress • Show commitment to PBIS by hiring PBIS-supportive administrators	District evaluation plan Implementation Blueprint
Community	• Keep a parent/guardian on the PBIS team • Support local business with PBIS products (expectations posters, "Caught Ya" tickets, etc.)	Parent satisfaction survey Increase in positive comments from area businesses and community members

teaching; show the behavioral matrix with the lesson plans; and share academic assessment scores (hopefully they've also improved), surveys, and SET and SAS scores. We recommend getting sound bites from parents and the guy who owns the convenience store next to the school. It would also make sense to remind the principal about the district commitment to PBIS and invite him or her to your next PBIS Leadership Team meeting. (Note: It is the district's responsibility to replace the principal with one who would commit to PBIS.) We know of schools that have lost funding and administrative support but have carried on with PBIS as best they can, knowing it is the best way to run a school. These teachers meet on their own time to sustain PBIS.

Buy-In and Support

At each stage of implementation, we recommend taking time to consider how to keep support for PBIS strong. Buy-in is just as crucial during ongoing sustainability as it is during the earlier stages of implementation. What steps need to be taken to continually achieve buy-in? Which team members need to take action? **Figure 10.1** outlines these tasks and responsibilities for stage 5, as you are working to sustain and improve PBIS in your school.

Telling Your School's Story

As your PBIS Leadership Team and school staff are working to sustain and improve how they use the PBIS framework, telling your school's PBIS story to others is especially important. Communicate what is going well and what aspects of the initiative you are working to improve. This may elicit ideas from others, too. We recommend that you develop a narrative based on your data as you prepare to sustain and improve PBIS in your school.

When schools prepare displays of their PBIS progress, they often use a format typically seen at science fairs: telling a story with data, images, and attention-grabbing headlines. Start by creating an outline of information you want to share, add graphic displays of progress, and include mottoes, photos, and other examples to create human interest.

Part Three

Setting the Stage for PBIS Tiers 2 and 3

Chapter 11
Are You Ready for Advanced Tiers?

As we have stressed repeatedly in this book, it can take three to five years, sometimes even more, to fully implement all eight key features of PBIS Tier 1 with fidelity. Now that your implementation of this tier is fully in place, one thing you probably have noticed is that most students do quite well with these supports. They follow the expectations, participate in the reinforcement systems, and strive to keep their school a safe and calm place to learn. But you probably have also noticed that some students—always the same ones—are being referred out of the classroom repeatedly for similar behaviors. You may also have noticed that a few of these same students lead the school in referrals and suspensions, as if someone had told them it was a competition to get the highest numbers. How can the PBIS continuum of supports in your school reach these students, as well? That is the purpose of PBIS Tiers 2 and 3.

PBIS follows a three-tiered model of prevention that comes from the field of public health. The tiers in this model represent a continuum of prevention strategies that depend on teaching and reinforcement to improve students' engagement in school as well as their successful social competence. These tiers are called primary, secondary, and tertiary prevention, or Tier 1, Tier 2, and Tier 3. In general, these intervention strategies are viewed on a continuum from least to most intensive:

- **Primary prevention** refers to those practices applied to the general population to avoid the development of social behavioral problems in the first place.
- **Secondary prevention** refers to activities used with members of the population who experience risks for developing social behavioral problems.
- **Tertiary prevention** encompasses activities designed to reduce the frequency or severity of social behavioral problems among students who have already exhibited these problems.

The Three-Tiered Prevention Logic of PBIS

Prevention logic suggests that systematic use of effective practices at each of these tiers prevents and reduces the occurrence of social behavioral problems and lessens the effects of those that do occur. At the end of the day, you have fewer new cases and better, more effectively handled existing cases. These outcomes benefit individuals, groups, and service systems. You may recall from Chapter 1 the three-tiered PBIS triangle. It is shown again in **Figure 11.1.**

Figure 11.1

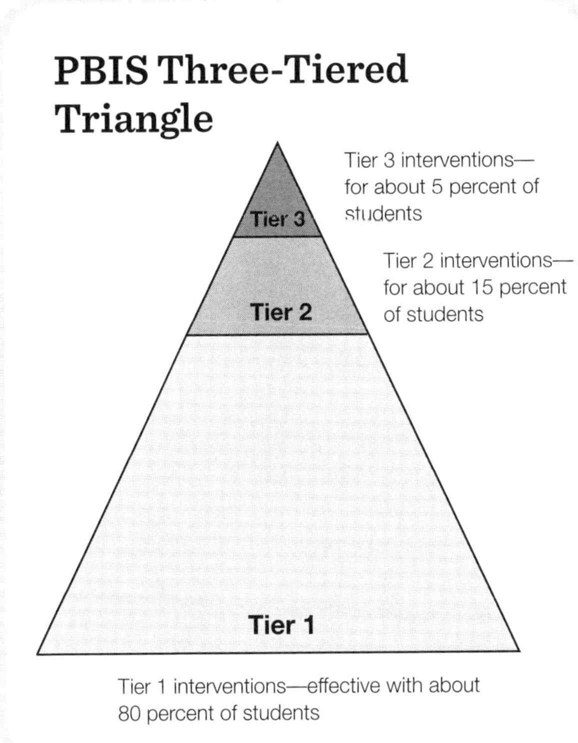

Viewing the prevention model as a triangle makes sense and fits the three-tiered logic. In PBIS, the triangle is made up of evidence-based practices that are essential for the whole school (Tier 1), for a few students who need some additional support (Tier 2), and for those students who need a great deal of support (Tier 3). The big idea is to organize a school intervention system that prevents as many problems as possible so there are fewer severe problems requiring extensive services. The challenge facing educators is to create a school environment that effectively and collectively promotes the success and well-being of all students and all staff.

As a general guideline, the bottom and largest zone (Tier 1) in Figure 11.1 is for primary prevention of student behavior. Interventions at this tier are universal; all students and all staff are involved. When this comprehensive and consistent set of universal interventions is applied schoolwide, about 80 percent or more of your entire school population knows and follows the expectations. They participate in the behavioral reinforcement activities (such as drawings for prizes, student of the month, wall of fame), and they have zero to one referrals during the course of a school year.

Tier 2, the middle tier, represents interventions for about 15 percent of students—those who need more support beyond the schoolwide interventions. These students may have two to five referrals in a year. Tier 2 interventions may include small social-skills groups (such as a girl's group, friendship group, calming strategies group, or maybe a lunch bunch) that are typically led by the school social worker, counselor, or behavior specialist; or there may be other interventions to help at-risk students. Intervention strategies for this tier may involve intensive teaching of prosocial behavior, and the use of behavior contracts or check-in and check-out systems.

Students need to see how their behavior not only affects them, but also ripples out and has an impact on others: teachers (who have to stop teaching to write the referrals), students (who have to stop learning while the teacher writes the referral), the behavior specialist (who has to process the behavior and do the data entry for the referral), the administrator (who has to call the student's parents), the parents (who may get interrupted at work because of the behavior), and so on.

Students need to see how their behavior not only affects them, but also ripples out and has an impact on others.

Beth remembers one student's eyes growing as big as the clock on the wall when she was told that every time she called her teacher a so-and-so, at least five people were involved in handling the incident (student, teacher, behavior specialist, parent, behavior room staff, and sometimes the school social worker). The girl explained that she felt like her teacher didn't listen to her, so she yelled at her teacher. This student, her teacher, and Beth had a sit-down conference during which the student could be honest, the teacher accepted the feedback and said her piece, and an agreement was reached to help each other out during a somewhat chaotic class period. Over a few weeks the problem gently righted itself.

Tier 3, the top tier, represents specialized interventions for students with the highest level of need. At this level, the behavioral team can do a functional behavioral assessment and create an individualized behavioral plan for this student. Some of these students may also be receiving special education services, or the data may show that an evaluation for special education may be in order. These students tend to be at high risk for challenging behaviors, which are the leading cause of expulsion. Generally, these interventions may be necessary for about 5 percent of the school population—students who may have six or more referrals.

Is Your School Ready to Implement Tiers 2 and 3?

So when is it time to implement Tiers 2 and 3? Before your school considers taking this step, be sure that all components of Tier 1 are soundly in place. It's best to give your team at least a couple of years for full Tier 1 implementation. That isn't to say that students with high needs are being ignored while you focus on the universal tasks of Tier 1 PBIS. Some schools will already have groups in place or have a behavioral team discussing students who have challenging behaviors. If that is true for your school, continue those efforts while you focus primarily on completing Tier 1 implementation. When your school believes it is ready for a formalized process to implement Tiers 2 and 3, consider these questions:

- What data sources document that Tier 1 is in place with fidelity? (for example, SET = 80/80; BoQ = 70)
- How many major and minor ODRs will trigger Tier 2 or Tier 3 strategies for students in your school? (for example, two to five referrals for Tier 2)
- Will your school weigh major ODRs against minor ODRs? (For example, will three minor referrals equal one major referral? Minor ODRs are often written for behaviors that could be managed in the classroom; teachers generally lose less instructional time when they handle these issues within the classroom.)
- How will you address students with internalized behaviors? (for example, sleeping in class, acting withdrawn, not participating in activities, experiencing failing grades, or visiting the nurse frequently—behaviors often ignored that could benefit from Tier 2 supports) Research demonstrates that Tier 2 interventions and supports can change the trajectory of problem behavior, lost instructional time, or school exclusion.[29]

A discussion on how to implement Tiers 2 and 3 is beyond the scope of this book, but the preceding guidelines and questions can begin your exploration stage of implementation for Tiers 2 and 3. Don't rush your school into implementing strategies for all the tiers on the first day of school or let staff pressure push you to do too much too soon. Give yourself and your staff time to make sure the features of Tier 1 are solidly in place with fidelity. You wouldn't build a house without a strong foundation. Hence, you shouldn't build up the PBIS triangle without a strong foundation

Big Idea: It is more efficient and effective to prevent problems from occurring or getting worse than to simply react to them. PBIS redesigns the school environment, not the students. In other words, PBIS changes adult behavior.[28]

[28]Sugai, 2013.
[29]McIntosh, Frank, and Spaulding, 2010.

in Tier 1. Take your time with the first tier. Build your foundation and build it well. That foundation will help you create a strong second tier, and then a third tier.

Coach's Tip from Beth

I remember trying to do all three simultaneously when I didn't have a good handle on what Tier 1 was all about. With Char's suggestions, I took a step back and focused my energies on implementing Tier 1 strategies. Thcro were still students participating in groups and teachers creating behavioral plans for the at-risk students, so there was support available for all students and staff. I took the necessary steps to implement Tier 1 in a way that would be sustainable. Besides the benefits that come with staying focused on one tier at a time, having the pieces of Tier 1 in place (the ODR procedure, teaching schoolwide expectations, a continuum of consequences, data collection and monitoring, and so on) will help you identify which students are not being reached through these universal prevention strategies.

Conclusion

Prevention has always been a hard concept to sell, because it's difficult to attach a dollar benefit to.* However, if your school is one that suffers from a lot of uncontrolled student behaviors, you know you need help. The intense needs for Tiers 2 and 3 might suggest you are operating in a crisis-intervention framework. But more than anything, you need a solid Tier 1 prevention system that successfully reduces the demand for higher tiers. Perhaps you don't have enough resources to support a three-tiered system right away. Perhaps staff and students are burned out. We believe in the value of establishing a strong first level prevention framework. That is why we chose, in this book, to explain the step-by-step process of Tier 1 implementation at fidelity. The process can be slow and not always complete, as Char explains from her experience as a trainer:

When I first began PBIS team training in Minnesota, PBIS cofounder George Sugai was our trainer. He did it all. Two days, all day. We gave every participant his or her own copy of a wonderful team training manual. That was in 2005. Nine years later, we have a whole team of homegrown trainers and still the same training manual that only covers Tier 1 implementation. Trainers, especially in year two, will talk about Tiers 2 and 3 so that it is not a foreign concept to teams, but this is merely previews of coming attractions. There is no formal team training, as of yet, on Tiers 2 and 3. Change is hard to create and sustain, even when focusing on adult behavior only. Every two years, we have a cohort of schools in our region graduate or complete two years of formal training. Not all of those schools have successfully achieved all of the features of Tier 1, but research shows that schools progress at their own pace.[30]

Just as prevention is a hard sell, so is change. As a PBIS coach, Beth was not sure what she was getting into, as she describes:

I loved PBIS from the get-go and was sure everyone would love it as much as me. However, that was not the case. As mentioned earlier, implementation of PBIS isn't so much about changing student behavior but changing the way adults respond to behavior. Some people climbed on the PBIS bus with me, others had one foot on the bus, and still others didn't want to go near the bus. I was lucky in that our principal was on the bus and she knew that forcing people onto the bus isn't the way to go. Start small and keep good data. People cannot argue with the data. As we went along, we implemented Tier 2 and 3 interventions because our school social worker saw they were necessary and was willing to do whatever was needed to help our students succeed. We also had a committed PBIS team.

So when you get frustrated with buy-in and the pace of change (and we are pretty sure you will), reach out to others who are on the "PBIS bus." They will understand. Take your time with implementation. Get on the bus and enjoy the journey. There will be bumps in the road; some people will get off the bus and others will get on. But stay the route and eventually you will arrive at the station where the logic of prevention prevails and you will find your school to be a calmer, safer, more peaceful place to be. Soon enough, people will be asking you, "How do I get on the bus?" It is our hope that you find this book to be a useful companion on your personal PBIS journey and that you share your knowledge and experience with others.

*The state of Maryland created a thoughtful spreadsheet that can calculate the savings in administrator time based on reduced ODRs. See www.pbismaryland.org for a DIY cost/benefit worksheet.

[30]McIntosh, et al., 2010.

Appendix

Contents

Coach's Self-Assessment

This self-assessment is designed to assist beginning coaches in identifying current strengths and professional development goals. It is organized to assess perceived knowledge and skills in the PBIS implementation areas of data, practices, and systems. The self-assessment may also serve as a data source schools and districts can use to identify the training and support a new coach might need.

Coach: ______________________________ Date: ______________________

School System/District: ______________________ State: ______________________

Beginning Coach

Coaches at this level should have fluency with universal (Tier 1) PBIS items involving schoolwide, classroom, and non-classroom settings. Coaches should be able to facilitate leadership team progress by guiding members through the PBIS implementation process.

3 = Fluent/Mastered 2 = Building skills, but not yet fluent 1 = Still learning

Area	Skill	Self-Assessment
Data	**1.** Familiar with multiple data collection systems and their uses with PBIS Leadership Teams; e.g., Team Implementation Checklist (TIC), Self-Assessment Survey (SAS), School-Wide Evaluation Tool (SET) and office discipline referrals (ODRs)	3 2 1
	2. Can assist schools to develop other data systems as needed; e.g., ISS, OSS, attendance reports, observations	3 2 1
	3. Can teach and support leadership team's use of data to guide decision making; e.g., PBIS assessments, ODRs, achievement, safety, attendance, suspension, expulsion	3 2 1
Practices	**1.** Knows and can define the essential features of schoolwide PBIS	3 2 1
	2. Understands features of effective classroom instruction and management	3 2 1
	3. Can guide schools in identifying and adopting evidence-based practices	3 2 1
	4. Knows strategies to increase appropriate behavior and decrease inappropriate behavior of groups of students	3 2 1
	5. Can provide schools with models and examples of other schools implementing PBIS	3 2 1
	6. Understands basic principles of applied behavior analysis; e.g., reinforcement, punishment, stimulus control, extinction	3 2 1
Systems	**1.** Can facilitate effective team meetings	3 2 1
	2. Can provide effective consultation and technical assistance to school teams	3 2 1
	3. Able to effectively communicate within and across schools, district, region, etc.	3 2 1
	4. Can assist schools to establish systems that support staff and increase sustainability of PBIS efforts	3 2 1

Coach's Self-Assessment Summary and Action Plan for Professional Development and Support

On your coach's self-assessment, add up your scores within each area (data, practices, systems). Add the three area scores together for a composite score; fill this in the blank. Use the scores to identify current coaching strengths as well as areas of need. Within each area (data, practices, systems), identify professional growth goals and the resources and support needed to accomplish each goal. Fill in the timeline for completion.

Current Coaching Level: ______________________ Composite Score: ______________

Area	Goal/Outcome statement: WHAT needs to be accomplished?	Resources/Support needed: HOW will this be accomplished?	Timeline
Data			
Practices			
Systems			

Self-Assessment Survey (SAS) for PBIS Leadership Teams

Schoolwide Systems

Current Status			Feature	Priority for Improvement		
In Place	Partially in Place	Not in Place	***Schoolwide systems involve all students, all staff, and all settings.***	High	Medium	Low
			1. Three to five student behavioral expectations have been defined and are stated positively and clearly.			
			2. Expected student behaviors are taught directly.			
			3. Expected student behaviors are rewarded regularly.			
			4. Problem behaviors (failure to meet expected student behaviors) are defined clearly.			
			5. Consequences for problem behaviors are defined clearly.			
			6. Distinctions between office- versus classroom-managed problem behaviors are clear.			
			7. Options exist to allow classroom instruction to continue when problem behaviors occur.			
			8. Procedures are in place to address situations that are emergencies or potentially dangerous.			
			9. A team exists to problem solve and plan behavioral supports.			
			10. School administrator is an active participant on the behavioral support team.			
			11. Data to evaluate problem-behavior patterns are collected and summarized within an ongoing data system.			
			12. Patterns of behavioral problems are reported to teams and on a regular basis (e.g., monthly) to facilitate active decision making.			

continued →

Self-Assessment Survey (SAS) for PBIS Leadership Teams, continued

Current Status			Feature	Priority for Improvement		
In Place	Partially in Place	Not in Place	***Schoolwide systems involve all students, all staff, and all settings.***	High	Medium	Low
			13. School has formal strategies for informing families about expected student behaviors at school.			
			14. Booster training activities for students are developed, modified, and conducted based on school data.			
			15. Schoolwide behavioral support team has a budget for (a) teaching students, (b) ongoing rewards, and (c) annual staff planning.			
			16. All staff is involved directly and/or indirectly in schoolwide interventions.			
			17. The leadership team has access to ongoing training and support from district personnel.			
			18. The school is required by the district to report on the social climate, discipline level, and/or student behavior at least annually.			

Non-Classroom Systems

Current Status			Feature	Priority for Improvement		
In Place	Partially in Place	Not in Place	***Non-classroom settings are defined as particular times or places where supervision is emphasized (e.g., hallways, cafeteria, playground, bus).***	High	Medium	Low
			1. Schoolwide expected student behaviors apply to non-classroom settings.			
			2. Schoolwide expected student behaviors are taught in non-classroom settings.			
			3. Supervisors actively supervise (move, scan, and interact) students in non-classroom settings.			

continued →

Self-Assessment Survey (SAS) for PBIS Leadership Teams, continued

Current Status			Feature	Priority for Improvement		
In Place	Partially in Place	Not in Place	***Non-classroom settings are defined as particular times or places where supervision is emphasized (e.g., hallways, cafeteria, playground, bus).***	High	Medium	Low
			4. Rewards exist for meeting expected student behaviors in non-classroom settings.			
			5. Physical/architectural features are modified to limit (a) unsupervised settings, (b) unclear traffic patterns, and (c) inappropriate access to and exit from school grounds.			
			6. Scheduling of student movement ensures appropriate numbers of students in non-classroom spaces.			
			7. Staff receives regular opportunities for developing and improving active supervision skills.			
			8. Status of student behavior and management practices is evaluated quarterly using data.			
			9. All staff is involved directly or indirectly in management of non-classroom settings.			

Classroom Systems

Current Status			Feature	Priority for Improvement		
In Place	Partially in Place	Not in Place	***Classroom settings are defined as instructional settings in which teachers supervise and teach groups of students.***	High	Medium	Low
			1. Expected student behavior and routines in classrooms are stated positively and defined clearly.			
			2. Problem behaviors are defined clearly.			
			3. Expected student behavior and routines in classrooms are taught directly.			

continued →

Self-Assessment Survey (SAS) for PBIS Leadership Teams, continued

Current Status			Feature	Priority for Improvement		
In Place	Partially in Place	Not in Place	***Classroom settings are defined as instructional settings in which teachers supervise and teach groups of students.***	High	Medium	Low
			4. Expected student behaviors are acknowledged regularly and positively reinforced (>4 positives to 1 negative).			
			5. Problem behaviors receive consistent consequences.			
			6. Procedures for expected and problem behaviors are consistent with schoolwide procedures.			
			7. Classroom-based options exist to allow classroom instruction to continue when problem behavior occurs.			
			8. Instruction and curriculum materials are matched to student ability (math, reading, language).			
			9. Students experience high rates of academic success (>75 percent correct).			
			10. Teachers have regular opportunities for access to assistance and recommendations (observation, instruction, and coaching).			
			11. Transitions between instructional and non-instructional activities are efficient and orderly.			

continued →

Self-Assessment Survey (SAS) for PBIS Leadership Teams, continued

Individual Student Systems

Current Status			Feature	Priority for Improvement		
In Place	Partially in Place	Not in Place	***Individual student systems provide specific supports for students who engage in chronic problem behaviors (1–7 percent of enrollment).***	High	Medium	Low
			1. Assessments are conducted regularly to identify students with chronic problem behaviors.			
			2. A simple process exists for teachers to request assistance.			
			3. A behavioral support team responds promptly (within 2 working days) to students who present chronic problem behaviors.			
			4. Behavioral support team includes an individual skilled at conducting functional behavioral assessments.			
			5. Local resources are used to conduct functional assessment-based behavior support planning (approximately 10 hrs/week/student).			
			6. Significant family and/or community members are involved when appropriate and possible.			
			7. School includes formal opportunities for families to receive training on behavioral support and positive parenting strategies.			
			8. Behavior is monitored and feedback provided regularly to the behavioral support team and relevant staff.			

School-Wide Evaluation Tool (SET) Overview

Purpose of the SET

The School-Wide Evaluation Tool (SET) is designed to assess and evaluate the critical features of schoolwide effective behavioral support across each academic school year. The SET results are used to:

1. Assess PBIS features that are in place
2. Determine annual goals for schoolwide effective behavioral support
3. Evaluate ongoing efforts toward schoolwide behavioral support
4. Design and revise procedures as needed
5. Compare efforts toward schoolwide effective behavioral support from year to year

Information necessary for this assessment tool is gathered through multiple sources including review of permanent products, observations, and staff (minimum of ten) and student (minimum of fifteen) interviews or surveys. There are multiple steps for gathering all of the necessary information. The first step is to identify someone at the school as the contact person. This person will be asked to collect each of the available products listed (see box) and to identify a time for the SET data collector to preview the products and set up dates for observations and interviews or surveys. Once the process for collecting the necessary data is established, reviewing the data and scoring the SET averages takes two to three hours.

Products to Collect

1. ________ Discipline handbook
2. ________ School improvement plan goals
3. ________ Action plan for meeting schoolwide behavioral support goals
4. ________ Social skills instructional materials and implementation timeline
5. ________ Behavioral incident summaries or reports (e.g., office referrals, suspensions, expulsions)
6. ________ Office discipline referral (ODR) form(s)
7. ________ Other related information

Using SET Results

The SET is designed to provide trend lines of improvement and sustainability over time. The results measure the proportion of schoolwide behavioral supports from the PBIS features that are (1) not targeted or started, (2) in the planning phase, and (3) in the implementation or maintenance phase of development.

School-Wide Evaluation Tool version 2.1, June 2005, © 2001 Sugai, Lewis-Palmer, Todd & Horner, Educational and Community Supports, University of Oregon

School-Wide Evaluation Tool (SET) Scoring Guide

School: ______________________ Date: ______________________

District: ______________________ State: ______________________

Pre: __________ Post: __________ SET data collector: ______________________

Feature	Evaluation Question	Data Source (circle sources used) P = Product; I = Interview; O = Observation		Score (0, 1, 2)
A. Expectations Defined	1. Is there documentation that staff has agreed to 5 or fewer positively stated school-wide behavioral expectations? *(0 = No; 1 = Too many or negatively focused; 2 = Yes)*	Discipline handbook Instructional materials Other ______	P	
	2. Are the agreed upon expectations publicly posted in 8 of 10 locations? (See interview and observation form for selection of locations.) *(0 = 0–4; 1 = 5–7; 2 = 8–10)*	Wall posters Other ______	O	
B. Behavioral Expectations Taught	1. Is there a documented system for teaching behavioral expectations to students on an annual basis? *(0 = No; 1 = States that teaching will occur; 2 = Yes)*	Lesson plan books Instructional materials Other ______	P	
	2. Does 90% of the staff asked state that teaching of behavioral expectations to students has occurred this year? *(0 = 0–50%; 1 = 51–89%; 2 = 90–100%)*	Interviews Other ______	I	
	3. Do 90% of team members asked state that the schoolwide program has been taught or reviewed with staff on an annual basis? *(0 = 0–50%; 1 = 51–89%; 2 = 90–100%)*	Interviews Other ______	I	
	4. Can at least 70% of 15 or more students state two-thirds of the school rules? *(0 = 0–50%; 1 = 51–69%; 2 = 70–100%)*	Interviews Other ______	I	
	5. Can 90% or more of the staff asked list two-thirds of the school rules? *(0 = 0–50%; 1 = 51–89%; 2 = 90%–100%)*	Interviews Other ______	I	

continued →

School-Wide Evaluation Tool (SET) Scoring Guide, continued

Feature	Evaluation Question	Data Source (circle sources used) P = Product; I = Interview; O = Observation		Score (0, 1, 2)
C. Ongoing System for Rewarding Behavioral Expectations	1. Is there a documented system for rewarding student behavior? *(0 = No; 1 = States to acknowledge, but not how; 2 = Yes)*	Instructional materials Lesson plans Interviews Other ________	P	
	2. Do 50% or more of students asked indicate they have received a reward (other than verbal praise) for expected behaviors over the past two months? *(0 = 0–25%; 1 = 26–49%; 2 = 50–100%)*	Interviews Other ________	I	
	3. Does 90% of staff asked indicate they have delivered a reward (other than verbal praise) to students for expected behavior over the past two months? *(0 = 0–50%; 1 = 51–89%; 2 = 90–100%)*	Interviews Other ________	I	
D. System for Responding to Behavioral Violations	1. Is there a documented system for dealing with and reporting specific behavioral violations? *(0 = No; 1 = States to document; but not how; 2 = Yes)*	Discipline handbook Instructional materials Other ________	P	
	2. Does 90% of staff asked agree with administration on what problems are office-managed and what problems are classroom-managed? *(0 = 0–50%; 1 = 51–89%; 2 = 90–100%)*	Interviews Other ________	I	
	3. In how many locations is the documented crisis plan for responding to extremely dangerous situations readily available? *(0 = 0–3; 1 = 4–5; 2 = 6–7)*	Walls Other ________	O	
	4. Does 90% of staff asked agree with administration on the procedure for handling extreme emergencies (e.g., stranger in building with a weapon)? *(0 = 0–50%; 1 = 51–89%; 2 = 90–100%)*	Interviews Other ________	I	

School-Wide Evaluation Tool version 2.1, June 2005, © 2001 Sugai, Lewis-Palmer, Todd & Horner, Educational and Community Supports, University of Oregon

continued →

School-Wide Evaluation Tool (SET) Scoring Guide, continued

Feature	Evaluation Question	Data Source (circle sources used) P = Product; I = Interview; O = Observation		Score (0, 1, 2)
E. Monitoring and Decision Making	1. Does the discipline referral form list (a) student/grade level, (b) date, (c) time, (d) referring staff, (e) problem behavior, (f) location, (g) persons involved, (h) probable motivation, and (i) administrative decision? *(0 = 0–3 items; 1 = 4–6 items; 2 = 7–9 items)*	Referral form (circle the items that are present on the referral form)	P	
	2. Can the administrator clearly define a system for collecting and summarizing discipline referrals (e.g., computer software, data-entry time)? *(0 = No; 1 = Collected, not summarized; 2 = Yes)*	Interview Other ________	I	
	3. Does the administrator report that the leadership team provides discipline data summary reports to the staff at least three times per year? *(0 = 0/year; 1 = 1–2/year; 2 = 3 or more/year)*	Interview Other ________	I	
	4. Do 90% of leadership team members asked report that discipline data is used for making decisions in designing, implementing, and revising schoolwide behavioral support efforts? *(0 = 0–50%; 1 = 51–89%; 2 = 90–100%)*	Interviews Other ________	I	

School-Wide Evaluation Tool version 2.1, June 2005, © 2001 Sugai, Lewis-Palmer, Todd & Horner, Educational and Community Supports, University of Oregon

continued →

School-Wide Evaluation Tool (SET) Scoring Guide, continued

Feature	Evaluation Question	Data Source (circle sources used) P = Product; I = Interview; O = Observation		Score (0, 1, 2)
F. Management	1. Does the school improvement plan list improving behavioral support systems as one of the top 3 school improvement plan goals? *(0 = Not listed at all; 1 = 4th or lower priority; 2 = 1st–3rd priority)*	School improvement plan Interview Other ______	P I	
	2. Can 90% of staff asked report that there is a schoolwide leadership team established to address behavioral support systems in the school? *(0 = 0–50%; 1 = 51–89%; 2 = 90–100%)*	Interviews Other ______	I	
	3. Does the administrator report that leadership team membership includes representation of all staff? *(0 = No; 2 = Yes)*	Interviews Other ______	I	
	4. Can 90% of leadership team members asked identify the team leader? *(0 = 0–50%; 1 = 51–89%; 2 = 90–100%)*	Interviews Other ______	I	
	5. Is the administrator an active member of the schoolwide leadership team? *(0 = No; 1 = Yes, but not consistently; 2 = Yes)*	Interviews Other ______	I	
	6. Does the administrator report that leadership team meetings occur at least monthly? *(0 = No team meetings; 1 = Less often than monthly; 2 = At least monthly)*	Interviews Other ______	I	
	7. Does the administrator report that the team communicates progress to the staff at least four times per year? *(0 = 0/year; 1 = 1–3/year; 2 = 4 or more/year)*	Interviews Other ______	I	
	8. Does the team have an action plan with specific goals that is less than one year old? *(0 = No; 2 = Yes)*	Action plan Calendar Other ______	P	
G. District-Level Support	1. Does the school budget contain an allocated amount of money for building and maintaining schoolwide behavioral support? *(0 = No; 2 = Yes)*	Interviews Other ______	I	
	2. Can the administrator identify an out-of-school liaison in the district or state? *(0 = No; 2 = Yes)*	Interviews Other ______	I	

Summary Scores	A = /4	B = /10	C = /6	D = /8	E = /8
	F = /16	G = /4	Mean = /7		

School-Wide Evaluation Tool version 2.1, June 2005, © 2001 Sugai, Lewis-Palmer, Todd & Horner, Educational and Community Supports, University of Oregon

Action Planning Sheet

Key Feature Number	Activities	Who Is Responsible?	Target Start Date	Target Completion Date	Review Date

Writing a Purpose Statement

A purpose statement for your school sets the climate for everything else. In the business world this is called a tagline. The statement should be printed and posted widely: on a big banner in the hallway; on school Web pages; and on the newsletter, school handbook, and programs for school concerts and athletic events. Incorporate the following into your process for creating a purpose statement:

1. State positively in two or three sentences *(We are . . . , We will . . . , Our purpose is to . . . , etc.)*
2. Focus schoolwide: All students, all staff, all settings
3. Relate to academic achievement
4. Agree upon by at least 80 percent of school staff

> *Evergreen School's Purpose Statement*
>
> *Evergreen School is a community of learners. We come to school to become our best selves by learning academics and becoming good citizens in a community that cares.*

Brainstorm some ideas for your purpose statement here:

Writing Schoolwide Behavioral Expectations

Your schoolwide behavioral expectations should expand on your purpose statement. They explain how your school will support the purpose statement. Expectations are better than rules because they allow more flexibility and expandability, and, unlike a rule, expectations can't be broken.

> *Evergreen School's Behavioral Expectations:*
>
> *We come to school to learn.*
> *We respect ourselves and others.*
> *We are responsible for our actions.*

Brainstorm some ideas for schoolwide expectations here:

Data Drill Down for Creating Precision Statements

- Choose a current schoolwide behavioral problem (versus an individual student problem).
- Create an example of a precision statement for the identified behavior. See below for examples.
- Be prepared to show and discuss how you drilled deeper into your data to define the problem with precision.

Drill Down Questions

1. Where (non-classroom) are the most problem behaviors in general occurring (top location)?
2. Who is receiving the most referrals in the identified location (top grade)?
3. What are the two most frequent problem behaviors for the identified group in the identified location?
4. When is the problem behavior most likely to occur for the identified group in the identified location (top time)?
5. Why is the problem behavior happening for the identified group in the identified location at the identified time (consider a 30-minute time span, including 15 minutes before and after the behavior)?

Primary versus Precise Statements of the Current Problem

Primary	Precise
Last year we had an increasing trend of problem behaviors during first 3 months (.5–2.2/day above national median) and .5–1.0/day above national median for remainder of school year.	Inappropriate language, disrespect, physical aggression, harassment, disruption, in class and common areas (hall, cafe, playground, commons) are taking place at 9:45, 12:45–1:30, 11:30–12:15 involving many 6th and 7th graders. Behaviors appear to be driven by a need to gain peer or adult attention.
Gang behavior is increasing.	Bullying (verbal and physical aggression) on the playground is increasing during the first recess, is being done mostly by four 4th-grade boys, and seems to be maintained by social praise from the bystander peer group.

PBIS Team Implementation Checklist (TIC 3.1)

This checklist is designed to be completed by the PBIS Leadership Team once a quarter to monitor activities for implementation of PBIS in a school. The team should complete the PBIS action plan at the same time to track items that are in progress or not yet started.

School:________________ Coach:__________ Date of Report:__________

District:________________ County:__________ State:__________

Person Completing Report:____________________

PBIS Leadership Team Members:____________________

PBIS Leadership Team Completes Quarterly (or more often) **Status: A = Achieved I = In Progress N = Not yet started**				
	Q1	**Q2**	**Q3**	**Q4**
Establish Commitment	**Status:**			
1. Administrator's support and active involvement • Admin attends PBIS meetings 80% of time. • Admin defines social behavior as one of the top three goals for the school. • Admin actively participates in PBIS training.				
2. Staff support • 80% of staff agrees that school climate/discipline is one of top three school improvement goals. • Admin/staff commit to PBIS for at least three years.				
Establish and Maintain Leadership Team	**Status:**			
3. Representative team established • Includes grade-level teachers, specialists, paraprofessionals, parents, special educators, counselors, bus drivers. • Team has established a clear purpose.				
4. Team has regular meeting schedule, effective operating procedures • Agenda and meeting minutes are used. • Team decisions are identified and an action plan is developed.				
5. Audit is completed for efficient integration of PBIS Leadership Team with other similar committees or initiatives • Team has completed an audit of existing school committees and initiatives.				

continued →

PBIS Team Implementation Checklist (TIC 3.1), continued

PBIS Leadership Team Completes Quarterly (or more often) Status: A = Achieved I = In Progress N = Not yet started				
	Q1	Q2	Q3	Q4
Conduct Self-Assessment	**Status:**			
6. Team completes self-assessment of current PBIS practices being used in the school • The team has completed the TIC (progress monitoring), BoQ (annual assessment), or SET.				
7. Team summarizes existing school discipline data • The team uses office discipline referral (ODR) data, attendance, and other behavioral measures for decision making.				
8. Team uses self-assessment information to build action plan for implementation of immediate areas of focus • The team has an action plan guiding implementation of PBIS with specific actions, assignments of responsibilities, and timetables for completion.				
Establish Schoolwide Behavioral Expectations and Prevention Systems	**Status:**			
9. Three to five schoolwide behavior expectations are defined and posted in all areas of building • Three to five positively and clearly stated expectations are defined. • The expectations are posted in public areas of the school.				
10. Schoolwide behavioral matrix developed • Behavioral matrix is used to define how schoolwide expectations apply to specific school locations. • Matrix is distributed to all staff.				
11. Teaching plans for schoolwide expectations are developed • Lesson plans are developed for teaching schoolwide expectations at key locations throughout the school. • Faculty is involved in development of lesson plans.				
12. Schoolwide behavioral expectations taught directly and formally • Schedule/plans for teaching the staff the lesson plans for students are developed. • Staff and students know the defined expectations. • Schoolwide expectations are taught to all students. • Plan is developed for teaching expectations to students who enter the school midyear.				

continued →

PBIS Team Implementation Checklist (TIC 3.1), continued

PBIS Leadership Team Completes Quarterly (or more often) Status: A = Achieved I = In Progress N = Not yet started				
	Q1	Q2	Q3	Q4
13. System in place to acknowledge and reward expected behaviors • Reward systems are used to acknowledge use of expected behaviors. • Ratio of reinforcements to corrections is high (4:1). • Students and staff know about the acknowledgment system and students are receiving positive acknowledgments.				
14. Clearly defined and consistent consequences and procedures for undesirable behaviors are developed • Major and minor problem behaviors are clearly differentiated and defined. • Clearly defined and consistent consequences and procedures for undesirable behaviors are developed and used. • Procedures define an array of appropriate responses to minor (classroom-managed) behaviors. • Procedures define an array of appropriate responses to major (office-managed) behaviors.				
Develop Classroom Behavioral Support Systems	**Status:**			
15. School has completed a summary of classroom systems • The teaching staff has completed a classroom assessment (e.g., SAS Classroom Survey, Classroom Systems Survey, etc.)				
16. Action plan in place to address any classroom systems identified as a high priority for change • Results of the assessment are used to plan professional development and support for staff.				
17. Data system in place to monitor ODR rates that come from classrooms • School has a way to review ODR data from classrooms to use in data-based decision making.				
Establish Information Systems	**Status:**			
18. Discipline data are gathered, summarized, and reported at least quarterly to all staff • Data collection is easy, efficient, and relevant for decision making. • ODR data are entered at least weekly. • ODR form lists (a) student/grade level, (b) date/time, (c) referring staff, (d) problem behavior, (e) location, (f) persons involved, (g) probable motivation, (h) consequences, and (i) administrative decision. • ODR data are available by frequency, location, time, type of behavior, motivation, and student. • ODR data summary is shared with staff at least monthly.				

continued →

PBIS Team Implementation Checklist (TIC 3.1), continued

PBIS Leadership Team Completes Quarterly (or more often) Status: A = Achieved I = In Progress N = Not yet started				
	Q1	Q2	Q3	Q4
19. Discipline data are available to the team regularly (at least monthly) in a form and depth needed for problem solving • Leadership team is able to use the data for decision making, problem solving, action planning, and evaluation. • Precision problem statements are developed and used for problem solving.				
Build Capacity for Function-Based Support				
20. Personnel with behavioral expertise are identified and involved • Personnel are able to provide behavior expertise for students needing Tier 2 and Tier 3 support.				
21. At least one staff member of the school is able to conduct simple functional behavioral assessments • At least one staff member can conduct simple behavioral assessments and work with a team to develop behavioral support plans for individual students.				
22. Intensive, individual student support team structure in place to use function-based supports • A team exists that focuses on intensive individualized supports for students needing Tier 3 supports. • The team uses function-based supports to develop, monitor, and evaluate behavioral plans. • The team delivering Tier 3 has a data system that allows ongoing monitoring of the fidelity and outcomes of individual behavioral support plans.				

Additional Comments and Information:

PBIS Action Plan

Include only those items from the Team Implementation Checklist (TIC) that are marked "in progress" or "not yet started."

Activity	Tasks/Action Steps (What)	Who	By When
1. Administrator's support and active involvement			
2. Staff support			
3. Representative leadership team established			
4. Regular meeting schedule and effective operating procedures in place for leadership team			
5. Audit is completed for efficient integration of PBIS team with other committees or initiatives addressing behavioral support			
6. Team self-assessment is completed to identify current PBIS practices used in the school			
7. ODR data is summarized by leadership team			
8. Self-assessment information is used to build action plan for implementation of immediate areas of focus			
9. 3–5 schoolwide behavioral expectations are defined and posted in all areas of building			
10. Schoolwide behavioral matrix developed			
11. Teaching plans for schoolwide expectations are developed			

continued →

PBIS Action Plan, continued

Activity	Tasks/Action Steps (What)	Who	By When
12. Schoolwide behavioral expectations are taught directly and formally			
13. System in place to acknowledge and reward behavioral expectations			
14. Consequences and procedures for undesirable behaviors are developed, clearly defined, and applied consistently schoolwide			
15. Classroom systems summary is completed by leadership team			
16. Action plan addresses any classroom systems identified as a high priority for change			
17. Data system is in place to monitor ODR rates from classrooms			
18. Discipline data are gathered, summarized, and reported at least quarterly to all staff			
19. Discipline data are available to team at least monthly in a form and depth needed for problem solving			
20. Personnel with behavioral expertise are identified and involved			
21. At least one staff member of the school is able to conduct simple functional behavioral assessments			
22. Intensive, individual student support team structure is in place to use function-based supports			

SUBSIST PBIS Sustainability Checklist

Self-Assessment and Action Planning Tool for PBIS Leadership Teams

Purposes: This self-assessment has been designed to assist leadership teams in identifying the presence of key PBIS features related to sustainability of schoolwide PBIS and to guide action planning for sustainability.

Guidelines for Use:

- Complete the self-assessment as a team.
- Consider existing efforts, initiatives, and programs that may be integrated with PBIS systems and structures.
- Use results to identify strengths and areas for action planning.

Date:

Team Members Completing Self-Assessment:

Instructions:

1. Identify the extent to which items are fully in place, partially in place, or not in place.
2. Circle items that will be priorities for the upcoming year (identify the smallest changes that will make the greatest impact).
3. Add each circled item to the action plan, identifying *who* will do *what* by *when*.

Feature		In Place?		
		Yes	Partially	No
Priority	**1.** There is agreement that PBIS serves a critical and shared need for the school.			
	2. PBIS addresses outcomes that are highly valued by school personnel.			
	3. A vast majority of school personnel (>80%) support PBIS.			
	4. PBIS is integrated into new school or district initiatives (e.g., renamed to new needs, shown how PBIS can meet the goals of the new initiatives as well).			
	5. Parents are actively involved in the PBIS effort (e.g., as part of leadership team or district committee).			

McIntosh, K., Doolittle, J. D., Vincent, C. G., Horner, R. H., & Ervin, R. A. (2013). *SUBSIST PBIS Sustainability Checklist (Version 1.1).* Eugene, OR: Educational and Community Supports, University of Oregon.

continued →

SUBSIST PBIS Sustainability Checklist, continued

Feature		In Place?		
		Yes	Partially	No
Building Leadership	**6.** The school administrators actively support PBIS.			
	7. The school administrators describe PBIS as a top priority for the school.			
	8. The school administrators actively support school personnel when implementing and aligning initiatives (e.g., shield staff from competing demands, change language to align PBIS with new initiatives) to allow PBIS to continue.			
	9. The school administrators ensure that the PBIS team has regularly scheduled time to meet.			
	10. A school administrator regularly attends and participates in PBIS team meetings.			
External Leadership	**11.** There are adequate district resources (funding and time) allocated for PBIS.			
	12. The district administration actively supports PBIS (e.g., describes PBIS as a top priority, provides clear direction).			
	13. State/provincial officials actively support PBIS (e.g., promotion, publicity, providing infrastructure).			
	14. PBIS is promoted to important organizations (e.g., school board, community agencies, businesses, parent groups) at least yearly.			
	15. PBIS is embedded into school and/or district policy (e.g., school improvement plans, mission/vision statements)			

McIntosh, K., Doolittle, J. D., Vincent, C. G., Horner, R. H., & Ervin, R. A. (2013). *SUBSIST PBIS Sustainability Checklist (Version 1.1).* Eugene, OR: Educational and Community Supports, University of Oregon.

continued →

SUBSIST PBIS Sustainability Checklist, continued

Feature		In Place?		
		Yes	Partially	No
Effectiveness	**16.** The practices and strategies implemented as part of PBIS are evidence-based (i.e., published research documents their effectiveness).			
	17. School personnel perceive PBIS as effective in helping them achieve desired outcomes.			
	18. School personnel celebrate the positive effects of PBIS at least yearly.			
	19. PBIS has a "crossover effect" in other areas (e.g., improved academic achievement scores, attendance).			
	20. PBIS is effective for a large proportion of students.			
	21. PBIS has been expanded to other areas (e.g., classrooms, buses, students with intensive needs, parenting workshops).			
	22. PBIS is implemented with fidelity (i.e., it is used as intended).			
	23. Data are collected that show the critical features of PBIS are being implemented fully.			
	24. The leadership team implementing PBIS is knowledgeable and skilled in PBIS.			
	25. The PBIS team is well organized and operates efficiently (e.g., regular meeting schedule, process, agenda, and minutes).			
	26. The school PBIS team meets at least monthly.			
Efficiency	**27.** PBIS becomes easier to use with continued experience.			
	28. PBIS is considered to be a typical operating procedure of the school (it has become "what we do here; what we've always done").			
	29. PBIS is viewed as part of system already in use (as opposed to being an "add-on" system).			
	30. Implemented PBIS strategies are cost-effective (in terms of money and effort).			
	31. PBIS is viewed as at least as cost-effective as other approaches to this problem or area of the building (e.g., zero tolerance policies, character education, social-emotional curriculum).			
	32. Data for PBIS are easy to collect and do not interfere with teaching.			
	33. Materials related to PBIS (e.g., handbook, lesson plans, posters) are used and adapted across school years.			

McIntosh, K., Doolittle, J. D., Vincent, C. G., Horner, R. H., & Ervin, R. A. (2013). *SUBSIST PBIS Sustainability Checklist (Version 1.1)*. Eugene, OR: Educational and Community Supports, University of Oregon.

continued →

SUBSIST PBIS Sustainability Checklist, continued

	Feature	In Place?		
		Yes	Partially	No
Data-Based Decision Making	**34.** Needs assessments (e.g., EBS/PBIS Self-Assessment Survey) are conducted.			
	35. Data on the fidelity of implementation are collected at least yearly (e.g., SET, BoQ, TIC, EBS Survey).			
	36. Student outcome data are collected at least yearly (e.g., ODRs, academic achievement data, school safety survey, student/parent satisfaction survey).			
	37. Data are reviewed regularly at each team meeting.			
	38. Data are presented to all school personnel at least four times per year.			
	39. Data are presented at least once per year to key stakeholders outside of the school (e.g., district officials, school boards, community agencies and groups).			
	40. Data are used for problem solving, decision making, and action planning (to make PBIS more effective or efficient).			
Capacity Building	**41.** All school personnel have a basic understanding of PBIS practices and how and why they work.			
	42. There is a high level of schoolwide PBIS expertise within the school.			
	43. The school PBIS team has regular access to district PBIS expertise (e.g., external/district coaches or consultants).			
	44. School teams and new personnel are provided with professional development in PBIS at least yearly.			
	45. The school team is connected to a "community of practice" (e.g., network of other PBIS schools, local/regional conferences).			
Over-coming Barriers	**46.** Efforts are taken to build consensus on the school's core values, beliefs, and goals as they relate to PBIS.			
	47. To overcome shifting priorities, the team and school administrators review new initiatives and identify how PBIS can contribute to or be integrated with those initiatives.			
	48. To address general school turnover, the PBIS team is representative and communicates with groups across the school (e.g., administration, grade-level teachers, specialists, staff, students).			
	49. To address "champion" turnover, the leadership and expertise for implementing PBIS is shared among a number of school personnel.			
	50. Administrators have created FTE positions with job descriptions for PBIS-related activities.			

McIntosh, K., Doolittle, J. D., Vincent, C. G., Horner, R. H., & Ervin, R. A. (2013). *SUBSIST PBIS Sustainability Checklist (Version 1.1).* Eugene, OR: Educational and Community Supports, University of Oregon.

Free or Inexpensive Rewards for Students

For Individual Students at the Elementary Level:

- Assist the custodian.
- Assist with morning announcements over the PA system.
- Be a helper in another classroom.
- Be featured on a photo recognition board.
- Be recognized during announcements.
- Be the first one in the lunch line.
- Be the leader of a class game.
- Be the line leader or the caboose.
- Be the scout (the person who goes ahead of class to tell the specialist teacher they are on the way).
- Be the teacher's helper for the day.
- Borrow the principal's chair for the day.
- Choose a book for the teacher to read aloud to the class.
- Choose any class job for the week.
- Choose music for the class to hear.
- Choose the game during physical education.
- Choose which homework problem the teacher will give the answer to for a freebie.
- Coupon for free test answer from teacher.
- Dance to favorite music in the classroom.

For Individual Students at the Secondary Level:

- Have an adult volunteer write you a job recommendation.
- Attend an all-school party on the weekend, sponsored and chaperoned by parents, with different areas for all interests:
    - Dance area
    - Basketball area
    - Game board area
    - Conversation pit
    - Graffiti wall (piece of sheetrock decorated with colored markers)
    - Karaoke area
    - Computer animation area
- Act as assistant coach for any sport.
- Assist PTO to develop ways to reward teachers who go out of their way to help students.
- Call in a request to a radio station, which the teacher will play in the classroom.
- Go to the grade school and teach students about a topic of interest.
- Present a PowerPoint for the class on a particular subject of interest.
- Choose what assignment the class does for homework.
- Design a theme for a school dance, ice cream social, or game night.
- Dress as the school mascot during a sporting event.
- Apprentice on a Saturday at a local store or business.
- Be the water/towel person at a sporting event.
- Do stagecraft for any school performance (lights, stage design, props).
- Assist with the scoreboard at a sporting event.
- Eat lunch with a preferred adult.
- Get free entrance to a dance or sporting event.
- Get a library pass to research a topic of interest.
- Paint a ceiling tile to go in the hallway.

Courtesy of Laura A. Riffel, Ph.D. Used with permission

continued →

Free or Inexpensive Rewards for Students, continued

For the Whole Class:

- Earn the "Golden Plunger Award" for the cleanest classroom.
- Earn the "Gold Record" for the best behavior in music class for the week.
- Earn the "Golden Maracas Award" for the best behavior in Spanish class.
- Earn the "Golden Mouse Award" for the best behavior in computer class.
- Earn the "Golden Paintbrush Award" for the best behavior in art class.
- Earn the "Golden Spoon Award" for the best behavior in the cafeteria.
- Earn the "Golden Sports Trophy" for the best behavior in physical education.
- For all of the above, the next level is the platinum award, which is even more prestigious.
- For the best manners in the library, have the "Shelf Elf" sit in the student's classroom for a week.

Group Incentives with Group Rewards:

1. If there is a zero ODR day, the next day "Zero the Hero," the good behavior mascot, visits classrooms and eats lunch with students.
2. If there are zero tardies, absences, or other issues that have been a problem, instate a homework-free night for the whole school.
3. If the school has ten days with zero ODRs, the principal does something silly, like sit on the roof, get taped to a wall, wear a funny costume, or dress in a competing school's colors.
4. Draw a giant football field on the wall in the hallway. Each class has a football on the field. Every day that a class has zero absences, zero ODRs, zero tardies, etc., its football moves forward five yards. As each class makes a touchdown, it earns a homework-free night or an extra recess. Its football size is then increased and it starts all over again, while others continue toward a touchdown.
5. Play appropriate student-chosen music during the class transition period. Continue with the reward as long as tardies or other issues remain low (set the criteria).

Courtesy of Laura A. Riffel, Ph.D. Used with permission

Sample Menu for PBIS Reinforcement of Positive Behaviors

	The Evergreen School Menu for "Caught Ya" Tickets
2 tickets	Choose a prize from the trinket box.
3 tickets	Wear slippers for the day (must be approved by principal for safety).
3 tickets	Wear your hat for the day.
3 tickets	Bring a stuffed animal to school for a day.
3 tickets	Gain special recognition—either a phone call home or a certificate.
5 tickets	Get a picture of you and two friends on the front bulletin board.
5 tickets	Trade chairs with your teacher for a day.
5 tickets	Move your desk to a different location in your classroom for one day.
5 tickets	Read aloud in class a book of your choice.
5 tickets	Assist the teacher of your choice for 15 minutes.
10 tickets	Sing a song or tell a joke at the beginning of a class.
10 tickets	Get 15 minutes of extra reading time as agreed upon with teacher.
10 tickets	Get 15 minutes of extra computer time as agreed upon with teacher.
10 tickets	Get 15 minutes of drawing time as agreed upon with teacher.
10 tickets	Eat lunch in the classroom with a friend.
10 tickets	Get a free homework pass on an assignment.
10 tickets	Eat lunch with a staff person of your choice.
10 tickets	Wear jeans on Friday instead of your school uniform khakis (must still wear uniform shirt).
10 tickets	Dance in the music room for 20 minutes with 2 friends and Ms. Maher. You choose the music.
12 tickets	Serve as a workroom assistant for 20 minutes.
12 tickets	Serve as a custodial assistant for 20 minutes.
12 tickets	Shoot baskets in gym with any staff member for 20 minutes.

continued →

Sample Menu for PBIS Reinforcement of Positive Behaviors, continued

12 tickets	Design a bulletin board with Ms. Woods for 20 minutes.
12 tickets	Listen to music during a class for 20 minutes during silent work time.
15 tickets	Make cookies with Ms. Carr after school.
15 tickets	Eat a snack and play a board game with Ms. Kaufmann after school.
15 tickets	Serve as a library clerk with Mr. Olson for 20 minutes.
25 tickets	Create a special welcome with sidewalk chalk for 30 minutes.
30 tickets	Have the assistant principal as your own personal assistant for one hour.
30 tickets	Enjoy a free restaurant lunch with the principal.
30 tickets	Get 15 minutes extra recess for your entire class.
50 tickets	Dye Mr. Anderson's hair with pink stripes.
50 tickets	Take Ms. Nowak's hamsters home for the weekend.

Tips for Creating a Reward Menu:

1. Include a variety of prizes—some kids want things, some kids want time with a person, some kids want to be special, etc.
2. Some schools equate tickets and trinkets with money. For example, 1 ticket may be worth $1 in trinkets, 5 tickets may be worth $5 of trinkets, etc.
3. Hand out the prizes once a week—any more than that and they may start losing their appeal.
4. Survey the staff in your building and see what they will contribute to the list of rewards.
5. Keep all of the prizes in one place and designate a specific "prize time" during the week, e.g., Fridays during advisory. Have students put their names in a bucket if they have tickets. Choose one student from each advisory to go to the prize room. The names stay in the bucket for the next week's drawing.

Glossary of Terms and Acronyms

action plan: A written plan that uses data to identify goals and determine specific action steps, timelines, and resources needed to reach each goal. The action plan includes *who* will do *what* by *when* and *where*, and *how* it will be accomplished and evaluated, or measured.

Benchmarks of Quality (BoQ) is an annual self-assessment tool for universal Tier 1.

big five: The five common data summary reports in the SWIS data tracking of office discipline referrals: referrals by average number per day, by type of behavior, by time of day, by location, and by student.

core reports: The big five behavioral data summary reports (see *big five*) aggregated in SWIS and displayed online on the main SWIS dashboard. The summary reports enable teams to monitor schoolwide patterns of problem behavior.

effective behavior support (EBS): An evidence-based practice that supports positive behavior.

fidelity: The extent to which the core features of PBIS are implemented according to their original design and focus. Fidelity measures whether everyone is doing the same intervention in the same way and whether that intervention aligns with one of the eight key features of PBIS.

implementation science: The science of a "specified set of activities designed to put into practice an activity or program of known dimensions" (Fixsen et al. 2005); includes the *what* and *how* of implementation.

office discipline referral (ODR): One of the primary outcome measures of student behavior in PBIS. An ODR represents and measures specific student behavior through the use of an electronic or paper behavioral incident report that contains specific defined fields.

PBIS assessment coordinator: A designated leadership team member (sometimes the coach) who obtains a PBIS online assessment account; assists leadership teams in using PBIS assessment tools and data to measure progress, to facilitate problem solving, and to determine what supports may be most beneficial; assessments include the TIC, SAS, SET, BoQ, and the forthcoming PBIS Implementation Inventory.

PBIS coaching: A set of responsibilities, actions, activities, and personnel resources (i.e., coaches) organized to train, facilitate, assist, maintain, and adapt local PBIS implementation.

PBIS Implementation Inventory is an assessment tool that can measure progress and fidelity across all three tiers of implementation. Some states will use this for their state recognition programs. Expected release spring 2014.

PBIS: Positive Behavioral Interventions and Supports

School-Wide Evaluation Tool (SET) is an assessment designed to evaluate the features of SW-PBIS across each academic year. It provides a good measure of implementation and fidelity. It is conducted by an outside evaluator and was created as a research tool.

Schoolwide Information System (SWIS): A Web-based application for efficient collection, analysis, and reports of office discipline referral (ODR) data.

Schoolwide Positive Behavioral Interventions and Supports (SWPBIS): A systematic framework and set of evidence-based practices for improving behavioral and academic outcomes for all students and all staff in all school settings.

Self-Assessment Survey (SAS) solicits feedback from all staff members on the status of SWPBIS implementation and the priorities for action planning (formerly known as EBS Survey).

sustainability: The ongoing, long-term practice of SWPBIS after formal training ends and at a level of fidelity that continues to produce valued outcomes.

Team Implementation Checklist (TIC) is a progress-monitoring tool completed monthly or quarterly by the school PBIS Leadership Team to measure implementation of the Tier 1 universal system.

References and Resources

Print

Algozzine, B., Horner, R. H., Sugai, G., Barrett, S., Dickey, S. R., Eber, L., Kincaid, D., et al. (2010). "Evaluation Blueprint for School-Wide Positive Behavior Support." Eugene, OR: National Technical Assistance Center on Positive Behavior Interventions and Support. Retrieved from www.pbis.org.

Algozzine, B., Barrett, S., Eber, L., George, H., Horner, R., Putnam, B., Swain-Bradway, J., McIntosh, K., & Sugai, G. (2013). "The Positive Behavioral Interventions and Supports Implementation Inventory." Version 1.1 (beta test).

Bandura, A. (1977). "Self-Efficacy: Toward a Unifying Theory of Behavioral Change." *Psychological Review.* 84(2), 191–215.

Barrett, S., & Duda, M. (2011). "Coaching for Competence and Impact." PBIS Leadership Forum.

Center of Positive Behavioral Interventions and Supports (2010). *Implementation Blueprint and Self-Assessment.* Washington, D.C.: Office of Special Education Programs, U.S. Department of Education.

Coffey, J. H., & Horner, R. H. (2012). "The Sustainability of School-Wide Positive Behavior Interventions & Supports." *Exceptional Children.* 78(3), Summer 2012.

Cotton, K. (1990). "Schoolwide and Classroom Discipline." *School Improvement Research Series: Close-Up #9.* Office of Educational Research and Improvement (OERI), U.S. Department of Education. Online at educationnorthwest.org/webfm_send/530.

Filter, K. J., & Sytsma, M. (2013). *Staff Buy-In to School-Wide Positive Behavioral Interventions and Supports.* Manuscript submitted for publication.

Fixsen, D. L., Naoom, S. F., Blase, K. A., Friedman, R. M., & Wallace, F. (2005). *Implementation Research: A Synthesis of the Literature.* Tampa, FL: University of South Florida, Louis de la Parte Florida Mental Health Institute, National Implementation Research Network (FMHI Publication #231).

Froelich, K., & Puig, E. (2007). "The Magic of Coaching: Art Meets Science." *Journal of Language and Literacy Education* [Online]. 3(1), 18–31.

Gilbert, T. (1978). *Human Competence: Engineering Worthy Performance.* New York: McGraw-Hill.

Goodman, S. (2013). "Implementation of a district-wide Multi-Tiered System of Supports Initiative through Stages of Implementation." *The Utah Special Educator.* 35, 20–21.

Horner, R. (2011). "Coaching for Effective Implementation." Third Annual KY PBIS Network Conference.

Horner, R., & Sugai, G. (2006). "Policy Brief: Scaling Up Effective Educational Innovation." Prepared at the request of the U.S. Department of Education, Office of Special Education Programs, Washington, DC.

Horner, R. H., Sugai, G., Smolkowski, K., Eber, L., Nakasato, J., Todd, A., & Esperenza, J. (2009). "A Randomized, Wait-Listed Controlled Effectiveness Trial Assessing School-Wide Positive Behavior Support in Elementary Schools." *Journal of Positive Behavior Interventions.* 11(3), 133–144.

Joyce, B., & Showers, B. (1995). *Student Achievement through Staff Development: Fundamentals of School Renewal.* White Plains, N.Y.: Longman.

Lohrmann, S., Forman, S., Martin, S., & Palmieri, M. (2008). "Understanding School Personnel's Resistance to Adopting School-Wide Positive Behavior Support at a Universal Level of Intervention." *Journal of Positive Behavior Interventions.* 10(4), 256–269.

Mathews, S., McIntosh, K., Frank, J. L., & May, S. (2013). "Critical Features Predicting Sustained Implementation of School-Wide Positive Behavior Support." *Journal of Positive Behavior Interventions.*

McIntosh, K., Doolittle, J. D., Vincent, C. G., Horner, R. H., & Ervin, R. A. (2013). *SUBSIST PBIS Sustainability Checklist (Version 1.1).* Eugene, OR: Educational and Community Supports, University of Oregon.

McIntosh, K., Frank, J. L., & Spaulding, S. A. (2010). "Establishing Research-Based Trajectories of Office Discipline Referrals for Individual Students." *School Psychology Review.* 39(3), 380–394.

Romano, N., & Nunamaker, J. F. (2001). "Proceedings of the 34th Hawaii International Conference on System Sciences."

Sailor, W., Dunlap, G., Sugai, G., & Horner, R., (Eds.) (2009). *Handbook of Positive Behavior Support.* New York: Springer.

School-Wide Evaluation Tool (SET) Implementation Manual, Version 2.0 (2012). University of Oregon.

Strickland-Cohen, M. K., McIntosh, K., & Horner, R. H. (2014). "Sustaining Effective Practices in the Face of Principal Turnover." *Teaching Exceptional Children.* 46(3), 18–24.

Sugai, G., & Horner, R. (2009). "Defining and describing Schoolwide Positive Behavior Support." *Handbook of Positive Behavior Support.* Sailor, W., Dunlap, G., Sugai, G., & Horner, R. (Eds). New York: Springer. 307–326.

Sugai, G. (2008). "RTI & SWPBS" PDF document retrieved from PBIS website: www.pbis.org/common/pbisresources/presentations/0708gsrtiandpbisDC.pdf.

Sugai, G. (2013). "Arranging for Seats at the 'School Reform Table.'" PBIS Leadership Forum. Chicago Plenary session.

Sulik, L. R. (2012). "Anxiety in Children: An Update for Professionals." Keynote. Minnesota Children's Mental Health Conference, April 2011.

Todd, A. W., Newton, J. S., Algozzine, K., Horner, R. H., & Algozzine, B. (2013). *The Team-Initiated Problem Solving (TIPS II) Training Manual.* Eugene, OR: University of Oregon, Educational and Community Supports. Online at www.uoecs.org.

Online

State PBIS Websites
Many websites represent the accomplishments and resources developed across the country in various states. Those presented in this listing have a long history of SWPBIS implementation and have developed resources that others can use.

CASEL
www.casel.org
This website promotes teaching social-emotional skills to students in all grade levels. The social-emotional learning domains are self-awareness, social-awareness, self-management, relationship skills, and responsible decision making. You will find videos about how teaching social-emotional learning has improved schools as well as the CASEL guide to many curriculums that teach social-emotional skills, rated according to the program design and the effectiveness of each curriculum according to resent research.

Florida's Positive Behavior Support Project
flpbs.fmhi.usf.edu/
This website offers multiple resources for schools, school and district coordinators, and PBIS coaches. Florida developed the Benchmarks of Quality (BoQ), an assessment that is now used across the country. You will find resources for teams (team development) and for coaches (knowledge, skills, entry information); a Microsoft Excel template for an ODR calculator; and a 2013 online publication: *Systems Coaching: A Model for Building Capacity.*

Illinois PBIS
www.pbisillinois.org
This is the official site of the Illinois PBIS Network. Besides illustrating how PBIS is scaling up in Illinois, this website provides many resources and includes a section for coaches.

Maryland PBIS
pbismaryland.org
The state website for PBIS Maryland has archived many resources and materials. In addition to illustrating examples for schools across Maryland, this website offers resources that can be used in other states. One example is a template for a Cost Benefit Worksheet that calculates the instructional and administrative time reclaimed as an outcome of PBIS implementation. In addition, Maryland has extensive online resources for PBIS coaches.

Michigan's Integrated Behavior and Learning Support Initiative (MiBLSi)
www.miblsi.cenmi.org
This website for the state of Michigan includes multiple resources of interest and value to others, including resources for PBIS coaches, for evaluation processes, and for implementation strategies. Among many valuable resources are a series of practice profiles, which serve as rubrics for various components of PBIS implementation, e.g., "Coaching the Building Leadership Team: Practice Profile."

Missouri PBIS
pbismissouri.org
This website represents the statewide efforts of Missouri. Among the various resources offered are complete team workbooks for Tier 1 and Tier 2.

OSEP Technical Assistance Center on Positive Behavioral Interventions and Supports
pbis.org
The Internet home for the Technical Assistance Center for Positive Behavioral Interventions and Supports, this national PBIS website is referenced throughout this book. You will find everything related to PBIS, such as research, information for parents and families, training videos and resources, and tools needed to successfully implement PBIS in your school or district.

PBIS Apps
www.pbisapps.org
This Web-based application includes a number of tools specifically designed to assist schools, districts, regions, and states in achieving high fidelity and sustained implementation of SWPBIS. This website is designed to support schools' use of data by improving the efficiency and accuracy with which assessment tools are used. Tools are included for all three tiers of PBIS.

Uboost
uboost.com/integrations/pbis
This website provides a PBIS recognition and rewards program. Teachers who sign up receive 250,000 free points to give to students. The students can spend their points on a variety of good deeds focused on making the world a better place, for example, by protecting the Amazon rainforest, helping earthquake victims in Haiti, providing fresh drinking water for a developing country, or giving dog treats to an animal shelter.

Index

Page references in *italics* refer to figures; those in **bold** refer to reproducible forms.

S

About the Authors

Beth Baker, M.S.Ed., is an independent behavioral consultant and an intervention specialist at Minneapolis Public Schools where she works to create positive behavioral environments for elementary students. She was formerly the lead PBIS coach for a school district in the Minneapolis metropolitan area, as well as a special educator for many years, working with students who have emotional behavioral disability (EBD) needs. Beth lives in Minneapolis, Minnesota. To arrange a consultation or workshop, contact Beth at beth@beyondthebasics.us. She enjoys presenting on all topics related to PBIS and social-emotional learning.

Char Ryan, Ph.D, is a PBIS coach, evaluation specialist, and statewide facilitator and trainer for SWIS in Minnesota. She is also a licensed psychologist and consultant with the Minnesota Association for Children's Mental Health. Formerly, Char was an assistant professor at St. Cloud State University and the state PBIS coordinator at the Minnesota Department of Education. She is a frequent conference presenter and has been published in numerous journals, including *Psychology in the Schools*. Char lives in Minneapolis, Minnesota. To arrange a consultation or workshop, contact Char at pbis.char@gmail.com.

Other Great Books from Free Spirit

No Kidding About Bullying
For educators, group leaders, and caregivers, grades 3–6. 296 pp., PB, 8½" x 11"

The New Bully Free Classroom®
For teachers, grades K–8. 192 pp., PB, 8½" x 11"

RTI Success
For teachers and administrators, grades K–12. 256 pp., PB, 8½" x 11"

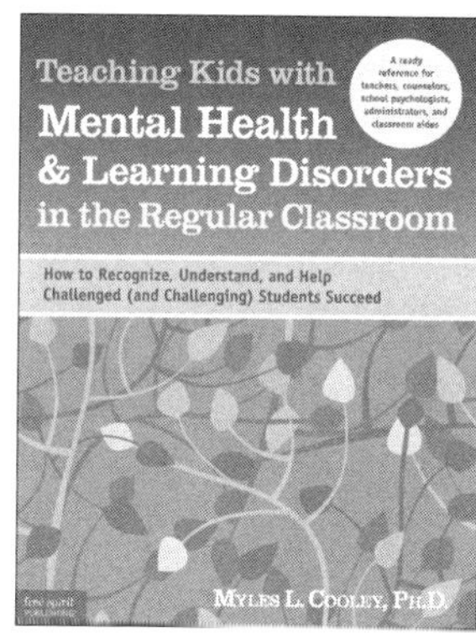

Teaching Kids with Mental Health & Learning Disorders in the Regular Classroom
For teachers and youth workers, grades K–12. 224 pp., PB, 8½" x 11"

Activities for Building Character and Social-Emotional Learning

Safe & Caring Schools® Series

Each book: PB, 8½" x 11". For educators, group leaders, and caregivers, grades PreK–8.

Grades PreK–K, 160 pp.

Grades 1–2, 208 pp.

Grades 3–5, 208 pp.

Grades 6–8, 208 pp.

Interested in purchasing multiple quantities and receiving volume discounts?
Contact edsales@freespirit.com or call 1.800.735.7323 and ask for Education Sales.

Many Free Spirit authors are available for speaking engagements, workshops, and keynotes.
Contact speakers@freespirit.com or call 1.800.735.7323.

For pricing information, to place an order, or to request a free catalog, contact:

Free Spirit Publishing Inc.
6325 Sandburg Road • Suite 100 • Golden Valley, MN 55427-3629
toll-free 800.735.7323 • local 612.338.2068 • fax 612.337.5050
help4kids@freespirit.com • www.freespirit.com